Commentary on the Letter to the Galatians
Bible Study Notes and Comments

by David E. Pratte

Available in print at
www.gospelway.com/sales

Commentary on the Letter to the Galatians
Bible Study Notes and Comments

ISBN-13: 978-1722417581
ISBN-10: 1722417587

Note carefully: No teaching in any of our materials is intended or should ever be construed to justify or to in any way incite or encourage personal vengeance or physical violence against any person.

Front Page Photo
The Street Called "Straight" in Damascus

Now there was a certain disciple at Damascus named Ananias; and to him the Lord said in a vision, "Ananias." And he said, "Here I am, Lord." So the Lord said to him, "Arise and go to the street called Straight, and inquire at the house of Judas for one called Saul of Tarsus, for behold, he is praying."
– Acts 9:10-12 (NKJV)
But when it pleased God, who separated me from my mother's womb and called me through His grace, to reveal His Son in me, that I might preach Him among the Gentiles, I did not immediately confer with flesh and blood, nor did I go up to Jerusalem to those who were apostles before me; but I went to Arabia, and returned again to Damascus. – Galatians 1:15-17

Other Acknowledgements
Unless otherwise indicated, Scripture quotations are generally from the New King James Version (NKJV), copyright 1982, 1988 by Thomas Nelson, Inc. used by permission. All rights reserved.

Scripture quotations marked (NASB) are from *Holy Bible, New American Standard* La Habra, CA: The Lockman Foundation, 1995.

Scripture quotations marked (ESV) are from *The Holy Bible, English Standard Version*, copyright ©2001 by Crossway Bibles, a publishing ministry of Good News Publishers. Used by permission. All rights reserved.

Scripture quotations marked (MLV) are from Modern Literal Version of The New Testament, Copyright 1999 by G. Allen Walker.

Scripture quotations marked (RSV) are from the Revised Standard Version of the Bible, copyright 1952 by the Division of Christian Education, National Council of the Churches of Christ in the United States of America.

Scripture quotations marked (NIV) are from the New International Version of the Holy Bible, copyright 1978 by Zondervan Bible publishers, Grand Rapids, Michigan.

Other Books by the Author

Topical Bible Studies

Growing a Godly Marriage & Raising Godly Children
Why Believe in God, Jesus, and the Bible? (evidences)
The God of the Bible (study of the Father, Son, and Holy Spirit)
Grace, Faith, and Obedience: The Gospel or Calvinism?
Kingdom of Christ: Future Millennium or Present Spiritual Reign?
Do Not Sin Against the Child: Abortion, Unborn Life, & the Bible
True Words of God: Bible Inspiration and Preservation

Commentaries on Bible Books

Genesis
Joshua and Ruth
Judges
1 Samuel
2 Samuel
1 Kings
Ezra, Nehemiah, and Esther
Job
Proverbs
Ecclesiastes
Gospel of Matthew

Gospel of Mark
Gospel of John
Acts
Romans
Galatians
Ephesians
Philippians and Colossians
Hebrews
James and Jude
1 and 2 Peter
1,2,3 John

Bible Question Class Books

Genesis
Joshua and Ruth
Judges
1 Samuel
2 Samuel
1 Kings
Ezra, Nehemiah, and Esther
Job
Proverbs
Ecclesiastes
Isaiah
Daniel

Gospel of Matthew
Gospel of Mark
Gospel of Luke
Gospel of John
Acts
Romans
1 Corinthians
2 Corinthians and Galatians
Ephesians and Philippians
Colossians, 1&2 Thessalonians
1 & 2 Timothy, Titus, Philemon
Hebrews
General Epistles (James – Jude)
Revelation

Workbooks with Study Notes

Jesus Is Lord: Workbook on the Fundamentals of the Gospel of Christ
Following Jesus: Workbook on Discipleship
God's Eternal Purpose in Christ: Workbook on the Theme of the Bible
Family Reading Booklist

Visit our website at www.gospelway.com/sales **to see a current list
of books in print.**

Other Resources from the Author

Printed books, booklets, and tracts available at
www.gospelway.com/sales
Free Bible study articles online at
www.gospelway.com
Free Bible courses online at www.biblestudylessons.com
Free class books at www.biblestudylessons.com/classbooks
Free commentaries on Bible books at
www.biblestudylessons.com/commentary
Contact the author at
www.gospelway.com/comments

Table of Contents

(Due to printer reformatting, the above numbers may be off a few pages.)

Notes to the Reader

To save space and for other reasons, I have chosen not to include the Bible text in these notes (please use your Bible to follow along). When I do quote a Scripture, I generally quote the New King James Version, unless otherwise indicated. Often – especially when I do not use quotations marks – I am not quoting any translation but simply paraphrasing the passage in my own words. Also, when I ask the reader to refer to a map, please consult the maps at the back of your Bible or in a Bible dictionary.

**You can find study questions to accompany these notes at
www.gospelway.com/sales**

**To join our mailing list to be informed of new books or
special sales, contact the author at
www.gospelway.com/comments**

Introductory Thoughts about Commentaries

Only the Scriptures provide an infallible, authoritatively inspired revelation of God's will for man (2 Timothy 3:16,17). It follows that this commentary, like all commentaries, was written by an uninspired, fallible human. It is the author's effort to share his insights about God's word for the purpose of instructing and edifying others in the knowledge and wisdom found in Scripture. It is simply another form of teaching, like public preaching, Bible class teaching, etc., except in written form (like tracts, Bible class literature, etc.). Nehemiah 8:8; Ephesians 4:15,16; Romans 15:14; 1 Thessalonians 5:11; Hebrews 3:12-14; 5:12-14; 10:23-25; Romans 10:17; Mark 16:15,16; Acts 8:4; 2 Timothy 2:2,24-26; 4:2-4; 1 Peter 3:15.

It follows that the student must read any commentary with discernment, realizing that any fallible teacher may err, whether he is teaching orally or in writing. So, the student must compare all spiritual teaching to the truth of God's word (Acts 17:11). It may be wise to read several commentaries to consider alternative views on difficult points. But it is especially important to consider the *reasons or evidence* each author gives for his views, then compare them to the Bible.

For these reasons, the author urges the reader to always consider my comments in light of Scripture. Accept what I say only if you find that it harmonizes with God's word. And please do not cite my writings as authority, as though people should accept anything I say as authoritative. Always let the Bible be your authority.

Notes on the *Ancient Christian Commentary*

The *Ancient Christian Commentary* is a compilation of comments on the Scriptures written by men who profess to be followers of Christ in the early centuries after the Scriptures were completed. Like any uninspired men, they may be mistaken at times. Many were part of groups that had departed from God's way, even as are many modern commentators. Nevertheless, I quote them at times because I find the viewpoints of those who lived so close to the first century to be especially interesting. I hope you also find the comments helpful.

"He who glories, let him glory in the Lord" – 1 Corinthians 1:31

Abbreviations Used in These Notes

ASV – American Standard Version
b/c/v – book, chapter, and verse
ESV – English Standard Version
f – the following verse
ff – the following verses
KJV – King James Version
NASB – New American Standard Bible
NEB – New English Bible
NIV – New International Version
NKJV – New King James Version
RSV – Revised Standard Version

Comments on Galatians

Introduction

The letter directly states that Paul wrote it – 1:1,2; 6:11. This is essentially uncontested.

Horne says:

> The genuineness of this Epistle was never doubted. It is cited by the apostolic fathers, Clement of Rome, Hermas, Ignatius, and Polycarp; and is declared to be authentic by Irenaeus, Clement of Alexandria, Tertullian, Caius, Origen, and by all subsequent writers.

The churches addressed

The epistle clearly states that it was addressed to the churches of Galatia (1:2; 3:1). These churches are also mentioned in 1 Corinthians 16:1 and 1 Peter 1:1. Galatia was a region in Asia Minor (see **map**). Apparently this region had been settled several hundred years before the time of Christ by Gauls who migrated into the area. As a result the region became known as Galatia.

However, there is some disagreement about which cities are addressed. Galatia is referred to in Acts 16:6,7 on Paul's second preaching trip, and in Acts 18:23 on his third trip. Some believe that, at these times, Paul preached in Galatia and established churches there.

More recent archaeological evidence, however, has indicated that Antioch of Pisidia, Iconium, Lystra, and Derbe may, in Paul's day, have been included in the region of Galatia. In this case, these churches, established on Paul's first trip, may be the ones addressed. If so, their origin is described in Acts 13 & 14.

Some scholars are convinced that Paul addressed the letter to the cities in southern Galatia which had been established in his first preaching trip. Others believed that the letter is addressed to the cities in northern Galatia which were established on his later trips. See the notes in front of Willis' commentary for a further discussion of the subject.

Page #9   *Commentary on Galatians*

This issue would affect the question of when the book was written. However, the proper understanding of the book, however, does not depend on which view is held.

The churches of Galatia consisted mostly of converts from the Gentile background. However, there was a Jewish element among them which insisted that the Gentile converts must obey the Old Testament law and be circumcised in order to be saved. This became the primary area of conflict that Paul addresses in the book.

Date and place of writing

Galatians is one of Paul's earliest letters, but the exact date is uncertain. The exact date one adheres to depends on whether he believes the book was written to the cities in southern Galatia or to the cities in northern Galatia. The date has been placed from 52-58 AD. The place from which Paul wrote it was probably Ephesus or Corinth.

Horne says:

> There is great diversity of opinion among learned men concerning the date of Saint Paul's Epistle to the Galatians. ... It is evident that the Epistle to the Galatians was written early, be cause he complains in it of their speedy apostasy from his doctrine (Galatians i. 6.), and warns them in the strongest and most forcible terms against the judaising teachers, who disturbed the peace of the churches in Syria and Asia Minor, (i. 7—9. iii. 1.) ... we are authorised to conclude that he wrote this letter from Corinth about the end of 52, or early in the year 53.

Theme

The theme of the book is: **Justification is by obedient faith according to the gospel, not by observance of the Old Testament law.**

The book quickly makes apparent that teachers had come to the churches of Galatia teaching that Gentiles could become Christians but must also observe the Old Testament law, especially circumcision. Such men were called "Judaizers," based on the references to Judaism as a religious system (1:13,14) and living like a Jew (this is called "Judaizing" in the Greek – 2:14). This is the same issue dealt with at the meeting in Acts 15 and in the books of Romans and Hebrews (as well as Ephesians, Colossians, and 2 Corinthians).

The Old Testament was both a spiritual and a civil law. Jesus removed it as a spiritual law, but it still continued as civil law in many places in Israel. The earliest converts to the gospel were, of course, Jews. They could properly continue to keep many aspects of the law as civil law and as national tradition. But some continued to view it as binding spiritual law as well.

When Gentiles became Christians, these Judaizers believed the Gentiles must also keep the Mosaic Law in order to please God and be saved. The issue became of major importance because the fundamental question was whether the gospel of Jesus was just an addition to the Old Testament law or whether it was a complete replacement of that law. Or put another way, the question was whether or not, in order to become a Christian, one first had to become a Jew by circumcision and submitting to the Old Testament law.

Paul had taught that the gospel had replaced the law as God's will for His people. He had taught the Gentiles salvation through the blood of Jesus according to the gospel, but had never required them to be circumcised or keep the Mosaic code. This caused repeated and serious conflict between him and the Judaizers in the church as well as with unconverted Jews. This is why so many of his epistles discussed this issue.

In order to convince people to accept their views, the Judaizers had to undermine Paul's authority as an apostle. They apparently tried to convince people he was not a real apostle since he was not one of the original twelve. Therefore, he did not have authority as an apostle, and his teachings could be disregarded.

They apparently claimed that Paul's teachings were not directly from Jesus and were therefore not as authoritative as those of Peter, James, etc. They claimed the original apostles agreed with the views of the Judaizers, not with Paul. To respond, Paul had to establish his authority as an apostle, show that the other apostles did agree with his view, and then disprove the specific doctrine of the Judaizers regarding the Old Testament. This is the purpose of the book of Galatians.

Willis summarizes the position of the Judaizers and their influence in the Galatian churches in the following way:

1. The apostasy occurred rather quickly (1:6).

2. The apostasy was an attempt to bind the Mosaic Law upon the Galatian converts (5:2; 2:16-17).

3. The heretics charged that Paul's gospel originated from man (1:10-21).

4. The apostates reverted to the observance of days, months, and years (4:9-10).

5. They charged that Paul preached circumcision (5:11).

6. They tended to use their new liberty for an occasion to the flesh (5:13).

7. They tried to circumcise Gentiles to avert persecution of themselves (6:12).

8. These heretics apparently thought that the circumcision of the Gentiles would bring glory to themselves (6:13). – Willis, p. xxi

Willis points out further that the Judaizers apparently bound, not the whole Old Testament, but only the parts they thought important (5:3,4; 6:13). This may have been motivated by the fact that Jews persecuted any Jew who associated with Gentiles. As a result, some

Jewish Christians insisted that Gentiles who were converted must also practice circumcision and follow the Old Law in order that the Jewish Christians, who associated with them, could avoid persecution.

But one consequence of this view was that the some Judaizers would require obedience, not to the whole Old Testament law, but only to enough of the law to avoid persecution. The result was that, like many people today, they observed only parts of the law, but ignored other parts.

It follows that the book still has great practical value today because many people still try to justify their practices by the Old Testament, yet they take only parts of it, not all of it. And the same immoral practices exist today that are rebuked in the book.

Outline of the book

I. The Source of the Gospel Paul Taught – Chapter 1,2
Chapter 1
The danger of other gospels (1:6-10)
Paul's conversion, revelations, and call to apostleship (1:11-24)
Chapter 2
The meeting at Jerusalem regarding circumcision (2:1-10)
Peter's refusal to eat with Gentiles (2:11-21)
II. Evidence that the New Testament Replaced the Old Testament – Chapter 3,4
Chapter 3
Justification by faith compared to the curse of the law (3:1-14)
The relationship between the law, the gospel, and the promise to Abraham (3:15-29)
Chapter 4
The status of the Galatians (4:1-20)
An allegory of the two covenants (4:21-31)
III. Applications of the Gospel – Chapter 5,6
Chapter 5
Consequences of heeding false teachers (5:1-15)
Works of the flesh vs. fruits of the Spirit (5:16-26)
Chapter 6
Reaping what we sow and concluding admonitions

Galatians 1

Chapter 1,2 – The Source of the
Gospel Paul Taught

1:1-5 - Introduction

1:1,2 – Paul wrote as an apostle whose authority came, not from men nor through man, but through Jesus and God the Father who raised Jesus from the dead. Along with all the brethren who were with him, he addressed the letter to the churches of Galatia.

In the introduction, Paul identifies himself as the inspired author and greets the brethren in the churches of Galatia (see introductory notes regarding these churches). Paul notes that there were brethren with him who also greeted those in the churches of Galatia. We are not told here who these other brethren were. Nor were these brethren co-authors of the epistle with Paul. However, they would have joined with him in greeting those in the churches of Galatia.

The fact that this epistle is addressed to churches (plural) in a region shows that it was intended to be circulated among the churches. God intended from the beginning that Paul's letters be used as authority for churches, not just private correspondence to certain individuals (compare 2 Peter 3:15,16).

Note that Paul immediately begins the epistle by affirming his apostleship. We will see that Paul's authority as an apostle and the inspired source of his teaching becomes a major issue in the letter. It is apparent that some objected to the doctrine Paul taught that the Old Testament law had been removed and Gentiles could become Christians without obeying the Old Law.

In order to defend their viewpoint, these Judaizing teachers had to deny the source of Paul's teaching. They had to undermine his authority as an apostle and the inspiration of his teaching. So Paul begins immediately by affirming and defending his apostleship thereby defending the authority of his teaching.

Historical facts regarding Paul

Consider a few facts we know about this man:

* He was present at Stephen's death (Acts 7).

* Before his conversion he had persecuted the church (compare 1 Timothy 1:12ff; Acts 8,9).

* He was converted as a result of Jesus' appearance to him on the road to Damascus. Ananias was sent to baptize him (Acts 9,22,26).

* He then preached in Damascus, then in Jerusalem, and later went on three preaching trips, preaching even in Rome (Acts 9-26).

* He especially preached to Gentiles and worked to prove that they need not be circumcised and obey the Old Testament to be saved (Acts 15; Galatians, Romans)

* He wrote more New Testament books than any other man.

Qualifications of apostles

Paul claims that he was an apostle, and that his apostleship did not originate with man. No man nor any body of men had appointed him to his position, nor had he been appointed by anyone acting on behalf of any body of men. He was appointed personally and directly by Jesus Himself and by God who raised Jesus from the dead (compare verses 11,12).

Note that this statement claims Deity for Jesus. Paul expressly denied that he was appointed an apostle by **man**, yet he was appointed by **Jesus** and God the Father. Therefore, Jesus cannot be a mere man. Instead, Jesus is classed with the Father: Paul was appointed by Jesus and the Father. If Jesus had been a mere man, not Deity, Paul's statement would have been a falsehood. See also verse 11.

The word "apostle" simply means one who is sent on a mission. It is similar to the concept of an ambassador or an official representative who has been assigned to act on behalf of someone else. It can have different significance, even in the Scriptures, depending on who does the sending and what the mission was (see notes on verse 19).

But Paul was not an apostle in just some general sense. He emphasizes that the one who chose him to be an ambassador and apostle was Jesus Himself. This was not simply some mission assigned by men. He was claiming to be an official representative specifically chosen by Jesus Christ even as were the other twelve apostles. In so saying, Paul was directly confronting the false views of the Judaizers who sought to belittle his authority.

True apostles of Jesus had the following characteristics or qualifications:

1) Apostles had to be chosen by Jesus' Himself.

He is the one who "sent" them on the mission, authorizing their work. They did not assume the office by their own choice, nor were they chosen by majority vote or political maneuvering. There was always clear evidence that Jesus Himself had personally chosen each individual who received the office. See Luke 6:12-16; Acts 1:24-26; 26:16; Galatians 1:1.

2) Jesus then sent the Holy Spirit to directly guide the apostles as they preached the gospel and bore their testimony (Acts 1:8).

This direct guidance came when the apostles received Holy Spirit baptism on Pentecost (Acts 2). (John 16:13; 14:26; 1 Corinthians 2:10-16; 14:37; Ephesians 3:3-5; Matthew 10:19,20)

3) This baptism also gave them the power to do miraculous signs to confirm that their testimony really was from God.

These constituted the "signs of an apostle" (2 Corinthians 12:11,12). (Acts 14:3; 2:43; 3:1-10; 5:12-16; 9:32-42; Mark 16:17-20; Hebrews 2:3,4)

4) Apostles could lay hands on other people and give them miraculous powers.

But those on whom they laid hands could not in turn pass the powers on to others – Acts 8:14-24; 19:1-7; Romans 1:8-11; 2 Timothy 1:6.

5) Specifically, an apostle had to be an eyewitness of Christ after His resurrection, so that he could testify that he had personally seen Jesus alive after He had died.

The apostles had been chosen personally by Jesus to serve as witnesses of His work, especially of the fact that He had been raised from the dead (see Acts 1:21,22; compare 1 Corinthians 15:4-8; 9:1; Luke 24:36-48; John 15:26,27; 19:35; Acts 1:8; 2:32; 3:15; 4:33; 5:32; 10:39-42; 13:31; 1 John 1:1-4).

Note that, since no men today can have these qualifications, we can have no apostles living on earth in the church today. This destroys the concept of the Catholic Pope and Mormon apostles as successors to the apostles.

Evidence that Paul was an apostle

Some Judaizers in the first century and some people today have doubted whether or not Paul was a true apostle. That Paul, however, was an apostle is clear because:

* He claimed it (verse 1).

* He spoke by direct guidance of the Holy Spirit – 1 Corinthians 14:37; 2:10-16; Ephesians 3:3-5; 2 Corinthians 12:7-10; etc.

* His claim to apostleship was confirmed by miracles, the signs of an apostle (2 Corinthians 12:12; Acts 14:3,8-18; 13:6-12; 19:8-20; etc.)

* He was an eyewitness of the resurrected Christ, (Acts 9:1-18; 22:14,15; 26:16; 1 Corinthians 15:1-8; 9:1). Note that Paul was an eyewitness "born out of due time" (1 Corinthians 15:8,9). Nevertheless,

he did see Jesus after His resurrection and could serve in that primary role of an apostle.

* He could lay hands on others to give them miraculous powers – Acts 19:1-7; Romans 1:8-11; 2 Timothy 1:6.

* Jesus chose him and commanded him to be a witness of His resurrection (Acts 26:13-19).

> "Apostle" (αποστολος) – "1. a delegate, messenger, one sent forth with orders ... 2. Specially applied to the twelve disciples whom Christ selected, out of the multitude of his adherents, to be his constant companions and the heralds to proclaim to men the kingdom of God ... With these apostles Paul claimed equality ... 3. In a broader sense the name is transferred to other eminent Christian teachers ..." – Grimm-Wilke-Thayer.

1:3-5 – Paul asked for grace and peace to the Galatians from God the Father and the Lord Jesus Christ, who gave Himself for our sins to deliver us from this present evil world according to the will of God the Father, to whom be the glory forever and ever.

Paul then, as he customarily did in his epistles, called for the grace (unmerited favor) and peace from God and Jesus be upon them. He sought that they would have God's favor and a peaceful, harmonious relationship with God. The grace of God through the sacrifice of Jesus will become a major theme of this letter. However, we will see that he was concerned that they had been led astray from this relationship that he desired for them to have.

He plainly states that Jesus gave Himself for our sins to deliver us from the wickedness of society. This was according to the will of God. Once again Paul here immediately enters into a primary point of contention in the letter. One of the main issues he will discuss is the question of whether or not Jesus' death according to the gospel is adequate to save, or whether we also need the requirements of the old law. So, at the very outset Paul affirms that the sacrifice of Christ occurred according to the will of God and is adequate to deliver us from sin. The application will be that we do not need the Old Law.

> "Now Christ by atoning for our transgressions not only gave us life but also made us his own, so that we might be called children of God, made so through faith. What a great error it is, therefore, to go under the law again after receiving grace." – Ambrosiaster (*Ancient Christian Commentary*)

For other passages regarding Jesus' sacrifice for our sins, see: Matthew 26:28; 20:28; Ephesians 1:7; 1 Peter 1:18,19; 2:24; Hebrews 2:9; Revelation 1:5; 5:9; 1 Timothy 2:4-6; Isaiah 53:5-9; 1 Corinthians 15:3; John 1:29; Hebrews 9:24-28; 10:9-13; 13:20,21; Romans 5:6-11; 2 Corinthians 5:14,15.

Notice that Jesus came to save us from this present evil age. The philosophies that are popularly accepted in society tend to change with time, yet in every age sin is common. Beliefs and ideas that are in vogue now may not have been accepted at all in some past ages and may come to be rejected in future ages. Even in my lifetime society has come to accept practices such as abortion, no-fault divorce, legalized gambling, and homosexuality including homosexual marriage. None of this was generally accepted in my youth, and much of it was illegal. What people accept may change with time, but Jesus came to deliver us from all of this. His word stands the same throughout time and is the absolute standard by which Christians determine what they believe and accept.

Paul then concludes that glory belongs to God forever because of His goodness and grace. It is interesting that Paul adds an "Amen" this early in the letter. He appears to want from the very outset to affirm and reemphasize that God has made the plan for our salvation through Jesus Christ. The application will be once again that the Old Law is not the means of forgiveness.

Once again notice that Paul's description of Jesus necessarily implies that Jesus possesses Deity. Not only did Jesus give the sacrifice for our sins, but the passage says that grace comes to us from God the Father and Jesus Christ. But no mere human could properly be said to be the source of grace along with the Father. This can be true of Jesus only if He possesses true Deity.

1:6-10 - The Danger of Other Gospels

1:6,7 – Paul marveled that they were removing themselves so quickly from the One who called them in the grace of Christ unto a different gospel, which is not another gospel but some were troubling them by perverting the gospel of Christ.

Paul immediately expresses his concern for the quickness and apparent ease with which the Galatians had been led from the true gospel. They had departed so quickly that he marveled. We all know that people can leave the truth, but we are amazed when it happens so quickly with some people.

> "The one who is carried away after a long time is worthy of blame, but the one who falls at the first attack and in the initial skirmish has furnished an example of the greatest weakness. And with this he charges them also, saying 'What is this, that those who deceive you do not even need time, but the first assault suffices to rout and capture you?'" – Chrysostom (*Ancient Christian Commentary*)

The danger of apostasy

"Turning away" (NKJV) is translated "removing" (ASV, KJV), "deserting" (NASB, ESV). It carries the idea of a turncoat or an apostate. See Acts 7:16; Hebrews 7:12; 11:12; Jude 4.

By accepting a different gospel, they were turning away from the One who called them in grace. God (Deity) is viewed in the Scriptures as the ultimate source of our calling. He calls us through the gospel (2 Thessalonians 2:14). Those who heed the call are His people and are often referred to in relationship to their calling – Ephesians 1:18; 4:4; Philippians 3:14; 2 Timothy 1:9; Hebrews 3:1. To turn away from the doctrine God teaches is to turn away from God.

People who accept a different gospel generally believe that they are still in God's favor. Even if they realize that they have changed their beliefs, Satan deceives them into thinking that they have simply accepted a new truth but have not departed from their relationship with God. Sometimes people who stand for the truth will even minimize the significance of error by saying that people have "left the church." Paul makes clear that those who accept a different gospel have departed from the **Lord**, and that is the primary concern.

We are called in grace in the sense that, only by the gospel can we receive grace to forgive our sins. Without Jesus' sacrifice (verse 4), there is no forgiveness. The gospel is a message of grace. This grace will be emphasized throughout the book, in contrast to the law which required sinless law keeping in order for the sinner to be justified before God under the law itself.

Consider some important consequences. First, a person can be in the grace of God, and therefore truly saved, and yet depart from the One who called him in grace. If he departs, is he still saved and destined for eternal life? Clearly not. So one who was truly in God's grace can so fall from grace as to be lost. "Once saved, always saved" is a false doctrine, clearly refuted in this epistle (compare notes on 5:4).

Further, if one follows a different gospel, he has departed from God. One need not renounce his faith in God or in Jesus to depart from God. Specifically, the error in this book was committed by people who still claimed to believe Jesus was the Son of God who died as the sacrifice for sins and rose again. They most likely still believed He is the head of the church, etc., and they still believed in baptism (immersion) for remission of sins. Yet they are clearly stated to be anathema (unless they repent) because they followed a different teaching. Specifically, they believed one must also be circumcised and keep Old Testament laws. These facts reveal the error of many who want to boil the list of "essential beliefs" down to a very few basics.

A different gospel or another gospel?

Verse 6 and verse 7 use contrasting terms. The English translations often try to convey the difference, but it is stronger in Greek than in many English translations.

The Galatians were turning to a "different" gospel, but it was not really "another" gospel. "Different" (ʽετερος) means something different in kind, quality, or character from the thing to which it is compared. "Another" (αλλος) means simply one more of the same or similar nature.

So Paul is saying the Galatians were turning to a gospel different in nature from the one he taught them, but it was not another one just as good as the one he taught. I may have a car, and I may buy "another" car – one that is basically similar in nature and can do the same job. But a house is not "another" car; it is "different." It will not do the same job.

The gospel means good news. But the gospel being taught by the Judaizers could not save because it depended on perfect law keeping, which no one but Jesus has ever accomplished. This was not good news at all but bad news. So the gospel they were following was not really a gospel in nature. It was not just another one as good as what Paul taught, because it would not do the same job. It could not save. To change the gospel makes it worthless.

"Unto a gospel which differs so radically from that which I preached to you that it is not another gospel, for it is not a gospel at all." – Hogg and Vine

So, those who taught this different gospel were causing "trouble" for the Galatians (disturbing, disquieting, agitating them). Those who teach differently from what God has revealed in His word cause trouble among God's people. This is the same word used to describe the Judaizers in the letter from the Jerusalem meeting in Acts 15:24. Like Ahab, they will often accuse those who oppose their errors as being the ones who are causing the trouble (1 Kings 18:17). But those who truly understand God's word will recognize that trouble is caused by those who teach error, not those who resist it.

They had "perverted" the gospel or "distorted" it (NASB, ESV). They had not turned it into something just a little different, but yet just as good as the original. They had changed it to something of a different character so that it had become worthless.

> "Pervert" (μεταστρεφω) – "'to transform into something of an opposite character' (meta, signifying 'a change,' and strepho,) as the Judaizers sought to 'pervert the gospel of Christ,' Galatians 1:7; cp. 'the sun shall be turned into darkness,' Acts 2:20; laughter into mourning and joy to heaviness, James 4:9." –Vine

1:8,9 – Though we or an angel from heaven or any man preach any other gospel than what we have preached, let him be accursed.

No man may preach differently from the revealed gospel.

Having expressed his concern for the fact the Galatians were accepting another gospel, Paul flatly states the consequence to anyone who would teach such a doctrine: he is accursed of God. First Paul states this consequence for himself, his associates, or even an angel from heaven who should teach such a different gospel. Then to emphasize the point, he repeats it regarding anyone who would teach a different gospel. The repetition shows how important this point is. (Hogg and Vine point out that the original language implies that Paul's reference in verse 9 to what he said before refers, not to verse 8, but to his past teaching to the Galatians.)

It is unlikely, of course, that Paul or an angel from heaven would preach another gospel (verse 8). Paul's point is that, even should someone of such high authority do such teaching, Christians should still reject their message. If so, it necessarily follows that **no one** has the right to teach a different gospel. Verse 9, however, may more directly refer to those who even at that time were teaching a different gospel.

This shows clearly that the gospel taught by Paul and other inspired men cannot be changed with God's approval, not even by those who first revealed it. The reason this is so is that the message was not originated by man to begin with (verses 11,12), therefore men cannot change it. The message came from Jesus; the men simply delivered it. To change it would be for man to take to himself the position of Deity. This is clearly forbidden. Man is not wise enough to alter or improve on God's revelation.

Yet men continually seek to do things different from what God said. Some overtly claim to have a new revelation. Some even claim it came from an angel (such as the Book of Mormon). Even so we must reject it if it differs from the gospel.

Others claim to follow the gospel, but they practice things not found in the gospel. This is likewise a violation of the passage. When a man claims God will accept a practice which is nowhere found in God's word, he has changed the message just as surely as if he claims that people do not have to do something the message instructs us to do. Whether more or less, either is a different gospel.

Notice that this must be applied regardless of who the individual is who teaches the error: any man, even an apostle or an angel. Truth must be applied without partiality or favoritism. Far too often people accept teaching because of their loyalty to a man when they might never accept that teaching from someone else. It may be a favorite preacher, perhaps the preacher who converted them, or it may be a family member or someone else they highly respect. But no matter who it is, one who teaches a different gospel is accursed, and we must have the honesty to recognize so.

No gospel/doctrine distinction

Note that "gospel" refers to the whole message of the New Testament. Some people claim that the gospel is just certain basic, fundamental truths – usually they say it refers to the basic principles by which one receives forgiveness and becomes a follower of Jesus Christ. This, they say, must be taught and believed properly. But then they say that doctrine refers to the teachings about how to live after one is forgiven of sins. We are then told that, when different people or different churches teach different doctrine, this does not necessarily lead to God's displeasure and so should not lead to a break of fellowship.

However, the New Testament makes no such distinction between gospel and doctrine. Both terms refer to all that God teaches in His word in the New Testament for us to follow, whether in order to become children of God or in order to live faithful lives as children of God (see 1 Timothy 1:8-11). Furthermore, many passages teach that we must follow truly the gospel and other passages teach we must follow truly the doctrine. Our goal must be to practice correctly all that God's word instructs us to do without change. See the Scripture references listed below.

So, this passage and many others like it condemn whole hosts of denominational practices that please the people who practice them, but which are nowhere found in the Bible. Those who seek to please God must make sure that their practices fit what is revealed in the word of God. It is not enough to claim that no Scripture directly forbids a practice. Rather, we must demonstrate that a practice does fit the Scriptures, and if we can find no such evidence, we should reject the practice or stand in danger of God's disapproval.

Note how strongly Paul, from the very outset, attacks the views of the Judaizers. He has said that those who teach such views are accursed (verses 8,9), and those who follow the views are departing from Christ (verses 6,7). Both the teachers and the followers are displeasing God. This is why Paul is so concerned. Followers cannot simply lay blame on the teachers. They too are responsible before God if they accept and follow error.

Many passages forbid men to change the message God has revealed or to practice anything different from it.

Other Passages about the Dangers of Changing God's Word

Matthew 15:9 – And in vain they worship Me, Teaching as doctrines the commandments of men.

Matthew 15:13 – ...Every plant which My heavenly Father has not planted will be uprooted.

2 John 1:9-11 – Whoever transgresses and does not abide in the doctrine of Christ does not have God. He who abides in the doctrine of Christ has both the Father and the Son. If anyone comes to you and does not bring this doctrine, do not receive him into your house nor greet him; for he who greets him shares in his evil deeds.

Colossians 3:17 – And whatever you do in word or deed, do all in the name of the Lord Jesus, giving thanks to God the Father through Him.

Jeremiah 10:23 – O LORD, I know the way of man is not in himself; It is not in man who walks to direct his own steps.

Proverbs 14:12 – There is a way that seems right to a man, but its end is the way of death.

Proverbs 3:5,6 – Trust in the LORD with all your heart, And lean not on your own understanding; In all your ways acknowledge Him, And He shall direct your paths.

Revelation 22:18,19 – For I testify to everyone who hears the words of the prophecy of this book: If anyone adds to these things, God will add to him the plagues that are written in this book; and if anyone takes away from the words of the book of this prophecy, God shall take away his part from the Book of Life, from the holy city, and from the things which are written in this book.

1 Timothy 1:3 – ... charge some that they teach no other doctrine

2 Timothy 1:13 – Hold fast the pattern of sound words which you have heard from me, in faith and love which are in Christ Jesus.

"Accursed" (αναθεμα) – "...1 that which is dedicated as a votive offering, *a votive offering* set up in a temple ... 2 that which has been cursed, *cursed, accursed* ... 3 the content that is expressed in a curse, *a curse...*" – Bauer-Danker-Arndt-Gingrich.

1:10 – Paul was seeking the favor of God, not man. He was not striving to please men; for if he were still pleasing men, he would not be a servant of Christ.

Having powerfully stated the danger of other gospels, Paul then affirmed his determination to please God and not men. The rest of us should, of course, have the same commitment.

Paul asked whether he was trying to persuade men or God (NKJV). Other translations say, "Am I now seeking the favor of men, or of God?" (ASV, NASB) or the "approval" of men (ESV). This seems to me to express the meaning better in light of the rest of the verse, where Paul clearly states he was not seeking to please men but God. He would not be a servant of Christ if he was pleasing men.

Many Scriptures warn us that our primary concern should be to please God, rather than pleasing men. There is great danger in allowing ourselves to be influenced by the desires of other people when those desires differ from the will of God. See John 12:42,43; 5:44; Matthew 6:1-18; 10:34-37; 23:5; 2 Corinthians 10:12,18; 1 Thessalonians 2:4; Acts 4:19; 5:29.

This does not mean it is always wrong to do what pleases ourselves or others. In fact, in 1 Corinthians 9:19-23 Paul expressly stated that he tried to please men whenever it would help him influence them with the gospel. The point is that the will of men must never take priority over the will of God. If it does, then men become our master instead of God, and we cease to be servants of God. Whenever God's will conflicts with man's will, as it often does, we must be sure that God's will prevails.

Why does Paul make this point here? Evidently either some were accusing him of seeking to please men, or else he believed the Galatians were in danger of seeking to please men. It is possible that they were following this different gospel (verses 6-9) in order to please the Judaizers and perhaps other family members.

Judaism, like a number of other religions, involves strong family traditional ties. That is, the religion is a strong tie within the family so there are strong pressures for people to maintain the family religion. If people leave the family religion, they are viewed as rejecting the family, and the family brings strong pressures upon them. This makes it very difficult for people to leave the family religion. Other verses in the book imply this problem (see 2:11-14; 6:12). The book of Hebrews discusses this problem at great length.

Paul understood this problem because he had left the Jewish religion to become a Christian, and so had many other Christians. So he says, that if he was still pleasing men, he would never have become a follower of Jesus Christ. Pleasing men would have led him to remain in the Jewish religion. But he left that religion because he realized that the gospel was true and that in fact it was a fulfillment of what God had revealed in the Old Testament.

1:11-24 - Paul's Conversion, Revelations, and Call to Apostleship

1:11,12 – Paul made known that the gospel that he preached was not after man. He did not receive it from man nor was he taught it from man, but he received it through revelation from Jesus Christ.

The doctrine of direct inspiration

Having stated that people must not follow any other gospel, Paul then begins a lengthy defense of the gospel in contrast to following the law of Moses. He begins by stating the source of the gospel he preached. He claimed that it did not come from man, it was not according to man, nor had any human taught it to him. Rather, it had been revealed to him directly by Jesus Christ.

This clearly states the Bible concept of direct revelation, and affirms that Paul had this ability as an apostle (see verse 1). Those of us, who do not have the miraculous gift of direct revelation or prophecy, must receive the message of the gospel by being taught it from other men. Today, in particular, it comes to us through the inspired record of Scripture, which in turn was written by other men. In contrast to that, Paul affirms that he had received the message directly from Jesus Christ, not from men or having been taught it.

It appears that, as in 2 Corinthians, the Judaizers were attacking Paul's apostleship and denying that his revelation was truly from God. Paul answered by stating that his teaching did not consist of ideas originated by himself or any other human. Man did not originate it, made did not teach it to him, and the ideas did not harmonize with man's way of thinking.

Direct inspiration involved God, through the Holy Spirit, directly revealing His will to chosen spokesmen. These people did not receive their message from other men, directly or indirectly. Rather, the message came to them directly from God, so they were enabled to speak the message to others.

In this sense, the role of the inspired apostles and prophets is somewhat similar to that of a mailman or an ambassador. The mailman does not write the mail. He simply delivers it. The message contained is not his message, so he has no right to change it. The same is true for an ambassador who speaks as an official spokesman for a nation or government. He does not make the rules or decisions, so he has no right to change the message given him. He simply delivers the message determined by those in authority.

Paul's statement here serves as an important expression of the true Biblical concept of direct revelation from God through inspired men.

Other Passages Expressing the Concept of Revelation

1 Corinthians 14:37 – If anyone thinks himself to be a prophet or spiritual, let him acknowledge that the things which I write to you are the commandments of the Lord.

1 Corinthians 2:10-13 – But God has revealed them to us through His Spirit. For the Spirit searches all things, yes, the deep things of God. For what man knows the things of a man except the spirit of the man which is in him? Even so no one knows the things of God except the Spirit of God. Now we have received, not the spirit of the world, but the Spirit who is from God, that we might know the things that have been freely given to us by God. These things we also speak, not in

---

words which man's wisdom teaches but which the Holy Spirit teaches, comparing spiritual things with spiritual.

Ephesians 3:3-5 – how that by revelation He made known to me the mystery (as I have briefly written already, by which, when you read, you may understand my knowledge in the mystery of Christ), which in other ages was not made known to the sons of men, as it has now been revealed by the Spirit to His holy apostles and prophets

John 16:13 – However, when He, the Spirit of truth, has come, He will guide you into all truth; for He will not speak on His own authority, but whatever He hears He will speak; and He will tell you things to come.

Matthew 10:19,20 – But when they deliver you up, do not worry about how or what you should speak. For it will be given to you in that hour what you should speak; for it is not you who speak, but the Spirit of your Father who speaks in you.

2 Peter 1:20,21 – knowing this first, that no prophecy of Scripture is of any private interpretation, for prophecy never came by the will of man, but holy men of God spoke as they were moved by the Holy Spirit.

1 Thessalonians 2:13 – For this reason we also thank God without ceasing, because when you received the word of God which you heard from us, you welcomed it not as the word of men, but as it is in truth, the word of God, which also effectively works in you who believe.

2 Timothy 3:16,17 – All Scripture is given by inspiration of God, and is profitable for doctrine, for reproof, for correction, for instruction in righteousness, that the man of God may be complete, thoroughly equipped for every good work.

Luke 10:16 – He who hears you hears Me, he who rejects you rejects Me, and he who rejects Me rejects Him who sent Me.

Consequences of the doctrine

The application of Paul's statement is that he did not make up the message that he was revealing. Specifically, he did not invent the doctrine he taught about the Old Testament law. He did not even receive it by teaching given him from other inspired men. He received it directly from Jesus Christ by revelation.

If the message had been human in origin, then Paul or others might think they had the right to change it. But no one has that right, because the message originated from God (verses 8,9). Or if the message was human in origin, then people might believe they had the right to reject it. If it was simply man's wisdom, then another man might have a different view based on wisdom just as good or greater. But if the message is from God, then no man has the right to reject it because God's revelation is infallible.

Those who do not possess the gift of direct revelation, including all of us today, simply receive the message revealed by these inspired men.

Commentary on Galatians

They served as Divinely guided intermediaries who spoke (wrote) the message to us. But they themselves had no intermediaries between them and Deity. This being true, no human has any right to change the message (verses 8,9). Nor do we have the right to reject it. It is not human in origin, therefore man must not change it nor reject it.

Again note the contrast between Jesus and men. If Jesus was a mere man, then the gospel would have been given to Paul by man. But it did not come from man but from Jesus. So, Jesus is Deity, not human (see verse 1).

"Therefore he shows plainly that Jesus was not a [mere] man; and if he is not a man then without doubt he is God." Pamphilus (*Ancient Christian Commentary*)

> "Revelation" (αποκαλυψις) – "1 making fully known, *revelation, disclosure* a of the revelation of truth ... b of revelations of a particular kind, through visions, etc. ...c of the disclosure of secrets belonging to the last days ... 2 as part of a book title Revelation ..." – Bauer-Danker-Arndt-Gingrich.

1:13,14 – They had heard of Paul's former manner of life, how he persecuted the church and advanced in the Jews' religion beyond many countrymen of his age, because he was very zealous for the traditions of the fathers.

Paul has stated his claim, that his message came to him directly from God. He then proceeds to give the history of his conversion. The purpose was to show that he had no motive to teach what He did except that God had revealed it, and that he was teaching these truths long before any human could have given him the message.

He began by recalling his life before he became a Christian, when he was still involved in Judaism. This showed the Judaizers that he knew and could identify with their views – he once held those views and zealously proclaimed them. He went to the extent even of persecuting the church of Jesus and trying to destroy it because Christians had left Judaism. See Acts 8:3; 9:1,13,21; 22:4,19; 26:10ff; 1 Corinthians 15:9; Philippians 3:6; 1 Timothy 1:13; etc.

Paul's convictions led him to surpass other contemporary Jews. He was so zealous he achieved much more in the cause than did others. The history recorded in the book of Acts confirms these claims.

Note that Paul now realized that he had been zealous, not for the truth, but for the traditions of the fathers. Tradition is that which has been handed down to us. The source from which it is handed down determines whether or not it is valid and true. Divine traditions must be followed, but human traditions must not be viewed as authority. They can be accepted only as they agree with God's word. Yet Jews considered them to be authority and bound them on others. (See 1 Corinthians 11:1,2; 2 Thessalonians 2:15; 3:6; Mark 7:1-13; Matthew 15:1-14; Colossians 2:8; 1 Peter 1:18,19; Galatians 1:14.)

These facts about Paul's past were so widely known that he was convinced the Galatians knew about them.

Paul's intent was to confirm that his revelations about Judaism were not from men but from God. Had he continued seeking to please men, he would still be a Jew and would never have become a servant of Jesus (verse 10). He started out as a Jew and would have had no reason to leave it had he not been convinced that God willed for him to change. Even after conversion, he would have been sympathetic to Jewish beliefs. He would have been quite open to the Judaizers' view that the law should still be bound on Christians. What was it that convinced him to change? The only explanation is that God revealed it to him, as Paul claimed (verses 11,12).

1:15-17 – When God was pleased to separate Paul from his mother's womb, to call him by grace and reveal Jesus to him so that he might preach among the Gentiles, Paul did not confer with flesh and blood nor did he go to the apostles in Jerusalem but went to Arabia and then returned to Damascus.

God revealed His Son.

Paul then affirmed that God chose him, by His grace, to reveal the message of Jesus to him. This was the message that he preached (verses 8-12). This revealing began, of course, on that Damascus road when Jesus appeared to Saul to convince him Jesus was alive and to qualify Saul to become an apostle (see Acts 9,22,26; 1 Corinthians 9:1; 15:1-8). The events listed here in Galatians 1 must be compared to those accounts and must harmonize with them.

Note that here again Paul is claiming the qualifications of an apostle. He is reminding them that Jesus did appear to him and that God had chosen him for this office – both of which were qualifications of an apostle – see notes on verse 1.

Paul claims that this separation was from his mother's womb. Similar statements are made about other prophets (Jeremiah 1:5; Luke 1; Isaiah 49:1), the idea being that God had a plan for such men even before they were born. This could mean simply that God foreknew the use He could make of Paul, or that God had a will for Paul all along. In any case, Paul is clearly claiming that he was not an apostle by his own choice or human ambition but by God's direct choice.

This does not mean Paul lost his free moral agency. He could have rejected God's call, as had Israel (Romans 11:11,12) and Jonah. Remember, especially, that this is a call to a special office. There is no Bible evidence that God chooses certain individuals to be saved or lost before they are born. And the idea that such a choice is unconditional, or that men have no power to resist it, is an idea quite contrary to Scripture.

Paul was then responsible to preach the gospel.

Paul stated that Jesus' intent in calling him was so he would preach the message of Jesus. He then proceeds to give specifics of how that message was given him, confirming that it came, not from men, but directly from Jesus (verses 11,12). Note that the purpose of God was especially (though not exclusively) that he should preach to Gentiles. This is confirmed in Acts 9:15; 22:21; Galatians 2:8.

Having seen Jesus and received His calling as an apostle, Paul did not confer with flesh and blood (i.e., with other men). The point is that his doctrine did not come from any man (verses 11,12). The Lord revealed it directly to Paul, so he did not need any man's confirmation of the truth of it.

Paul did not even, at that time, go up to Jerusalem to visit the apostles there. Rather, he went into Arabia and returned to Damascus. Where he went in Arabia is not stated, nor are we told exactly why. Acts does not record the event. The point here is simply that he did not meet any apostle or inspired man who taught him or gave him his message of the gospel. It came directly from Jesus (perhaps including revelations received in Arabia, though this is not stated).

Let us compare this account to the conversion of Paul in Acts 9. In 9:18 he was baptized. After that he stayed "certain days" with the disciples in Damascus (verse 19). How long is not stated. But "straightway" or "immediately" (NKJV) he preached Jesus in the synagogues (this seems to mean "straightway" after the "certain days," but could mean immediately after his conversion). He then preached "many days" (verses 22,23) but was finally compelled to leave because of Jewish persecution.

The trip to Arabia could have come as an interruption during the "certain days" he was with the disciples in Damascus. Or it could have come as an interruption of the period of "many days" when he was preaching in the synagogue. We are not told. If this were important, the Scriptures would tell us. The point that is important is that Paul did not receive his doctrine from other men.

Note that preaching the message about Jesus is here referred to as preaching **Him.** This is true because the gospel message focuses on Jesus. The foundation of the message rests on who Jesus is (compare 1 Corinthians 15:1-3).

However, some become confused and think this means that the message we preach should consist only of things about Jesus and who He is and what He did, or at least that this is all that really matters. They tell us that specifics about how we ought to live do not really matter as long as we believe who Jesus is.

The truth, however, is that preaching Jesus includes preaching the will of Jesus for our lives as well as preaching who Jesus is. In Acts 8:5-12 Philip preached Jesus in Samaria. The result was that people were baptized, so preaching Jesus includes preaching the need for baptism. Furthermore, in preaching Jesus, Philip preached about the kingdom, which is the church. So preaching Jesus includes preaching what Jesus instructs us to do.

1:18-20 – Three years later Paul did go up to Jerusalem to visit Peter and stayed with him fifteen days. Even then, however, he did not see any other apostle except James the Lord's brother. Paul affirms before God regarding these things that he was not lying.

Paul's first trip to Jerusalem

Paul then describes the first time he ever met an apostle. This came after three years – presumably three years after his conversion. He then went up to Jerusalem, where he met Peter and stayed fifteen days with him.

This must surely refer to the trip to Jerusalem recorded in Acts 9:26-30, when Paul left Damascus because of persecution. The Acts 9 trip could not have occurred before the event Paul describes here, since Paul says that, when he made the trip referred to here, the church did not know him. Besides Paul's whole point here is that this is the first time he met an apostle. The main point is that Paul had known and preached the gospel as an apostle of Jesus Christ for three whole years before he ever met any other apostle. His message did not come from men.

Acts 9 shows that, on this trip to Jerusalem, the church at first did not accept Paul because they doubted his conversion. But Barnabas took Paul to the apostles and explained about his conversion. Then the church accepted Paul and he was working among them. It was apparently after this explanation by Barnabas that Peter let Paul stay 15 days with him. Exactly how long Paul was then in Jerusalem is not clear, but, of the time he was there, he spent 15 days with Peter. However, he soon had to leave because of persecution again. See also Acts 22:17-21.

James the Lord's brother

Perhaps the most difficult point of all to explain is the reference to James, the Lord's brother. Paul says he saw none of the other apostles except James the Lord's brother. This might seem to imply that Jesus had a brother named James who was an apostle. This would agree with the fact Paul took Barnabas to the "apostles" (Acts 9:27).

Jesus did have a brother named James (Mark 6:3). He is apparently referred to in Acts 12:17; 15:13; 21:18; 1 Corinthians 15:7; Galatians 2:9,12; James 1:1 (?). The problem is that he does not appear to have been an apostle. There was an apostle named apostle James, but he was the son of Alpheus (Acts 1:13). This man might have been a

Commentary on Galatians

cousin to Jesus, but not a brother. So we still do not have a "brother" of Jesus who was an apostle.

Some claim "brother" here means cousin, but that makes little sense. Jesus definitely did have a brother in the flesh named James (Mark 6:3). This man was Jesus' "brother" just like the other men named in that passage, and just like certain women were his "sisters," and Jesus was Mary's "son" (compare Matthew 12:46ff). But that James was not an apostle.

Since Jesus did have a brother named James, why would Paul refer to another James as his brother, when he was really only a cousin? It makes no sense, and such language is simply nowhere else used in the New Testament. Incidentally, the above reasoning clearly proves Jesus had brothers and sisters in the flesh, so Mary was not a perpetual virgin, as Catholicism claims.

"The theory that James and his brothers were really cousins of the Lord ... is without adequate support in Scripture." – Hogg and Vine.

But if this James is Jesus' literal brother, then he was not an apostle in the sense Peter was (verse 17). So, some commentators claim that the language may not mean that James was an apostle. Rather, Paul is saying that he did not see any other apostle, except he did see James the Lord's brother. A similar use of "except" occurs in Luke 4:25-27 – an exception to one part of what was previously stated, but not to all of it. In that case, James was not an apostle, but Paul did see him. And since this James was clearly very prominent, Paul simply wanted to make sure he mentions that he did see James.

If that explanation is valid, then Paul is clearly claiming that he saw only *one* true apostle – Peter. That is fine, except how do we then explain Acts 9:27, which says Barnabas took Paul to see the apostles (plural)? Hogg and Vine offer one explanation, which is that Peter acted as representative of the apostles. The others may have been out of town at the time, but by introducing Paul to Peter, Paul was in effect being introduced to the apostles, Peter acting on their behalf.

Another explanation is that, either in the Acts account or else here in Galatians 1, "apostle" is being used in a more general sense, not meaning those few men especially chosen as witnesses (as discussed in verse 1 above). Rather, the word in one place (or both) must be simply refer to messengers of the churches (compare Acts 14:14; Philippians 2:25; 2 Corinthians 8:23). Or perhaps it is used simply as designating one with a special place of influence, like an apostle. Perhaps Acts 9 uses the word generally to include Peter and other leading men, without bothering to distinguish the sense in which they were apostles. Another reason for specifically mentioning James is that he took a leading role in the meeting Paul will mention in chapter 2 and mentioned in Acts 15.

In any case, Paul clearly states that he is speaking the truth before God, not lying. Doubtless there were others living who could confirm his story, so aside from his inspiration, we must conclude his account is accurate. There must be some such explanation as that given above, though I am not sure what exact explanation is correct.

1:21-24 – Then Paul came to the area of Syria and Cilicia but was still unknown by face to the churches in Judea. They had simply heard that the one who had been persecuting the church was now preaching the faith of which he had previously made havoc, so they gave glory to God.

After this visit in Jerusalem, Paul went to Syria and Cilicia. This is also described in Acts 9 and 11. In Acts 9:30, because of persecution from the Jews, the church at Jerusalem sent Saul to Tarsus, which is in Cilicia (see **map**). In Acts 11:25,26, Barnabas was preaching in Antioch of Syria, and went to Tarsus to bring Paul back to work with him in Syria.

So limited was his contact in Jerusalem that Paul was unknown by face to the churches of Judea. There were a number of churches in the region of Judea. Of course, some people in the church in Jerusalem would have known Paul by face, even if he stayed only 15 days. But he would not have had time to become known to other churches in the area or even to some members in the church in Jerusalem.

But the people did hear about him that he was preaching the gospel, which he had once been trying to destroy. This led them to glorify God because of Paul's work. This shows that, though they did not know Paul well personally, they surely were not in opposition to his conversion and work. On the contrary, they glorified God for it. This also would confirm that Paul's preaching and work had been accepted as valid by other Christians in Judea, almost all of whom would have been Jewish in their background. Like the leaders in the church in Jerusalem, these Jewish Christians approved of Paul's work in contrast to the Judaizers who rejected it.

So, Paul's point here is that his contact with any apostle or other leaders of influence was very limited. He spent some time with Peter and with James, the Lord's brother, but this was only after he had been a Christian for three years and had been preaching the gospel. And even then the contact was very limited.

All this is intended to show that Paul's message was inspired by God and revealed directly to him. He did not get it from others (verses 11,12). This fact had special application to Paul's teaching about the Old Testament law and the fact that it had been removed and replaced by the New Testament. This in particular was a message that he received by direct inspiration from Christ. He did not get it indirectly from some other man; had that happened, some might wonder if he had misunderstood what he was taught. But there was no human element in the revelation of the message to Paul. It came directly from God, and therefore must be inerrant. No one should reject it.

Galatians 2

2:1-10 - The Jerusalem Meeting about Circumcision

2:1,2 – After fourteen years Paul again went to Jerusalem with Barnabas, taking Titus with them. He went up by revelation and showed to them the gospel that he had preached among the Gentiles. He did this privately among those of repute lest he might be running or had run in vain.

At this point Paul has established that the gospel he taught among the Gentiles was what he had believed and taught long before he came in contact with the apostles or leaders in Jerusalem. His doctrine came by revelation directly from Jesus, not through any man.

The next point he had to establish was that, though his doctrine did not come from the apostles, yet they agreed with it. Apparently the Judaizers were claiming or at least implying that the original apostles did not teach the same about this as Paul did. So Paul dealt next with this concern.

He discusses a time, fourteen years later, when he went to Jerusalem to discuss the specific issue regarding circumcision and the law with the leaders at Jerusalem. Presumably this is fourteen years after his conversion (as in 1:18), not fourteen years after the previous visit mentioned in 1:18-24.

Note that Barnabas went with Paul. This is natural since Barnabas and Paul had been closely associated in the work in Antioch in Acts 11 and in their first preaching journey. Together they had converted many Gentiles without requiring them to be circumcised or to keep the Old Law. So the issue concerned them both, and they had both been sent to Jerusalem by the church in Antioch.

Though Paul had not been well known in Jerusalem, Barnabas certainly had been well known there. He had been involved in the care for the needy saints in Acts 4:36,37. He had been the one to introduce Saul to the church in Jerusalem – Acts 9:26. He had been sent by the church in Jerusalem to encourage and strengthen the new church in Antioch – Acts 11:22. His relationship with the leaders and members in Jerusalem would no doubt help in achieving harmony on the issues involved.

Commentary on Galatians

Is this the same meeting as in Acts 15?

Surely this must refer to the same meeting in Jerusalem mentioned in Acts 15. There are simply too many coincidences for these to be two separate meetings. Although each of the two accounts gives some details that are omitted in the other account, that is to be expected, and there are no real contradictions.

Notice how the two records agree in such a way as to identify the same meeting:

* Both passages refer to meetings in Jerusalem.

* Both involved Paul, Barnabas, and others going to Jerusalem. Though not directly stated, it is implied that they went from Antioch, since that was where Paul and Barnabas were working together.

* In both cases, other people accompanied them (Acts 15:2; Galatians 2:1).

* Both involved meetings with the leaders of the church in Jerusalem, specifically Peter and James.

* In both cases the issue was whether or not circumcision should be bound on Gentiles.

* In both cases the meeting was necessitated by people who had agitated the view that circumcision was necessary.

* In both cases Paul and Barnabas defended the view they taught.

* In both cases the decision was that circumcision and obedience to the Old Law was not necessary.

* In both cases the leaders in the Jerusalem church specifically commended and endorsed Paul and Barnabas as being faithful teachers (compare Acts 15:25,26 to Galatians 2:6-10).

The chances are minuscule that two such conferences occurred in close approximation. Why would a second meeting be needed? Both accounts show clearly that the meeting concluded with complete agreement among the inspired men. To have a second such meeting so soon afterward would be senseless. I conclude that these are two accounts of the same meeting.

One question about this conclusion is that Acts 11:27-30 and 12:25 shows that Paul had been to Jerusalem another time between his visit in Acts 9 and the meeting in Acts 15. Why did Paul not mention this in Galatians?

I believe the answer is not difficult. In chapter 1, he gave his history to answer a particular argument or complaint. He demonstrated that his doctrine came from Jesus, not from men (the apostles in particular). That was thoroughly established in chapter 1 by showing he had been preaching for three years before he even met an apostle.

No further evidence was needed on that point, so Paul has moved on to another aspect of the subject – something that happened, he said, fourteen years after his conversion. He now begins to discuss the question of whether or not the other apostles agreed with his view. That is answered by the Acts 15 meeting as also described in Galatians 2.

The visit in Acts 11,12 is irrelevant to Paul's discussion. The purpose of that visit was to deliver gifts for needy saints, not to discuss circumcision. Paul and Barnabas delivered funds to various churches in Judea, not just to the Jerusalem church. It is possible in that visit that he did not even meet with any apostles.

The trip in Acts 11 was perhaps ten years after Paul's conversion and came after he had already met Peter and James. Such a trip would prove nothing more about the source of his teaching, so it was irrelevant to the point of chapter 1. Furthermore, it would prove nothing about whether or not the apostles agreed with his teaching, so it was irrelevant to the point of chapter 2. He did not discuss it because it was not relevant to the discussion.

Some commentators assume that the visit in Galatians 2 is the same as the visit in Acts 11 and 12, rather than the visit in Acts 15. But this assumes that a meeting and discussion occurred in Acts 11 and 12 despite the fact that nothing whatever is said there about it, while at the same time overlooking the numerous similarities between Galatians 2 and Acts 15.

An argument offered to defend the view that the meeting in Galatians 2 is the same as that in Acts 11 is the fact that, after the record of the meeting to discuss circumcision, Paul then records the sin of Peter in Antioch. This event involved Barnabas, but Acts 15 records that Paul and Barnabas separated soon after the meeting in Jerusalem. It seems unlikely that Peter would visit Antioch and change his conduct so soon after the meeting in Acts 15.

A possible response is that we must remember Peter's volatile nature. He had been known to change quickly and easily, as when he denied Jesus so soon after plainly insisting he would never do so.

However, a more likely explanation is that the account of Peter's inconsistency is not in chronological order, but in fact the event happened before the meeting in Acts 15. Hogg and Vine point out that the original language implies the events are not in chronological order.

In fact, it is possible that Peter's conduct in Galatians 2 was actually part of the controversy in Antioch at the beginning of Acts 15 and contributed to the meeting in Jerusalem. It is interesting that Peter, Barnabas, and James were all directly or indirectly involved in Peter's inconsistent conduct, Paul confronted them, and then they were all involved in the meeting in Jerusalem that resolved the issue. This would help explain the situation and why they were all willing to meet and be sure others in Jerusalem were corrected.

A powerful argument against the Galatians 2 Jerusalem meeting occurring during the visit of Acts 11 is that Paul plainly says the event occurred after the space of fourteen years. But the visit in Acts 11 occurred before the death of King Herod in Acts 12. But Hogg and Vine explain that Herod is known to have died in A.D. 44. Fourteen years before that would be A.D. 30, which would be far too soon for Paul's conversion. This point alone appears to me to conclusively demonstrate that the Jerusalem meeting in Galatians 2 is the same as that in Acts 15.

Paul's purpose in attending the meeting

Paul states first that he took Titus with him. His purpose in this will become clear in the next few verses. Acts 15 does not name Titus, but verse 2 says "certain others" went with Paul and Barnabas.

Then he states that he went up by revelation. Acts 15:2,3 says that he and Barnabas were sent to Jerusalem by the church in Antioch, but that does not change the fact he received a revelation instructing him to go. God sometimes gave revelations to His prophets in order to inform them how they should respond to requests that had been made of them (compare Acts 10, 13; etc.). In fact, it is even possible that the church agreed to send Paul after it heard he had received his revelation.

Paul mentions the revelation to show that his going did not mean that he had any doubts about his teaching. He has abundantly shown that he believed and taught confidently his view with no need for confirmation from the apostles. And when he got to Jerusalem, he defended his view with complete confidence that it was correct (verses 4-6). It is even possible that he did not even see any need to go until the revelation informed him to do so.

When he arrived, he communicated to certain of the leaders (people of reputation) of the Jerusalem church what he had been preaching. He did this lest he had run or might run in vain. Again, this should not be taken as an indication that he doubted his teaching. His whole point is that he had no doubt about it.

The point of the meeting, from Paul's view, was that such a meeting should help settle once and for all that the original apostles did agree with his teaching. He had no doubts about his teaching, but others did. They were claiming that the other apostles did not agree with Paul (see Acts 15:1,5,24).

If this doctrine became widely accepted, it could cause people to turn away from Paul's teaching. Many might go into error in the matter, and others might become discouraged and fall away. And many Gentiles might refuse to be converted if they were taught, in effect, that they had to become Jews. This would cause Paul to run in vain, not in the sense that he was teaching error, but that many people he taught may be influenced by this false doctrine and be lost.

So Paul's concern was, not that he might be proved wrong, but that he might have an opportunity to prove to the apostles, the Jerusalem church, and thereby to all Christians everywhere, that he was really teaching truth. Note that this is exactly Paul's argument regarding the meeting here and in Acts 15 (compare 16:4). Paul sought the opportunity to defeat any efforts to undermine the truth he taught.

A private meeting

Note that Paul states expressly that he met with those of reputation in private.

"Reputation" is not meant critically, but simply that the leaders in the Jerusalem church would be the ones the Judaizers would most lean on for their teaching. It is even possible that Paul was describing these leaders in the church the way the Judaizers themselves described them in order to emphasize the authority of their teachings.

Jerusalem was the headquarters of Judaism and the beginning point of the preaching of the gospel and the conversion of Jews. If the apostles and elders in that place agreed with Paul, how could anyone who claimed to be a Christian possibly withstand the conclusion that Paul really was speaking truth?

Now it is interesting that this was a private meeting to discuss a matter of major doctrinal concern to the church. Apparently only men were present: elders, apostles, and other men. Everyone in this meeting as named in Galatians 2 and in Acts 15 was a man.

We today have some who claim such meetings are without Divine approval. They claim that decision-making meetings must include the whole church and must, in particular, permit the presence and even vocal participation of women. They even claim this Jerusalem meeting, as recorded in Acts 15, proves their position.

Yet here is a clear statement regarding that very Jerusalem meeting, making clear that it involved a **private** meeting of church leaders, and none are mentioned as present except men. Close reading of Acts 15 confirms this. When Paul and Barnabas first arrived, they met with the **church** and apostles and elders (verses 4,5). Some in that meeting claimed circumcision was necessary.

Then in verses 6-21 a **different** meeting was held to make a decision about the issue – "the **apostles and elders** came together to consider this matter" (verse 6). These, of course, were all men. Everyone who spoke was a man. No mention is made that this meeting involved the whole church, let alone women. It was this meeting that decided the issue.

Later, in verses 22-29 a letter was sent confirming and publicizing the decision made in the verses 6-21 meeting. The whole church (verse 22; "brethren" – verse 23) with the apostles and elders, were pleased by the decision and joined in sending the letter. But the decision had already been made in a private meeting of leaders and authority figures. Paul removes all doubt in Galatians 2 by clearly stating that a **private** meeting of those of reputation met and reached the decision.

To claim, as some are doing, that it is unscriptural for decisions to be made on behalf of the church in a private meeting of the men or elders of the congregation is to miss the Bible teaching entirely. 1 Corinthians 14:34,35 shows that women may not even ask a question in meetings of the whole church. So if, as some claim, decisions should be made in a meeting of the whole church with women present, the women would not even be able to speak. Galatians chapter 2 confirms what is revealed in Acts 15: the claim that women must be allowed to be present and to speak in meetings where decisions are made for the whole church is simply an invalid claim which is not substantiated by Scripture.

2:3-5 – In that meeting Titus, who was a Greek, was not compelled to be circumcised. The problem was created by false brethren who privately came in to spy out our liberty in Christ and bring us into bondage. Paul gave place by way of subjection not for an hour that the truth of the gospel might continue.

Paul summarized the result of the meeting.

Acts 15 shows clearly that the apostles and elders had agreed with Paul that Gentiles did not need to be circumcised. Paul confirms that here, stating it in a different way.

First, he says that Titus, who attended the meeting with him, was not compelled to be circumcised. This explains why, in verse 1, he mentioned Titus being there. We are plainly told Titus was a Greek, but he was not required to be circumcised. The use of the term "compel" would imply that the Judaizers in the Jerusalem church attempted to insist that Titus be circumcised (Acts 15:5). But the attempt was not successful.

In Acts 16:1-3, Paul had Timothy circumcised, but that was different situation. Titus was simply a Greek – not even Jews would expect him to be circumcised. Timothy's mother, however, was a Jew and his father a Greek. Jews would expect him to be circumcised and would not be likely to even discuss God's word with him so long as he was not.

Timothy's case was a matter of becoming all things to all men, including becoming a Jew to the Jews (1 Corinthians 9:19-23). Paul there clearly stated that he was not under the law but would submit to its customs if doing so would help him convert Jews. But he would not allow the Old Testament to be bound as law, and surely not on Gentiles. To Gentiles he would be as one who was not under the law. To bind circumcision on Gentiles would violate the principle of being "all things to all men," as well as other principles.

Paul did not object to circumcision as a matter of custom, but he definitely opposed its being bound as a requirement for salvation, including binding it on Gentiles and thereby turning many of them from the faith.

Paul then explained that indeed there were some who sought to "compel" Gentiles like Titus to be circumcised. Titus became, in effect, a test case. Paul brought an uncircumcised Gentile Christian with him to see if the apostles would insist that he be circumcised. When they did not, that ought to have settled the matter once for all.

However, there were some, even at Jerusalem (Acts 15:5), who did want to require circumcision and the keeping of the Old Testament. Paul refers to these as false brethren who came in stealthily to spy out the liberty we have in Jesus and bring us into bondage. The expression compares these Judaizers to spies sent into a foreign land to see how it can be defeated and enslaved.

So Paul viewed the Judaizers as those who would bring Christians – especially Gentiles – into slavery. He elsewhere speaks of the law as bondage compared to the freedom of the gospel (see notes on 3:19-25; 5:1,13; Acts 15:10). To accept the efforts of those who sought to bind the Old Law would be to destroy the liberty in Christ and bring us into bondage to a law that cannot save and that, we will see, Jesus has removed. While those who teach such doctrines may not be aware that their doctrine will bring others into bondage, nevertheless this is the effect of such conduct from the view of God.

Paul refused to give way to this doctrine or to submit to it even for an hour, so the truth of the gospel might continue with God's people. Clearly he viewed the doctrine of binding the Old Testament and circumcision to unquestionably be a violation of the gospel. This means that it is a specific example of "another gospel" that causes the teachers of it to be accursed and the followers of it to depart from Jesus (1:6-9).

Notice that Paul has established here how we should deal with those who would attempt to bind the seventh-day Sabbath or other Old Testament laws on Christians today. All such laws, which were part of the Old Testament but are not included in the New Testament, are no more in effect today than circumcision is. Those who seek to bind them are seeking to spy out our liberty in Christ, and we should not submit to this even for an hour. Those who teach such doctrines are preaching another gospel.

Note however, that the teachers of this other gospel did not deny Jesus' Deity or authority, nor did they deny the necessity for believing in Jesus and being baptized. They simply added other requirements as necessary which the gospel itself did not teach. And Paul opposed their views with absolutely no compromise. This is how false teaching should be handled.

So at this point in the epistle, Paul has established that his teaching came directly from Jesus, and not from any man. Paul had held to this teaching firmly, and he had allowed it to be tested in the crucible of apostolic teaching. Yet the result was that his teaching not only was not defeated, but in fact even Titus remained uncircumcised. The "test case" demonstrated Paul's teaching to be valid.

Other passages regarding false teachers: Matthew 7:15-23; 15:14; 2 Corinthians 11:13-15; 1 Timothy 4:1-3; Acts 20:28-30; 1 John 4:1; 2 Timothy 4:2-4; Titus 1:9-14; 2 John 9-11; Romans 16:17,18; Galatians 1:6-9; 2 Peter chap. 2

2:6-8 – People of reputation imparted nothing to Paul but rather they saw that he had been entrusted with the gospel to the uncircumcised and Peter with the gospel to the circumcised.

Paul here begins a statement, then completes it after he interrupts himself. He states that those who seemed to be important added nothing to him – i.e., to his doctrine and knowledge of truth. The parenthetical statement says that it made no difference to him who they were because God shows no favoritism to man.

God shows no personal favoritism.

Why state this here? Surely he was not being disrespectful to the other apostles, nor was he denying their authority as apostles. He was surely not saying that as apostles they had no authority. There would be no reason to say such. He had no conflict with the apostles – his whole point is that they agreed with him. To deny their authority would be to undermine his own authority, for he was claiming to be an apostle like they were.

The reason he said this must, therefore, have been to correct improper attitudes held by the Judaizers. In what sense might they have viewed men with respect of persons? Well, the whole point is that they thought God had special favoritism for Jews – they believed people of one nation should continue to receive special status with God as they did under the Old Testament. This issue becomes a specific point of controversy between Peter and Paul as revealed in verses 11ff.

So it appears that Paul is saying that, although these men agreed with his teaching, he is not attaching any specific importance to the fact they were **Jewish** apostles. Of course, he too was a Jew, but his ministry was especially to Gentiles. The fact these apostles were Jews, ministering especially to Jews, did not in any way make their doctrine more authoritative than doctrine taught by any other inspired man, regardless of nationality. God and Paul did not accept the Judaizers' view of favoritism. Nevertheless, he wanted them and everyone else to know that these Jewish apostles did agree with what he was teaching.

These apostles did not add anything to his teaching.

As shown in 1:11,12ff, his doctrine had been revealed to him by Jesus. As such, it could not possibly conflict with anything taught by any other inspired man, for they all taught the same gospel (1:8,9). Since he was inspired as an apostle, he did not need other apostles to prove his teaching to be valid. Nevertheless, he wanted it clear that they added nothing to his teaching but agreed with it.

In fact, the other apostles recognized his ministry to the Gentiles (uncircumcised) as being valid, just as Peter's ministry to the Jews (circumcised) was valid. As noted in 1:16, Paul had been especially called to preach to Gentiles. He did preach to Jews, just as Peter did preach to Gentiles (Acts 10). But he emphasized preaching in Gentile territories, whereas other apostles (Peter in particular) emphasized preaching in Jewish regions. And each had worked effectively in that area of special calling.

Note that Jews and Gentiles are distinguished on the basis of circumcision. This was the token of the covenant with Abraham (Genesis 17) and therefore of the Old Testament law. It follows that to be circumcised identified one as Jewish. To bind this on Gentiles then would mean that, in order to be saved, it was not enough that they believe in Jesus and be baptized, but they also had to be identified as Jews. This would turn away many Gentiles and limit salvation in a way God never intended.

Clearly Paul is not saying he and Peter taught two different gospels – one to Jews and another to Gentiles. The whole point is they both taught the same. Yet some folks foolishly persist is claiming there was a distinction or conflict of some kind between their teachings. The whole point is there was no difference and could be no difference. Other passages confirm this (1:8,9; Acts 15:7-11; 2 Peter 3:15-16).

The difference was, not in the **message** they taught, but in the **subjects** whom they emphasized teaching. Peter emphasized taking the gospel to Jews and Paul emphasized taking it to Gentiles (compare verse 9). This does not mean that Paul only taught Gentiles. On the contrary, in nearly every city where he entered, he first attempted to teach Jews. Likewise, the point is not that Peter never taught Gentiles. On the contrary, he was the first to teach the gospel to the Gentiles in Acts 10,11.

Note the word "apostleship." We have used this term numerous times, but here we see it plainly used regarding the work or office of these two great apostles. And notice that Paul affirmed that, like Peter, he had worked effectively in his service as an apostle. Both men had accomplished important works of service, and taught many people, and many had been saved.

And with both of the men, the Holy Spirit had confirmed their teaching by miracles. The Holy Spirit would not have confirmed their doctrine had they been teaching error or had they been teaching doctrine which contradicted what other inspired man were teaching. Both taught the same doctrine, both did so effectively, and in both cases their teaching was confirmed by God miraculously. This should show that Paul's doctrine was not different from that of the apostles in Jerusalem nor was it in any way inferior to theirs.

2:9,10 – The reputed pillars in Jerusalem perceived the grace given to Paul, so they gave to him and Barnabas the right hand of fellowship to go to the Gentiles as the others were going to the circumcision. They did ask Paul and Barnabas to remember the poor, which Paul was zealous to do.

Here Paul, for the first time, names the men to whom he referred as "pillars" or men of reputation, etc. They were Peter (Cephas), James (the brother of Jesus as in 1:19, not the son of Zebedee since he was slain in Acts 12), and John (the son of Zebedee and brother of James). Note that the reference here to the prominence of James explains why Paul identified him as being in Jerusalem on his first trip there (1:19).

Note that, contrary to Catholic doctrine, nothing here gives any preeminence in this meeting to Peter. If Peter was the first Pope and head of the church, as Catholicism claims, why did Peter not resolve this issue? Or, why did he not at least take the dominant leading role over everyone else in the meeting? Catholicism claims that he did, however there is nothing here or in any other passage that so indicates. Rather, he was simply listed along with several others as being among the pillars in the church in Jerusalem, but nothing gave him dominance over the others.

The right hand of fellowship given to Paul

These men perceived the grace given to Paul – i.e., the grace to serve as a true apostle, as Paul had stated at the outset in 1:1,15. These other apostles and leaders recognized that Paul truly was an apostle and they gave to Paul and Barnabas the right hand of fellowship. They recognized that Paul was chosen of God to spread the gospel to the Gentiles, even as they had been chosen especially to spread it to the Jews.

The "right hand" is here used as a symbol of fellowship. As in 2 John 9-11, they would never have bid Godspeed to Paul had they considered him to be teaching error (1:8,9). In short, they completely agreed with Paul's teaching.

This conclusion destroyed any attempt by the Judaizers to claim the original apostles agreed with them and disagreed with Paul. Paul had expressly discussed his teaching with the other apostles, and not only did they add nothing to his teaching, but they extended fellowship to him and recognized his ministry! See other references on verses 6-8 above showing Peter endorsed Paul's apostleship and preaching.

Note that this result explains why God had given Paul the revelation to go to Jerusalem. It was not that Paul needed to learn the truth or to have confirmation of his teaching for his own sake. It was to remove any possible questions or doubts in the minds of others as to whether or not his teaching and ministry had the agreement and endorsement of the other apostles. Never again could anyone validly claim that there was a disagreement among the apostles on these matters.

The reference to the "right hand" demonstrates that shaking hands was a common custom in that day. It often was used as an expression of agreement or binding a pledge. See 2 Kings 10:15; 1 Chronicles 29:24 (footnote); Lamentations 5:6; Ezekiel 17:18. This is still a common practice among us today. The kiss in that day was also a common custom. But neither is binding to the exclusion of the other.

The same gospel meets the needs of all men.

Note further that, if the same gospel can serve the needs of both Jews and Gentiles, as widely different in culture and background as they were, then the same gospel will surely serve the needs of all men of all ages and all places. We do not need a new gospel today, as some claim. If the gospel met the needs of both Jew and Gentile, it will surely meet the needs of all men today.

The one thing that these Jewish leaders did request of Paul was that he remember the poor, and Paul was already eager to do this. This surely refers to the poor in Jerusalem, as described in 1 Corinthians 16:1-4. It refers to the same need discussed in Romans 15:25ff and 2 Corinthians 8&9. The men agreed that the Gentile churches should help the needy saints in Jerusalem and that this would help bond the Gentile and Jewish Christians together (note Romans 15:25-28). Apparently this problem in Jerusalem was an ongoing need of relatively long standing, since it is mentioned so often in so many places.

Note that there are those even today who claim that Paul's teaching differed from that of Peter and the other apostles. However, those who claim this today generally do not argue that people today should keep the Old Testament law. Rather, they argue that Peter taught that baptism is necessary to salvation, but Paul taught that it was not. Variations of this view exist, but the purpose typically is to claim that baptism is not necessary based on a supposed difference between the teaching of Paul and Peter.

We can offer many reasons for denying this view. Among those reasons is the plain fact that Paul himself was baptized to receive the washing away of sins – Acts 22:16. And he also taught that baptism is necessary to receive the benefits of the death of Christ, to come into

Commentary on Galatians

Christ, and to walk in newness of life – Romans 6:3,4. And we will see that he taught the same even here in the letter to the Galatians in 3:26,27. So the claim that Paul did not believe baptism is necessary to salvation is simply an invalid claim.

Furthermore, Peter himself expressly endorsed the doctrine of Paul both here and in 2 Peter 3:15-16. In any case, the claims Paul makes here in chapter 2 show clearly that he and the other apostles taught the same gospel and the same doctrine.

No authority for conferences of uninspired men today to establish church doctrine

Some people attempt to use the account in Acts 15 and in Galatians 2 as authority for church leaders to meet today to establish church doctrine. Such reasoning is invalid for a number of reasons:

* Paul expressly stated that he received a revelation from God that this meeting should occur – Galatians 2:1. Men who meet today to establish church doctrine have received no such revelation from God, and we will see that such revelations have ceased.

* This was a meeting of apostles and other inspired men directly guided by the Holy Spirit (Acts 15:28). Church conferences today, which attempt to determine doctrine, are meetings of uninspired men acting by human wisdom. The conclusions they reach are the doctrines of men, which churches are expected to follow in addition to the inspired revelation of God. This is exactly what Paul has already forbidden in Galatians 1:8,9. See also Matthew 15:9,13; 2 John 9-11; Colossians 3:17; Jeremiah 10:23; 26:2; Proverbs 14:12; 3:5,6; Isaiah 24:5; 30:1; Revelation 22:18,19; 1 Timothy 1:3; 2 Timothy 1:13; John 5:43; 1 Chronicles 15:13.

* God's word in that day was revealed through the spoken word of inspired men, before the Holy Spirit had guided men to completely record the will of God in writing. But God's intent, which was accomplished in the first century, was to completely and perfectly reveal His will in writing in the Scriptures. Since we now have that complete revelation in the Scriptures, the gift of direct guidance of the Holy Spirit has ceased. No such meetings of inspired men, as are here described, are possible nor are they needed. 2 Timothy 3:16,17; John 16:13; 14:26; Acts 20:20,27; 2 Peter 1:3; 1 Corinthians 13:8-11; Jude 3.

* The meeting involved representatives of only two churches – Antioch in Jerusalem – not a universal meeting of churches everywhere. The account in Acts 15 records that the reason the Jerusalem church and elders were involved was that the Judaizing teachers, who had been troubling Antioch, came from there and were claiming authority based on the teachers in Jerusalem.

2:11-21 - Peter's Refusal to Eat with Gentiles

2:11,12 – When Peter came to Antioch, he ate with Gentiles until certain people came from James. Then he drew back and separated from the Gentiles because he feared those who were circumcised. As a result, Paul resisted him to the face because Peter was condemned in this.

Paul has now established the following points: (1) He met all the requirements of an apostle, and he received his teaching directly from God, not from the other apostles. (2) Nevertheless, his teaching had been specifically examined by the other apostles, and not only had they not opposed it, but they had determined to fellowship Paul and support his ministry.

Peter's conduct

Now Paul turns to an event which shows, not only that his own teaching was from God, but that in fact one of the apostles, whom the Judaizers looked up to, had been wrong regarding this issue. He describes an occasion in which an apostle had acted according to the Judaizers' views, but in doing so that apostle – not Paul – was the one in error! This clearly contradicts the Judaizers, who apparently thought the Jerusalem apostles disagreed with Paul, so Paul was in the wrong and the Jerusalem apostles were right.

This event occurred on one occasion when Peter (Cephas) came to Antioch. As discussed earlier, this event may have occurred before the meeting in Jerusalem, but it may simply have served Paul's purpose to discuss them in this order. Hogg and Vine defend this view as agreeing with the original language.

In any case, Paul had to withstand Peter to his face because "he was to be blamed" (NKJV, KJV) or he "stood condemned" (ASV, NASB, RSV). Peter did something that was clearly wrong, so much so that Paul said he was guilty of hypocrisy because he knew better than to do what he did.

What Peter had done was that he would eat with Gentiles so long as no Jews were present, but when some Jewish brethren came from Jerusalem, he separated from the Gentiles and then refused to eat with them, because he was afraid of what the Jews would think of him.

The fact that these Jewish men came from James does not prove that James agreed with their doctrine or their conduct in this case. The passage simply says that they came from James. They knew him and had presumably been sent by him for some task. But there is no reason to assume that James taught what they practiced in this case.

Peter's knowledge

Peter surely knew better than to do this. When he had taught the gospel to Cornelius, he had eaten with Gentiles and had been confronted by Jewish brethren about it. He had explained and defended his action then (Acts 10:1-3). But later when he was in Antioch, he still was willing to eat with Gentiles, but he refused to do so when he thought Jewish Christians might object to it. Note that Peter's inspired preaching was correct and reliable, but his personal conduct did not live up to that preaching.

Jews traditionally refused to eat with one of another race or nationality. Perhaps this had originated because there were so many foods that were forbidden as "unclean" for Jews, but Gentiles would eat them. In any case, Jews came to refuse to eat with Gentiles as a sign of spiritual separation from them, whereas to eat with them would be taken as a sign of spiritual acceptance and unity with them. Perhaps the Jewish Christians were also concerned that eating with Gentiles would be viewed as an indication that the laws of uncleanness were no longer binding. For other passages see Genesis 43:32; John 4:9; Acts 10:28; 11:1-3; Matthew 18:17; 1 Corinthians 5:11.

Peter clearly knew that it was acceptable to eat with Gentiles; in fact, he had practiced it both in Antioch and at Cornelius' house. But he then refused, not because he believed it was wrong, but because he feared the Jews who objected to it. Nor can this be justified on grounds of "becoming all things to all men" (1 Corinthians 9); refusing to eat with Gentiles might please the Jews, but how would it make the Gentiles feel?

Principles of influence must be applied with understanding of the effect on everyone involved. While we may go along with certain traditions where we do not thereby displease God, yet this cannot be used as an excuse to hurt people. The effect was to indicate that these Gentile converts were not acceptable to be fellowshipped or associate with.

One wonders how formal this "withdrawing" and "separating" was? It does not appear to have been a church action, as described in 1 Corinthians 5 or 2 Thessalonians 3:6-15. Yet the implications were much the same. The effect was to imply that the Gentile converts were spiritually unfit to associate with until they obeyed the Old Testament, especially circumcision. That was surely the basis on which Jews refused to associate with Gentiles, and if the solution required keeping the Old Testament law, that was a religious or spiritual issue.

The effect of this on Gentiles was to imply they simply were not saved and not fit to be accepted as faithful Christians until they kept the old law. The impact was much greater than simply a matter of not inviting someone to your house for a meal. The effect of Peter's conduct was to make it appear that these brethren were condemned as sinners, even though Peter knew this was not true (note verse 15). This is why the issue was of such concern to Paul.

Peter's error

Willis points out that some Catholic writers attempted to rationalize Peter's conduct here in order to avoid the harm this event does to their doctrine that Peter was the first Pope. But no such rationalization is possible, nor is it needed. Peter never was Pope nor head of the church. He never claimed any such position, nor did any inspired writer ever claim it for him. Jesus was head over all things to the church (Ephesians 1:22,23). And Jesus Christ alone is the foundation on which the church was built (1 Corinthians 3:11).

Apostles and inspired men received direct revelations from God in the age when the Scriptures had not been completed. This was how Peter received the knowledge that Gentiles could be converted – Acts 10,11. But receiving a revelation did not assure that a man would obey God's word, not even the revelation he himself had received. Peter obeyed the revelation in the case of Cornelius, but he failed in the case recorded here in Galatians 2.

Some might wonder at Peter's failure here, knowing that he had first preached the gospel to Gentiles and had eaten with Gentiles at the household of Cornelius. But we must remember that Peter had always been an impetuous person. He made some courageous stands for truth, but he also failed miserably at other times. This was one of the times when he failed.

Willis correctly points out, however, that Peter's doctrine was not wrong. His error was that his conduct did not live up to his doctrine. This is important to Paul's point. Paul has established that he and Peter agreed in their doctrine. The Judaizers were wrong when they claimed that Peter and other Jerusalem apostles were teaching different from Paul.

Both Peter and Paul taught the same gospel, but in this case Peter failed to live up to what he knew to be the truth. That is why Paul accused him of hypocrisy, rather than accusing him of teaching error. Paul's point is that he and Peter taught the same truth about the salvation of the Gentiles; but when Peter failed to live up to what he taught, Paul had corrected him. Contrary to what the Judaizers would have expected, Peter was the one who was wrong, and Paul was the one who was right.

2:13,14 – The other Jews joined Peter in this hypocrisy, so that even Barnabas joined them. But Paul saw they were not walking uprightly according to the gospel. So he asked Peter, if he was willing to live as a Gentile even though he was a Jew, why did he compel the Gentiles to live as the Jews do?

Peter's influence

Not only did Peter commit this sin, but the other Jews went along with him, including even Barnabas. In this they played the hypocrite till Barnabas was carried away with the "hypocrisy" (NKJV, NASB) or "dissimulation" (KJV, ASV) or "insincerity" (RSV). This was hypocritical because Peter knew it was right to eat with Gentiles, yet he still insulted them by refusing to do so. He knew the Gentiles could be saved without the old law, but he acted as though these people who were really his brethren were yet unfit for his association!

Note also the power of influence. Peter did wrong because of the influence of the other Jews. Other Jews who were present likewise followed Peter. And finally even Barnabas was influenced to join the error. Barnabas surely knew better than to follow Peter in this. He had been involved with Paul in teaching and converting Gentiles in Antioch and on the first preaching trip. Yet even so, he allowed Peter and other leaders to influence him to practice what he had to know was wrong.

This too was part of Paul's concern. It was bad enough that Peter himself had acted in a way that spiritually insulted the Gentile converts, but his conduct also influenced other people to think and act wrongly. We need to seriously consider the impact of our influence when we are considering the conduct in which we will or will not participate.

Paul's response

Seeing their conduct, Paul realized they were not being straightforward about the truth. He simply called Peter to account for it, because his conduct was unbecoming the truth of the gospel. Note that Paul did not consider this to be some minor infraction. He said they were not walking according to the truth of the gospel.

If such a practice was allowed to spread in the early days of the church, the Jews and Gentiles would surely have ended up in different congregations, probably not even in fellowship with one another. Acts that were entirely unnecessary would be bound on the early church, and the result would be foolish divisions. People who were true and faithful Christians, acceptable to God, would be treated by other Christians as though they were in error and unworthy of association.

Paul said to Peter before them all, "If you, being a Jew, live in the manner of Gentiles and not as the Jews, why do you compel Gentiles to live as Jews?" Peter lived as a Gentile, not a Jew, in that, previously he had been willing to associate with Gentiles, even eating with them. Jews would not do this, but Gentiles would. So, in this Peter had acted like a Gentile, not like a Jew. But suddenly he changed and acted in a way that would naturally make the Gentiles feel compelled to live like Jews – be circumcised and keep the law, etc. This was completely inconsistent and pointed out Peter's hypocrisy.

We note that Paul rebuked Peter publicly. This passage is helpful in our understanding regarding when a matter should be dealt with privately and when it should be dealt with publicly. Jesus taught that personal sins between brethren should be dealt with at first privately and resolved as privately as possible. It becomes a matter for congregational knowledge and action only if the matter cannot be resolved privately (Matthew 18:15-17).

However, some issues, like the one being discussed here, are openly known issues from the outset. This was not a private act to be discussed and resolved privately This was a public act in which Peter had sinned in such a way as was known by a number of other people and was known to be influencing other people to commit sin. As a result, a number of people became involved in the error. Such a matter required those involved to be rebuked in a way that everyone realized it was wrong. It would then require them to make correction in such a way that everyone knew the act was wrong (1 Timothy 5:20).

Note also the courage that Paul needed to stand for the truth in this case. Not only was he required to rebuke an inspired apostle, but a large number of others were involved including even his close companion Barnabas. There are times when faithfulness to God requires us to be willing to stand even alone in the face of influential people, even influential people in the church, if necessary.

2:15,16 – *Those who were Jews by nature, not Gentiles, nevertheless knew that man is justified, not by the works of the law, but through faith in Christ. So they had believed on Christ because no one will be justified by the works of the law.*

A contrast between two systems or fundamental principles of justification

Paul speaks to Peter as one Jew to another, referring to them as Jews by nature – i.e., by birth, ancestry, and background. They were Jews in contrast to sinners of the Gentiles. Gentiles were viewed by Jews as sinners, because they did not have or keep the law, did not offer sacrifices at the temple, and above all were not circumcised. Paul is using the word as the Jews would use it. In particular, this is what Peter's conduct implied about the Gentiles – they were "sinners" unless they were circumcised, etc.

Commentary on Galatians

Yet even Peter and Paul, as Jews, knew that people could not be justified by works of the law but could be justified only by faith in Christ. They knew no flesh would be justified by the law, and that is why they had believed in Jesus. Peter knew and preached this, just as Paul did. The point then is, why should Peter act as though Gentiles should keep the law, which he knew could not save them.

Paul is describing how people can be "justified." This term refers to standing right or just before God and His holy will. How does this happen? Paul says it does not happen by works of the law but by faith in Jesus.

Note that "the law" in this context clearly refers to the Old Testament law – the law which Jews kept and which some were attempting to bind on Gentiles, including circumcision. The context requires this conclusion. However, the principles being discussed would apply to any system similar in nature to that law.

Willis rightly points out:

> "A study of the usages of the word *nomos* (**law**) from a Greek concordance will demonstrate that one cannot determine from the use of the definite article whether the word means 'law' understood qualitatively [generically] or the Mosaical law. Only the context can determine that."

Some people mistakenly read passages like this and conclude that no one needs to obey commands to be saved, but all they need to do is believe in Jesus. This is not what Paul said, believed, or taught, here or elsewhere.

To understand statements like these, we need an overview of gospel teaching about works, law, faith, grace, etc. Peter and Paul, in this discussion, of course, both had the knowledge of this information – Paul said they both "knew" this. To understand the point, we too must know it.

> "Justify" (δικαιοω) – "1 to take up a legal cause, *show justice, do justice, take up a cause* ...2 to render a favorable verdict, *vindicate.* ... of humans *justify, vindicate, treat as just* ... of God *be found in the right, be free of charges* ... 3 to cause someone to be released from personal or institutional claims that are no longer to be considered pertinent or valid, *make free/pure* ... 4 to demonstrate to be morally right, *prove to be right...*" – *Bauer-Danker-Arndt-Gingrich*

> "...primarily, 'to deem to be right,' signifies, in the NT, (a) 'to show to be right or righteous;' in the Passive Voice, to be justified, Matthew 11:19; Luke 7:35; Romans 3:4; 1 Timothy 3:16; (b) 'to declare to be righteous, to pronounce righteous,' (1) by man, concerning God, Luke 7:29 ...; (2) by God concerning men, who are declared to be righteous before Him on certain conditions laid down by Him." – Vine

Works of law was one system of justification

Works of law refers here to a fundamental principle by which a man might attempt to be justified before God. In this system one attempts to keep commands as a means, in and of itself, to stand righteous before God. This was the kind of law the Old Testament was. Note these characteristics of this system:

* It requires a lifetime of sinless perfection to really justify – Galatians 3:10-12. If you don't continue in all things written in the law, you are accursed. (Ezekiel 18:20; Deuteronomy 27:26; James 2:10; Romans 10:5; Leviticus 18:5)

* It provides no lasting forgiveness – Hebrews 10:1-4,11. Sins were eventually remembered, so the conscience was never permanently cleansed of guilt. So "works of law" is a system of justification by **law-keeping alone without forgiveness**. One stood justified before God only and entirely because he never did anything wrong.

* Justification therefore was earned by works of merit. If anyone ever achieved righteousness under this system, it would be a matter of **debt** – Romans 4:4. He would deserve to be considered right (justified) simply because he never did anything wrong. This system would justify, however, only if a person never sins. If he ever sins, he deserves punishment and cannot be saved by this system (Romans 6:23).

* The power or source behind justification would then be human ability – Romans 4:4.

* A man who was justified in this way could boast in his achievement – Romans 4:2; 3:27; Ephesians 2:8,9

* Such a man trusts in himself to be justified. Christ and His sacrifice are not needed – Galatians 3:21

* Since all men sin, this system will save no one – Romans 3:20,23. This is exactly what Paul affirms about the system here in Galatians 2:16. Compare 3:10-12 Acts 13:38,39.

Paul is not denying that obedience to the gospel is necessary to salvation. He is denying that men can be saved by the system or principle requiring perfect law-keeping without forgiveness.

Grace through faith in Jesus' sacrifice was another system of justification.

This is a different system or fundamental principle for justifying men. In this system one can be made righteous before God even though he has sinned.

* Even those who have sinned can be justified – Romans 3:23,24. So, a life of sinless perfection is not required. (Romans 5:1,2; Titus 3:3,7)

* Forgiveness is offered through a sacrifice that can truly forgive sins, but men must meet certain conditions to be forgiven – Ephesians 1:7; Hebrews 10:11-14,17. Jesus died as the sacrifice, paying the penalty

for man's sins. Unlike animal sacrifices, this sacrifice can permanently remove sins. However, men must be willing to meet conditions to receive the forgiveness (Acts 15:7-11; 2:38; 10:34-48; 22:16; Romans 10:9-17; chapter 6; etc.)

* Meeting these conditions does not earn or merit justification. It is reckoned as a matter of grace, not of debt – Romans 4:4-7. "Works," in contexts that contrasts these two systems of justification, refers to a life of sinless perfection. Righteousness by grace through faith means justification for those who have not lived a sinless life but are forgiven by the sacrifice of Jesus.

* The source or power that provides forgiveness is Jesus' death, not human ability – Ephesians 1:7; 2:8,9; Titus 3:5; 2 Timothy 1:9; Romans 3:24,25. These passages say we are not saved by works, but the meaning in context is that we do not earn it by a sinless life. This does not deny, however, that conditions are necessary. Note parallel ideas in Judges 7:2; Ephesians 2:5,6; Colossians 2:12,13; Romans 6:3,4.

* God receives the glory; human boasting is excluded – Ephesians 2:8,9; Romans 3:27; 1 Corinthians 1:29-31.

* Faith in Christ is required, not trust in self – Ephesians 2:8,9; Romans 3:22,26; 4:24; John 3:16; Luke 18:9-14. One realizes that his own effort has failed, so he needs the blood of Jesus to forgive him.

* This system of justification places salvation in the reach of all men, even those who have sinned – Acts 13:38,39; 15:10,11; etc.

Note that justification by faith in Jesus does not exclude obedience. In fact, it requires it. But the point is that, even though one has sinned, he can still be saved through having his sins forgiven if he is willing to become obedient. Whereas under the law system, once a person committed a sin, his case was hopeless.

Paul says that Peter knew all this, like Paul did. He knew people could not be saved by that old law. They can only be saved by the New Testament. So why compel people to go back to the Old Testament? It is foolish to treat people like sinners because they seek salvation by the New Testament without the old, yet that was what Peter was doing to the Gentiles.

Note that the phrase "justified by faith in Christ" can refer to the fact that we must believe in Jesus in order to be saved. Or it can refer to that teaching in which we place our faith in order to be saved – that is, the gospel as in Jude 3.

When one understands that the belief we must have in order to be saved according to the gospel requires us, not just to believe properly, but also to obey properly, and when we understand that what we must believe and obey is the teaching revealed in the gospel, it appears to me that there is no significant difference. Both views end up teaching the same thing. The problem is that some do not realize that we must believe the proper things in order to have a proper faith and we must also obey in order to have a proper faith.

See our addendum for further discussion about the sense in which we are or are not justified by law.

2:17-19 – While seeking to be justified in Christ, if we are found to be sinners, does that make Christ a minister of sin? Surely not. If I rebuild what I once destroyed, I prove myself to be a sinner, because through the law I died to the law that I might live to God.

Is Christ a minister of sin?

Verse 17 states a general truth. If we seek to receive justification through Jesus and His sacrifice, but at the same time we are guilty of sin, does that mean Christ is the one responsible for our sin? Does He or His ministry make us sinners? Of course not. He does not cause sin but died to remove it.

However, in this context the verse seems to carry more specific significance that may be somewhat difficult to understand. It seems to me that Paul refers to Peter's inconsistency regarding the gospel – this surely fits with verse 18. Peter sought to be justified by the gospel, because he knew the Old Testament could not really justify (verse 16).

Peter had also taught Gentiles to be justified by the gospel without circumcision or submission to the Old Testament, just like Paul had done. He did this with Cornelius in Acts 10. He had also defended it in Acts 11. He had stated it again in the Jerusalem meeting in Acts 15:10,11. And even in Antioch he had associated with converted Gentiles until the Jews came.

The reference then to sinners may refer to the way Peter had treated the Gentiles, whom Jews considered sinners (verse 15). By disassociating from them, Peter was treating them as if he agreed that they were sinners. But they had been justified by Christ by the very kind of teaching that Peter himself had done.

Now if, in attempting to be justified by the gospel, the Gentiles still ended up being sinners and unworthy of association, wouldn't that make Christ a minister of sin? They had obeyed His gospel. If they were still sinners, wouldn't that make Jesus somehow responsible? Instead of being cleansed or purified, they still ended up lost. Such is the consequences of Peter's conduct. It makes Jesus out to be a minister of sin. Peter's conduct led to a conclusion about Jesus which is clearly false, therefore Peter must be wrong.

One problem with the above explanation is that Paul speaks regarding "we." But "we" refers to Jewish Christians in the previous verses, rather than to Gentiles (verses 15,16). So, perhaps a variation, which teaches the same conclusion, is that Peter and Paul sought justification themselves through the gospel (verse 16). Yet both of them had associated freely with Gentiles in the past because Jesus' gospel had taught them to do so. But if associating with Gentiles was wrong to do, as Peter's conduct in the presence of Jews implied, then Jesus' gospel had made both Peter and Paul sinners. So again, the consequence of Peter's conduct is to imply that Jesus caused people to be guilty of sin. Paul is showing Peter the hypocrisy and inconsistency of Peter's position (compare verses 11-14).

Building again what we have destroyed

Paul then speaks in the first person about one who would build up again what he had previously destroyed. That would surely be a contradictory and hypocritical thing to do. One must be wrong either when he built it up or when he destroyed it. This is a general truth. When a person contradicts himself, one time or the other he must be wrong. This is a useful point in teaching. When people teach a doctrine that causes them to contradict themselves, then they convict themselves as transgressors.

The application in context is to Peter who had taught Cornelius and others that they could be saved by the gospel, but he did not require them to be circumcised. In doing this, he had destroyed the idea that the law was necessary, and he had worked to destroy the barrier between Jew and Gentile Christians. He had shown that they could associate together. He himself had made this very argument to the Jews in Acts 11. Now, by refusing to associate with Gentiles, he was rebuilding the Old Testament as a requirement to salvation and rebuilding the barrier between Jews and Gentiles.

Clearly, one time or another Peter was a transgressor. Of course, Peter and everyone present knew which time it was. All of this demonstrates that Peter was acting hypocritically in the situation for which Paul was rebuking him. So, he was proving himself a transgressor both by contradicting the true teaching of the gospel and by being hypocritical.

Through the law I died to the law that I might live to God.

In verse 19 Paul speaks in the first person, but the application is to Peter as well as to all Christians. We must die to the law to live to God.

Death here carries the idea of separation (as in James 2:26), just as life refers to union or oneness. In order to live or be united with God, we must die to or be separated from the law. Why is this so, and how does one "through the law" die to the law?

The law itself condemned men to be guilty of sin, but then it could not remove the sins for which it proved them to be guilty (Romans 3:20-23; chapter 7; Galatians 3:19-25; Hebrews 10:1-18). So the law itself made it necessary that men be separated from the law. So long as men remained subject to the law, the law itself proved them to be under condemnation. In order to be saved they therefore needed to escape that law with its condemnation (see notes on verse 16).

Peter and Paul both had realized this (verse 16). So they had died to the law by accepting the gospel (which gives true forgiveness and union with God). They had both taught that men no longer needed to obey its precepts.

This shows the complete inconsistency and hypocrisy of then binding the law on others. It constitutes putting them back under the very thing that separated them from God! They had to leave their obligation to the law in order to have fellowship with God, so to bind the law again would separate them from God! This is a horrible consequence which shows why Paul is so concerned about the issue.

Note that "law" here is used, as explained under verse 16, to refer to the system or principle of justification by law-keeping without forgiveness. This was the kind of system the Old Testament was. This does not mean we are free to disobey the New Testament or that we are no longer subject to any commands.

But what Paul here states about Peter is also true of all those who would seek to bind the seventh-day Sabbath and other aspects of the Old Testament law on Christians today. Like Peter and Paul, people seek to receive salvation by the sacrifice of Jesus Christ under the gospel. And as with Peter and Paul, this amounts to a recognition that no one can be saved by keeping the precepts of the Old Testament law. That law simply could not save. If so, why go back and bind it? To do so is to build again that which they have destroyed and to return to that to which they have died. In so doing, they make themselves transgressors.

2:20,21 – *I have been crucified with Christ, so it is no longer I who live but Christ who lives in me. The life I live is lived by faith in the son of God who loved me and delivered himself for me. I do not nullify the grace of God, for if righteousness came through the law then Christ died for nothing.*

Paul has discussed how the law cannot justify, therefore we must die to the law and live to God (verses 16,19). In verse 20 he appears to simply be enlarging on the significance of this death and life with Jesus. Notice that Paul states that Jesus died personally for him. Many Scriptures show that Jesus died for all, but each of us should take this personally, realizing that the sacrifice of Jesus applies directly to us.

We die to the law when we are crucified with Christ, then Christ lives in us, because we live by faith in Him. This is a fascinating and important concept.

Crucified with Christ

What does it mean to die with Christ and live with Him? There are several senses in which it is true. Clearly Christ's death removed the

Old Testament law, and we too must die to that law. Notice other ways the New Testament says we must die with Christ:

We must die to self.

Matthew 16:24-27 – To come after Jesus, we must deny self, take up our cross, and follow Him. The cross was a *place to die*. We must take our cross and follow Jesus, but where was He going? He was going to *die* (verse 21).

Verse 25 – The issue regards losing or gaining life. In order to live, we must die!

Verses 26,27 – If we live so we gain the whole world, we may lose our soul at the judgment. The lesson is that, to gain our life in eternity, we must die now. Deny self. This means ***total commitment*** to serving God. Give up what you want and live your life to please God.

Galatians 5:24,25 – Crucify the flesh with its passions and lusts. We all have natural desires, which are not necessarily wrong. But sometimes they lead us to disobey what is taught by the Spirit in the word. We must put to death these desires and follow the Spirit.

2 Corinthians 5:15 – Jesus died for us so we should no longer live for our***selves***, but for Him who died for us. Most people prefer to please themselves. "I don't want anybody telling me what to do!" This attitude must be killed so we let God tell us what to do. (2 Corinthians 8:5)

Luke 9:23 – The parallel to Matthew 16:24 adds to take up your cross *daily*. Crucifying self means denying your desires every day. It is a continual struggle to achieve total commitment to the Lord.

Galatians 2:20 – All these other passages help us understand this passage in Galatians. I have been crucified with Christ. It is no longer I who live, but Christ who lives in me. ***Self*** must be slain, because our desire to please self is what causes spiritual problems.

See Romans 12:1,2.

We must die to the will of men.

Colossians 2:8,20 – We die with Christ from the basic principles of the world. This refers to submitting to human laws (verse 22). Instead we follow Jesus the head (verse 19).

Matthew 15:9 – Worship based on human commands is vain. Why should we not submit? Because we died with Christ. Death often refers to separation. We separate ourselves from man-made laws, refusing to obey them.

Galatians 6:14 – Because Jesus died for me, the world has been crucified to me and I to the world. The context shows this means that I do not allow the pressures of the world to lead me to disobey Christ (compare verses 12,13).

Matthew 10:34-39 – Losing our life, taking our cross and following Jesus, requires us to serve Jesus even when this alienates us from our dearest loved ones. If we are not willing to make this sacrifice, we are not worthy of Jesus.

We must die to sin.

1 Peter 2:14 – Jesus bore our sins on the cross so we might **die to sin** and live to righteousness.

Romans 6:3-7 – The old man was **crucified** so the body of sin might be done away (verse 6). He who has **died** is justified from sin (verse 7). In physical death, the spirit departs from the body (James 2:26). In baptism, the body of sin is cut off from our soul.

Verse 17,18 – This happens when we obey from the heart the form of teaching delivered and are then made free from sin. His death then forgives our sins (death to sin) and we are raised to walk in newness of life.

Romans 6:1,2 – If we have **died** to sin (the guilt is removed), why return to the practice of sin? That is what some want to do. What good would it be to receive forgiveness if we return to sin?

Romans 8:13,14 – To live after the flesh leads to spiritual death. To avoid that death, we must **put to death** the deeds of the body (sin).

Colossians 3 – Verses 3-11 – We died to sin, so we should **put to death** these earthly members because they cause God's wrath to come upon us. Verses 12-14 – All these sins must be replaced with good habits.

2 Timothy 2:11 – To **live** with Jesus, we must **die** with Him. Before you can live, you must die. Eternal life comes only after we die to self, to the will of others, and to sin.

If righteousness is by the law, Christ died in vain.

Finally, Paul concluded his discussion of Peter's error by showing that Paul's position did not set aside, frustrate, nullify, or make void the grace of God. But the implication is that the Judaizers' position did do so.

Jesus died so men can be forgiven of their sins. This was the ultimate demonstration of the grace of God. But if people can be saved by the Old Testament law, what purpose would Jesus' death serve? He would have died in vain, and no one would need the grace of God. Why did Jesus make such an incredible sacrifice, if people already had the means of salvation? He died because the Old Testament cannot save.

But if the Old Testament law cannot save, then why require people to go back to it? To do so is to frustrate God's grace revealed in Jesus' death. It implies that Jesus died in vain. This is the effect of Peter's conduct. People were saved by Jesus apart from the law, yet Peter treated them as though they were sinners because they did not keep the Old Testament. This implies that the sacrifice of Jesus and His gospel are not enough to save, but people must go back to the Old Testament law. Such implies Jesus died in vain.

Although the account does not state Peter's reaction to Paul's rebuke, we can only conclude that he repented, since he later so plainly commended the teachings of Paul in 2 Peter 3:15,16.

Paul has now showed that his teaching was received directly from Jesus, not from the apostles or any other man. Further, his doctrine had been examined by the other apostles, and they had agreed it was correct. Finally, when an apostle acted contrary to what Paul taught, he was acting contrary both to the truth and to what he himself knew to be correct. Paul had resisted Peter's conduct and had defended his conclusion adequately.

The clear conclusion is that the Judaizers were as wrong as Peter and for the same reasons. Likewise, the same is true of the modern-day Judaizers who seek to bind the seventh-day Sabbath and other Old Testament teachings today.

But Peter did not continue to defend his error. We must conclude from 2 Peter 3:15 that Peter repented. By continuing to oppose Paul's teaching, however, the Judaizers were continuing to oppose the truth. Modern-day Judaizers need to realize that they cannot continue seeking to bind the Old Testament law and still maintain the grace of God. Like Peter and the Judaizers in the first century, they must make a choice either to accept salvation by the gospel alone and abandon their insistence on following the Old Testament, or they will cease to receive God's grace.

This concludes Paul's historical account of his teaching and prepares the way for a discussion of its doctrinal foundation.

Galatians 3

Chapter 3,4 – Evidence that the New Testament Replaced the Old Testament

3:1-14 - Justification by Faith Compared to the Curse of the Law

3:1-5 – The gospel confirmed by the Holy Spirit

3:1,2 – Paul asked who had bewitched the Galatians before whose eyes Christ had been openly set forth as crucified. Then he urged them to consider whether they had received the Spirit by the works of the law or by the hearing of faith.

In chapters 1 and 2 Paul had defended his authority as an apostle, showing that what he taught had been revealed to him by Jesus and was approved by the other apostles. Now he begins to examine specifically the doctrine he taught about the Old Testament as compared to the New Testament. He explains the doctrine and proves that it is valid.

The Galatians were leaving the truth despite the evidence that Jesus had been crucified for them.

First, Paul begins with a direct rebuke of the Galatians for leaving the truth on this point. He directly addresses them (see on 1:2), clearly showing that he is no longer summarizing what he had told Peter (chapter 2).

He calls them foolish, indicating that they were using very poor judgment. They were not acting wisely according to the evidence of the case. On the contrary, they appeared to be bewitched, under some kind of spell. This is exaggeration, of course. But the point is that the truth seems so obvious that people who knew the truth and left it are as though they are no longer in control of their minds. They seem as though they have lost their senses. He asks who had done this to them; and of course no one had literally done it, but the Judaizers were responsible for this harmful influence on the Galatians.

Paul explains that the Galatians had received the evidence that Jesus was crucified and raised from the dead. They had been taught this by one who was an eyewitness that Jesus had been raised (see 4:13). Paul had, in effect, drawn them a clear picture of the event and its meaning. How could they possibly turn from it?

Note the clear implication that acceptance of Judaistic teaching had the effect of turning one's back on Jesus' crucifixion (see 1:6-9). This is true because Jesus' death is the sacrifice of the gospel that really can forgive sin, unlike the Old Testament which could not forgive sin (2:16,21). To go back and bind the Old Testament would be to leave the system that could truly forgive sin in order to return to the system that required perfect law-keeping and could not save. This would have the effect of belittling the necessity for Jesus' death.

The Galatians had received the Holy Spirit through the gospel, not through the law.

Then Paul asked a specific question about the Holy Spirit. Did the Galatians receive Him by the works of the law or by the hearing of faith (i.e., the message of faith in the gospel)? This contrast between law and faith is the same as in 2:16, and contrasts the two different systems of justification. The hearing of faith confirms the fact that one must be taught the gospel before one can believe (Romans 10:17; 1:16; etc.). But hearing of faith stands for the complete response one must give to the gospel, just as faith does elsewhere.

But which system had given the Holy Spirit to the Galatians? This seems to be exactly parallel to verse 5, except that there Paul specifies that he is talking about the doing of miracles by the Holy Spirit. Clearly the Old Testament had not given the Holy Spirit or done miracles among the Galatians – Old Testament miracles had ceased when God had ceased revealing Old Testament teaching.

Miracles had been done among the Galatians by Paul and other New Testament teachers who delivered the gospel. Almost certainly some of the Galatian Christians have received miraculous gifts of the Spirit. This was the obvious answer to Paul's rhetorical question. The Galatians had received the Holy Spirit by the gospel, not by the Old Testament law. (Paul might also be implying that the teaching of the Judaizers had not been confirmed by miracles like Paul's teaching had been confirmed.)

What is the point? This is explained when one understands the purpose of miracles. Miracles were given to confirm the message of the one through whom the miracle was done (Mark 16:20; John 5:36; 20:30,31; Acts 2:22; 14:3; 2 Corinthians 12:11,12; Hebrews 2:3,4; 1

Kings 18:36-39). But Paul and his associates had done miracles, and they were the ones who laid hands on people to give them the gifts of the Holy Spirit (as in Acts 19:1-7). So, the point is that the miracles and coming of the Holy Spirit confirmed Paul's apostleship (2 Corinthians 12:11,12) and thereby confirmed his message to be from God.

Specifically, the miracles done through Paul confirmed what he taught. But what he taught was that the gospel had replaced the Old Testament, so the law is no longer in effect (compare Acts 15:12). God had likewise done miracles at Cornelius' household, when Peter baptized them without requiring circumcision (Acts 10,11). So the coming of the Holy Spirit and the associated miracles confirmed the message of Paul regarding the Old Testament. The Galatians knew this. Why then did they doubt the validity of his message? This was folly indeed.

Willis argues at length that Paul is referring in verse 2 to the fact that the Galatians received the indwelling of the Holy Spirit by the gospel. He points out that miracles are specifically mentioned in verse 5 but not in verse 2. So why would Paul make the same point twice in the context? Of course, Paul might make the same point twice for the sake of emphasis, as is often done in Scripture. Verse 5 could be the conclusion and restatement of an argument begun in verse 1.

Willis' view could be correct and surely does no violence to Scripture. It surely is true that all Christians receive the indwelling of the Spirit when they are converted. However, since the indwelling of the Spirit cannot be confirmed by any observable evidence, it seems to me to be a more convincing argument if receiving the Spirit in verse 2 refers to miracles.

3:3-5 – Having begun in the Spirit, were they so foolish as to think they would be perfected in the flesh? Did they suffer so many things in vain, if it was in vain? So, He who supplies the Spirit to them and works miracles among them, does He do it by the works of the law or by the hearing of faith?

Spirit or flesh?

Paul then again describes them as foolish. When they had heard and accepted the gospel, they had received the Spirit and His miraculous evidence for the gospel. Did it make sense, after this beginning, to end up emphasizing the flesh, as is done in circumcision? The gospel often contrasts the Spirit to the flesh – see Galatians 5:16-26; 6:7; 4:9; Romans 2:28,29; 8:1-6; Hebrews 7:16.

To walk by the Spirit is to follow the message revealed by the Holy Spirit and confirmed by His miracles. This is how the Galatians had begun their service to God. This message emphasizes proper spirit and attitude in all that we do in service to God. The old law, however, also

Commentary on Galatians

had significant outward or fleshly emphasis – especially in this case an emphasis on physical circumcision.

Most of them were Gentiles, who had never served God under the old law. They had begun a true relationship with true forgiveness by means of the gospel given by the Spirit and emphasizing that which is spiritual. Did it make sense now to turn from that Spirit-breathed and confirmed message and go back to emphasize the flesh in a system that required perfect outward obedience?

Note the distinction between the spiritual emphasis in the New Testament as compared to the fleshly or physical emphasis of the Old Testament:

Fleshly Old Testament	Spiritual New Testament
"carnal ordinances" (Hebrews 9:10)	spiritual law (John 6:63,27,68; Eph. 6:17)
physical nation	spiritual nation (1 Peter 2:9)
earthly kingdom	spiritual kingdom (John 18:36; Romans 14:17)
physical birth	spiritual birth (John 3:3,5; 1 Peter 1:23)
physical circumcision (Romans 2:28,29)	spiritual circumcision (Romans 2:28,29)
physical temple (Hebrews 9:1-5,24)	spiritual temple (1 Peter 2:5; Eph. 2:21,22)
physical priesthood	spiritual priesthood (1 Peter 2:5,9)
physical sacrifices (Hebrews 10:1-4; 9:13)	spiritual worship (1 Peter 2:5; Heb. 13:15) sacrifices/songs (1 Cor. 14:15; Eph. 5:19)

Perhaps the meaning here goes further than the above. Surely Paul is referring back to the point of verse 2 and verse 5. Perhaps he is saying that the gospel he preached was revealed by the Spirit and confirmed by miracles to be from the Spirit. But the Judaizers were not only emphasizing the flesh (circumcision), but flesh is all they had. Their message was not from the Spirit, nor did they have any proof from the Spirit for what they taught. Why turn from Paul's Spirit-revealed-and-confirmed message to that which had nothing from the Spirit to approve it?

Willingness to suffer persecution

Further, all who live for God will suffer persecution (2 Timothy 3:12). Apparently the Galatians had suffered when they became Christians. Much of this persecution came at the hands of Jews who, like the Judaizers, were trying to convince people to keep the Old

Testament law. In fact, the Judaizers taught as they did largely to avoid persecution. See 5:11; 6:12; see 4:29; Hebrews 10:35. The book of Acts records many examples in which Paul and other Christians were persecuted by Jews in city after city.

Having suffered past persecution, did it make sense for the Galatians to go back to keep the Old Testament? This would make their suffering for the gospel vain. It implies that they did not need to endure it – the suffering was worthless, unnecessary. To turn from the gospel back to the Old Law now, in order to avoid persecution, would be to imply that they never should have followed a message that led to persecution. But if they were right in following that message to begin with, then they should stay with it now regardless of persecution that may come.

In fact, this proved that, one time or the other, they were wrong. Either they were wrong when they stood for the gospel message as taught by Paul, even though persecuted for it. Or else they would be wrong now if they left it.

Verse 5 seems to repeat the point of verse 2 for emphasis, as was done in 1:8,9. It seems to conclude the argument of verses 1-5.

3:6-9 – Justification by faith confirmed by the case of Abraham

3:6,7 – Abraham believed God, and it was reckoned unto him for righteousness. So we can be sure that those who are of faith are sons of Abraham.

Abraham an example of faith

Next Paul uses the example of Abraham to defend the principle of justification by faith, rather than by the law. The power of this argument ought to be overwhelming to those who considered themselves descendants of Abraham.

Paul will show that Abraham was justified by faith and, in particular, that this was part of God's promise to Abraham. This principle ought to be important for every Bible believer, but it should be especially so for the Judaizers. Every Bible believer respects Abraham and seeks to learn about him, but to the Jews he was the patriarch of their nation and religion.

Jews held to the Old Testament because of their misplaced emphasis on their relationship to Abraham and to Moses. Paul will show that both of these are reasons to accept salvation by faith through the gospel, not by perfect keeping of the old law. He masterfully turns their arguments against them.

Jews magnified and rallied round their relationship to Abraham. They believed they were God's people just because of physical lineage to Abraham. The law was theirs because he was their ancestor, so they held to the law. See Matthew 3:9; John 8:33,39.

But Abraham was justified by *faith*, as stated in Genesis 15:6. He was not justified by the law of Moses, for it had not been given yet. Nor was he justified by circumcision, for it too had not been ordained at the time this statement was made (circumcision was not ordained until Genesis 17).

Rather, Abraham was accepted by God because he had faith in God to leave his homeland and travel to a place he had never seen, trusting simply in the promise God gave him regarding his descendants (compare Genesis 12). This promise had just been repeated in Genesis 15, then the record said that he trusted God (according to that promise) and so was justified on the basis of trusting in God. See also Hebrews 11:8-10; Romans chapter 4; James 2:14-26.

As such, Abraham became an example of the kind of faith we need to be justified under the gospel. This does not mean he was under the gospel, of course. But he placed his faith in the promises which were the basis of the gospel and salvation through Jesus (see verse 8).

And the particular force of Paul's statement is that Abraham was not justified by the Law of Moses nor by circumcision. He was justified before he was circumcised and many years before the coming of the law of Moses. Surely this disproved the argument of the Judaizers. Their great hero and the founder of their race was himself justified without the very things the Judaizers said were necessary. He needed forgiveness, just as we do, and he received it ultimately through the sacrifice of Jesus, who was promised to be his descendant. This is an example to us.

Children of Abraham

The Jews thought God should accept them because they were sons (descendants) of Abraham and had been circumcised. But Paul has just demonstrated that Abraham himself was justified, not because of circumcision, but because of faith. It follows that those who are true children of Abraham spiritually are, not those who are physical descendants of Abraham or who have been circumcised, but those who have faith like Abraham. But Gentiles could be justified by faith as well as Jews could. So, Jew and Gentile both can be spiritual sons of Abraham by faith. Note verse 9 below. See also Galatians 3:29; Romans 2:28,29.

Note that nothing here denies the need to obey commands in order to be saved by faith under the gospel. Abraham obeyed God, and his obedience was essential to his acceptable relationship to God by faith (see Genesis 12, 22, etc.). Specifically, Hebrews 11:8-10 and James 2:14-26 assert that his obedience was necessary for him to be justified by faith.

John 8:39 – Jesus said to them, "If you were Abraham's children, you would do the works of Abraham." Note that Jesus himself said that being a true child of Abraham is not simply a matter of what we believe.

It requires a faith that **works**. We must **walk** in the **steps** of Abraham – Romans 4:12.

So, "faith" is again used here referring to the principle of justification described in 2:16, not just for a conviction in one's heart without obedience. Nowhere do the Scriptures teach, as modern denominations often do, that one is forgiven of sins simply by being convinced that Jesus is the Savior so that he "prays the sinner's prayer in order to accept Jesus into his heart."

No passage of Scripture anywhere describes an alien sinner, who is not a child of God, being instructed to pray for forgiveness or receiving forgiveness on the basis of a prayer or on the basis of faith only. Rather, the Scriptures teach that one who truly believes must repent of sins, confess Christ and be baptized for the remission of sins (Acts 2:38).

This passage says that Abraham believed God and it was accounted to him *for* righteousness. Was he saved before he believed, or did he need to believe in order to receive righteousness? We realize that his faith did not earn righteousness as a matter of debt, but surely all would agree that "for righteousness" means it was a condition he must meet in order to receive it.

But Acts 2:38 says one must repent and be baptized *for* (same Greek word as in Galatians 3:6) remission of sins. So, is a person saved before he is baptized, or does he need to be baptized in order to receive forgiveness? Baptism does not earn righteousness as a matter of debt any more than faith does, but the Scriptures clearly teach that baptism is a condition one must meet in order to receive forgiveness, just as surely as faith is.

3:8,9 – Foreseeing that God would justify Gentiles by faith, the Scripture preached the gospel beforehand to Abraham when it said that all the nations of the earth would be blessed in him. So those who are of faith are blessed with Abraham who had faith.

Not only did Genesis say Abraham himself was justified by faith, but the promise in which Abraham trusted was a promise that offered the same blessing to all people, Jew and Gentile. It was the promise to Abraham, "In you all the nations shall be blessed." See Genesis 12:3; 18:18; 22:18; 26:4; 28:14.

Paul says this promise actually preached the gospel to Abraham. In what way? Because the significance of the promise was that Jesus would be a descendant of Abraham (the "seed" through whom the promise was fulfilled – Galatians 3:16). And the blessing Jesus would bring would be forgiveness or justification from sin through His sacrifice – Acts 3:25,26. But that is the essence of the gospel!

So, while the details were not spelled out and the system of justification was not yet in effect, nevertheless, the promise in which

Abraham believed was the promise of the gospel – the very promise the Judaizers were rejecting!

But this promise offered this blessing to "all nations" – not just one nation (Israel), but all nations. "Gentiles" means "nations." The promise specifically offered the blessing to "all" nations. Yet the Jews and Judaizers wanted to monopolize the promise for Jews only by insisting that, in order for Gentiles to receive the promised blessing, they in effect had to become Jews.

The Judaizers' position denied and contradicted the very promise to Abraham, in which they claimed to trust! It would have condemned Abraham, because he himself had not yet been circumcised at the time God justified him! Their position stood in direct defiance of the authority they cited to defend it!

So again Paul concludes, as in verse 7 (see there) that Abraham himself proves that the only principle on which anyone has been or can be justified is the principle of justification by faith, not by the old law or perfect law-keeping of any law. It follows that, in order to be blessed as Abraham was, all people must accept salvation through the death of Jesus Christ on the basis of faith. This is what it means to be sons of Abraham in the sense of children of faith (verse 7).

3:10-14 – The Law does not justify but condemns

3:10-12 – As many as are of the works of the law are under a curse, since the law itself said that anyone who did not continue in all things written in the book of the law to do them would be accursed. So no one is justified by the law. In fact, the law itself said that the righteous should live by faith, whereas the law required doing in order to live by it. So the law did not justify on the basis of faith.

Paul now turns to the "law" that the Judaizers so wanted to bind upon people, and he shows what the law itself says would be the consequence of binding it. This is a fuller explanation of the summary statement of 2:16 – see notes there.

The law condemns.

The problem with the law was that it brought a curse on everyone who did not keep it perfectly. This is quoted from Deuteronomy 27:26, perhaps combined with Psalm 119:21; Jeremiah 11:3; etc. (compare James 2:10-12). This is the principle of justification by law-keeping.

The law itself cannot justify unless one keeps it sinlessly. One must **do all** things written in the law, or he is accursed. Only if one obeys all things perfectly can one stand before the lawgiver, claiming a right standing according to the law because he never violated it. But the problem is that, once one has violated the law, he stands under the curse of penalty of it. But with regard to the law of God, that is the case of **everyone**. No one kept the law sinlessly (Romans 3:9-23).

Then, as explained under 2:16, the law could do nothing to bring about justification, because it did not have sacrifices that could really forgive sins. So, no one was justified by the law – verse 11, as discussed in 2:16.

These verses give a fundamental statement of the issue Paul is teaching regarding the law. ***The very nature of the Old Testament law was such that no one could ever be justified by it.*** All the law ever did for anyone as regards justification was to condemn them. It plainly stated that anyone who violated the law was accursed. But everybody who lived under the law violated it, so everyone who lived under it was accursed! Of itself, the law offered no solution for the problem, because the sacrifices under that law could not ultimately forgive sin.

The law said faith was needed.

The law furthermore confirmed that it could not justify from sin when it stated that justification must ultimately come on the basis of faith. The law said "the just will live by faith." The law leads to death, but faith is what is needed for life! This is what the law itself said. See Habakkuk 2:4 (compare Romans 1:17; Hebrews 10:38).

The law said that, in order to live spiritually before God, people must have faith. But law itself was not of faith. Instead, the law said people must ***do*** the law to live – Leviticus 18:5; Nehemiah 9:29; Ezekiel 20:11,13,21; (Romans 10:5).

This did not mean that people under the law lacked faith or were not taught to have it. On the contrary, people who pleased God under the law did have faith (Hebrews 11). But Paul is contrasting the two ***systems*** of justification.

The system of justification on the basis of law keeping, on which the Old Testament was based, could save only when one kept the law perfectly. If one sinned, the law itself could not save him. What was needed then was faith in a substitutionary sacrifice. The law had sacrifices, but they could not permanently forgive. So, the law said faith in a sacrifice was needed, but did not of itself provide that needed sacrifice! (See on 2:16.)

Nor does this mean that salvation under the gospel is by "faith only" without obedience to commands. The point is explained further in verses 13,14: the blessing predicted was justification by one who suffered in our place. If we have faith in Him, we can be saved even though we have not lived sinlessly. But the faith must be obedient faith.

3:13,14 – Christ redeemed us from the curse of the law, becoming a curse for us as it was written that everyone who hangs on a tree is cursed. As a result, the Gentiles might receive the blessing of Abraham in Christ and then might receive the promise of the Spirit through faith.

Here is the explanation of what the law lacked. It condemned everyone who disobeyed it, and it even said faith was needed to save, but it did not provide the sacrifice in which people need to place their faith.

The sacrifice people needed was the death of Jesus. Jesus became a curse for us when He died on the cross. Men were under the curse of the law for disobedience. Jesus committed no sin, yet He became a curse for us when He died. Deuteronomy 21:23 said that anyone who died by hanging on a tree was under a curse, because that was a punishment for disobeying God.

Jesus did not sin, so He did not deserve to die. Yet He bore the curse of the punishment of sin, which curse we deserved to bear. He bore it in our place and thereby paid the price to redeem us from the curse of the law. He paid the penalty for our sins.

Note that the passage does not say Jesus was guilty but only that He bore the curse or the punishment for us. Calvinism claims that the sins of mankind were actually transferred to Jesus so that he became guilty before God. This is nowhere stated here or anywhere else in Scripture. The Calvinistic concept of transferring guilt or righteousness is totally unscriptural, not found anywhere in Scripture. The guilt of Adam's sin is not transferred from Adam to his descendants by inheritance (Ezekiel 18:20). The righteousness of Jesus' sinless life is not transferred to the believer. Nor was the guilt of sin transferred from sinners to Jesus. What He bore was the curse – that is the punishment for sin, not the guilt of sin.

The term "redeem" means to liberate or secure the deliverance of someone or something. The idea is that one has been taken captive or brought into bondage or slavery. He was redeemed when a purchase price was paid so he could be set free. Paul has explained that sin puts us under the bondage or captivity of the curse of the law. Jesus provided the sacrifice that can set us free.

This sacrifice is what the law did not provide. And this sacrifice is that in which we must place our trust. The system of salvation by faith does not excuse people who live as they please, disregarding God's law. But it does offer forgiveness to those who, by faith receive the forgiveness of Jesus' sacrifice.

This, in fact, was the blessing that God had promised to Abraham would come on all nations through his seed (compare verse 8). The seed was Christ (verse 16), and the blessing was forgiveness through a sacrifice that could truly forgive sins so they would be remembered no more. This is what must be the object of our "faith," according to the promise of the Holy Spirit.

But to whom was this promise offered: to "all nations" (compare verse 8). That is what the Spirit had said to Abraham. But that includes the Gentiles!

So the conclusion of Paul's argument is that the Judaizers sought to bind a system that admitted it could not solve the problem of sin but only placed people under the curse of their own disobedience. It taught the need for faith in a sacrifice but could not give the sacrifice.

But the promise to Abraham pointed to the coming of the sacrifice in which we must believe. That sacrifice was offered when Jesus died on the cross, granting salvation to Gentiles as well as Jews, just like God promised. And now the Judaizing Christians sought to deny that the sacrifice alone was good enough to save the Gentiles. They wanted to require them to go back and keep the law that condemned but could not save!

"Redeem" (εξαγοραζω) ... "1 to secure deliverance of, *deliver, liberate...*" – Bauer-Danker-Arndt-Gingrich.

3:15-29 - The Relationship Between the Law, the Gospel, and the Promise to Abraham

3:15,16 – Even a covenant made by men, when it has been ratified, no one can make it void or add to it. The promises that God made to Abraham and to his seed spoke, not of many seeds, but of one seed which is Christ.

No one may modify a covenant that has been confirmed.

Paul here uses the term "covenant" to refer to the promise regarding the seed of Abraham. We usually think of a covenant as involving mutual agreements between two parties. However, the term used here does not necessarily involve mutual obligation. It may simply refer to a commitment made by one party to another. That is the case here, since Paul uses it interchangeably with the promise of God. It follows that no conditions were required – that is, God was going to use the nation of Israel to bring Christ into the world to give a blessing on all nations regardless of the faithfulness of the nation of Israel.

The Judaizers greatly emphasized the covenant with Abraham and the blessings promised to his descendants. So, Paul turned to a discussion of the promise to Abraham in order to show that it demonstrated his point, contrary to the teaching of the Judaizers.

The Judaizers apparently concluded that the law was part of the covenant with Abraham, or at least was tied to it, so that in order to receive the blessings of the covenant, one had to keep the law. Paul here disproves that view by showing that the covenant/promise and the law were two separate things. When Paul claimed the law was no longer binding, he was not saying people could no longer receive the blessing promised to Abraham.

Paul first showed that the covenant, as given by God to Abraham, could not be modified. He based this on the fact that even a man-made covenant cannot be modified, once it has been confirmed. Neither party can annul the agreement or add to it. (When Paul says that he spoke after the manner of men, he meant simply that he was speaking about affairs as practiced by humans but which in this case served as an illustration of divine covenants.)

We may illustrate this with a contract to purchase a house. Once the contract has been signed by both parties, neither one can set it aside or change it without the agreement of the other. It is binding until it has been fulfilled. Depending on the covenant, the parties might mutually agree to make a new covenant superseding the old, or they might make some other covenant. Or, if the covenant itself so allowed, they might fulfill its terms so that it ceases to be binding. But they cannot simply set aside the original covenant, contrary to its terms.

> "Covenant" (διαθηκη) – "... freq. used in legal and commercial discourse of disposition of things ... w. implication of promissory obligation. Disposition of one's personal effects would naturally come under testamentary law, hence 1 *last will and testament* ... 2 ... in LXX δ. retains the component of legal disposition of personal goods while omitting that of the anticipated death of a testator. ... Hence a δ. decreed by God cannot require the death of the testator to make it operative. Nevertheless, another essential characteristic of a testament is retained, namely that it is the declaration of one person's initiative, not the result of an agreement betw. two parties, like a compact or a contract. ... In the 'covenants' of God, it was God alone who set the conditions; hence *covenant* ... 3 The mng. *compact, contract* seems firmly established for Gr-Rom. times..." – Bauer-Danker-Arndt-Gingrich.

Seed singular

Paul applies this concept to the promise or covenant made to Abraham. The promise was made to Abraham and to his seed. This refers to the promise "in thy *seed* shall all nations of the earth be blessed" – see verse 8. The "seed" here referred to was Christ. It is singular in force, referring to a particular individual, rather than plural in force, referring to the whole nation of Jews.

Note that Willis discusses at length the fact that the original Hebrew word here, like our word "seed," can be either singular or plural in force. So, it would be a weak argument to claim (as I myself have in the past) that Paul is making an argument from necessary inference based on the number of the noun.

However, Hogg and Vine point out that God could have chosen a word that was clearly plural if he meant to refer to the descendants of Abraham, rather than using a word that was singular in form. So, Paul is giving an inspired interpretation in which he points out that it was a deliberate choice to use a singular word because the intent of God was to make a statement whose fulfillment would be found in one man, Jesus, not in the whole nation. So, the blessing to come on all nations (Jews and Gentiles) was something to come through Jesus.

Acts 3:25,26 explains specifically that this blessing was justification from sin by Jesus' sacrifice. This blessing came to all men through Jesus because of the promise to Abraham. Paul's point will be that the law was not inherently a part of that covenant, so the law did not have to continue in effect in order for people to receive the promised blessing.

A confirmed covenant needs no more confirmation.

Note an important point that can be made here. A covenant, once ratified or confirmed, does not need to be repeatedly confirmed afterwards to stay in effect. It remains in effect on the basis of its original confirmation. A legal contract, for example, does not need to be repeatedly signed every year to be binding. The original signing maintains the force of the contract for as long as the terms of the contract require.

This was true, as well, of both the Old and New Testaments. They were confirmed by the miracles that proved they were from God. While the covenants were in the process of being revealed, miracles were needed to confirm the terms as being from God. Once they were complete, however, no further miraculous confirmation was needed. Specifically, the New Testament has been confirmed and there is no need for further confirmation by miracles today.

To claim, as some do, that we still need miracles today, is to misunderstand the purpose of miracles. The miracles of the Old Testament served to confirm that the Old Testament message was from God. When that message had been completely revealed and confirmed by miracles, there was no longer a need for miracles to confirm that covenant.

Likewise, the New Testament was confirmed by the miracles done by the Holy Spirit through inspired men in the first century. That covenant has now been completely revealed and completely confirmed, so miracles are no longer needed. They have ceased and will not be repeated. To argue that miracles are needed today is to show a lack of faith in the New Testament as a completed and confirmed covenant between God and man.

See Mark 16:20; John 5:36; 20:30,31; Acts 2:22; 14:3; 2 Corinthians 12:11,12; Hebrews 2:3,4; 1 Kings 18:36-39; Exodus 4:1-9; 7:3-5; 14:30,31.

3:17,18 – Since the law came four hundred and thirty years after God confirmed the covenant to Abraham, it cannot nullify the promise. If the inheritance came through the law, then it would not come by the promise, but God granted it to Abraham by promise.

The law could not annul the covenant that God confirmed to Abraham.

Applying the principle of verse 15 to the covenant with Abraham, Paul shows that the law, which came four hundred and thirty years after the promise, could not change the effect or power of the promise. It could not annul it or make it of no effect.

Nor – and here is the main application – nor could the law provide the inheritance that the promise offered. The promised inheritance (justification from sins) could only be provided by that which was the fulfillment of the promise – i.e., Jesus' death.

The law was not the fulfillment of the promise, nor any inherent part of it. There was nothing about the promise to Abraham that necessarily included the law given by Moses. The law was not inherently necessary to the promise nor vice versa. Therefore, to conclude that justification requires the law or is provided by the law is to misunderstand the promise. Justification comes by the fulfillment of the promise (Jesus' death), not by the law. Justification was never the ultimate purpose of the law, but it was the ultimate purpose of the promise.

Since Paul uses human agreements to illustrate his point, let us expand on that idea with specific modern examples. Suppose in the year 2010 a man purchases a house and signs a thirty-year mortgage to pay for it. Later, in the year 2015 he purchases an automobile and signs a five-year loan. The two agreements are essentially separate. They began at separate times and end at separate times and they served separate purposes. No one would have the right to tie the car loan to the house mortgage as though they were inseparable.

In the same way, the promise God made to Abraham was made long before the coming of the Law of Moses, and one of its benefits (redemption through Christ) continued long after the end of the Law of Moses. The two covenants served two entirely different purposes. So no one had the right to continue to bind the Law of Moses after it expired. In particular, no one had the right to bind the law on people simply because they want the benefits of the promise made to Abraham.

The law and the covenant or promise were two separate items.

It is not clear to me that Paul's argument necessarily follows from the promise to Abraham. It may simply be an inspired explanation of the promise. That is, I am not sure that one could have been expected to know all this simply by studying the promise in Genesis. Rather than Paul's argument being a necessary inference which has to follow from what Genesis stated, perhaps Paul is giving an inspired explanation, showing how his teaching harmonized with and explained the real fulfillment of the promise.

This does, however, show how thoroughly mistaken the Judaizers were in claiming the law was necessary to justification. They appealed to their heritage on the basis of the promise to Abraham and believed Jesus was the sacrifice that gave justification, but then in turn they bound the law as being required in order to receive justification. In so doing they confused the law and the promise. Paul is saying this is not correct.

The blessing (promise) and the law were separate and distinct items. The promise given to Abraham granted a blessing to all nations, which would include Gentiles as well as Jews. That promise granted forgiveness through Jesus. The law, however, was a separate covenant given to the nation of Israel (not to all nations) four hundred thirty years after the promise to Abraham. Since the promise was separate and independent from the law, it does follow that the law was not necessary in order to grant the promised justification from sin. To claim that people need to keep the law in order to receive the promise of justification would be to confuse the law with the promise to Abraham, not recognizing the distinction between the two.

This is not to say that the law was a violation or contradiction to the promise. God had the right to add any arrangement He wanted for the guidance of the descendants of Abraham till the blessing promised to Abraham was fulfilled (verse 19). But the law and promise were independent, so then He could remove the law while still giving people the blessing of the promise through Jesus.

The term "inheritance," as used here, does not mean that the parent had to die in order for the child to receive the blessing intended by the parent. It may simply refer to a possession or property that one receives from someone else. In this case, it is the Father who grants the possession, but there is no implication in the word that the father must die for us to receive it.

Note: Willis discusses at length the 430 years mentioned here. There is considerable controversy regarding how this time is measured. Paul seems to state here that it was the time from the promise to Abraham till the giving of the law. Yet other passages seem to indicate a different measurement of the time. See Willis' notes for a fuller discussion.

"Inheritance" (κληρονομια) – 1 *inheritance* ... 2 *possession, property..."* – Bauer-Danker-Arndt-Gingrich.

Commentary on Galatians

3:19,20 – So, what purpose did the law serve? It was added because of transgressions till the seed should come to whom the promise had been made. It was ordained through angels by the hand of a mediator. But a mediator does not serve for just one party, but God is only one.

Why did God give the law?

Having explained that the law was not an inherent part of the promise, Paul then proceeds to answer the question that would naturally follow. What was the purpose of the law? If it was not part of – or a fulfillment of – the promise to Abraham, why did God give it? This is a good question. One might wonder why God gave the law at all. If the promise was to be fulfilled in Jesus, why not just go ahead and send Jesus centuries before the time when He did come? Why bother with the law and all the years people served under it, if it could not even justify?

Paul says the law was added because of transgressions. First, note that "added" shows it was not part of the covenant with Abraham. It was something separate that came later after the covenant had been made with Abraham, as has already been explained.

"Because of transgressions" could mean it was added because people were sinners and needed something to guide and restrain them till Jesus came to bring the solution to sin. Or it could mean it was added to show men how sinful they were so they would accept Jesus' sacrifice when it came. Both of these ideas are true, and the latter is emphasized in context. Which is meant here, I am not sure. Perhaps both are included.

Then Paul says it was added "till the Seed should come." The "seed" in this context can only mean Christ, as in verse 16. The law was added till He came and offered His sacrifice. It ended as a result of His death (compare notes on verses 24,25). Jesus was the one "to whom the promise was made," not just the one about whom it was made. It was made to Him in the sense that He received the opportunity to fulfill it.

Notice that the intent of God from the very beginning was for the law to be temporary. The effect of the promise to Abraham would continue to benefit mankind throughout all ages, because the blessing was forgiveness through the blood of Jesus Christ. The law, in contrast, was given till the seed should come. So the law was planned from the very beginning to be temporary, but the gospel which granted salvation through Christ is intended to be lasting.

Ordained through angels by the hand of a mediator

The law was appointed by angels. The law itself does not emphasize the involvement of angels in the revealing of it, but the New

Testament plainly states that this was the case as described also in Acts 7:38,53; Hebrews 2:2. Angels were clearly used in the revealing of it.

"By the hand of a mediator" refers to Moses, through whom the law was revealed. The people feared to approach the mountain, so Moses went to God to receive the law and deliver it to the people. Moses was the mediator through whom the people received God's words (Exodus 20:19; Deuteronomy 5:5). The reason Paul mentions this will be explained in verse 20.

The gospel also was revealed through a mediator, that is Jesus Christ. But it was not ordained through angels. And the mediator through whom it was revealed was not a human like Moses, but the Divine Son of God. The book of Hebrews uses this distinction to make clear one of the many advantages the gospel has over the Law of Moses (Hebrews 3:5,6; 9:15).

Verse 20 is difficult but appears to be a general statement about mediators. The existence of a mediator implies the existence of two parties who seek to resolve an alienation or negotiate a difference of viewpoint between them. But if only one party acts in a matter, why would there be need for a mediator?

However, God is one party, not two. What is the point? This is a further contrast between the law and the promise to Abraham. God did not need a mediator in making the promise to Abraham because there was no negotiation or resolution needed to. God simply spoke His promise and revealed it directly to Abraham. No mediator is needed if one party simply makes an unconditional promise. A mediator is needed only if two parties need to discuss a matter in order for it to bind themselves to an agreement.

The promise did not require a mediator, but the law did. So here is another difference showing the law and the promise to Abraham were two separate items.

3:21,22 – Did the law then contradict the promise of God to Abraham? Surely not? If God had given a law that could impart life, then the law could have resulted in righteousness. But the scriptures confined all people under sin that the promise by faith in Christ might be given to those who believe.

Was the law contrary to the promises of God?

Then Paul answers another question that would naturally arise from what has been said: Is the law somehow in violation of the promises to Abraham? If it is not part of the promise, was it an unauthorized addition? Was Paul saying there was something evil about it? Was he casting unfavorable reflections on it?

No, actually this law was as good as any law could be that functioned according to the principle of justification by works of law (as discussed in 2:16). If any law could have given life or righteousness (justification), then the law that God gave through Moses could have done it. It was not a bad law, nor was it a mistake, nor did God violate the promise to Abraham when He gave the law.

The problem was not that the law was a bad law. The problem was that no law, no matter how good it was, could have saved, so long as it acted on the principle of justification by works of law – i.e., so long as it required sinless perfection and had no real sacrifice that could remove guilt. The problem, as discussed under 2:16, is that no law can save so long as it has no forgiveness and people must earn justification by a sinless life.

What did the law accomplish?

What the law did do was to confine everyone under sin. That is, it convicted all people of being guilty of sin; and being guilty, they were slaves of sin without hope. The law required perfect obedience or else people were under the curse of disobedience. But all people disobeyed. So rather than justifying people, the law condemned everyone subject to it because they all violated the law. Those who commit sins are bondservants of it (Romans 6:12ff; John 8:31ff). They stand condemned by it, unable by their own human power to free themselves.

So, the law proved all men were guilty of sin, and therefore were subject to its curse (3:10-12). Having demonstrated that all men were guilty of sin, the law itself could do nothing about the problem, because the only sacrifices it had could not permanently remove guilt (Hebrews 10:1-18). See again notes on 2:16.

So, one purpose the law served was to prove to men that they were sinners in need of a sacrifice to be saved. Had God not sent the law, men would never have appreciated their need for Jesus' sacrifice. They would have believed they could save themselves by sinless living. By giving the law, God proved for all time that no one will be saved without Jesus' sacrifice because no one lives sinlessly. See Romans 3:19,20; 11:32.

"Law without grace, then, can expose disease but cannot heal. It can reveal the wounds but does not administer the remedy." – Fulgentius (*Ancient Christian Commentary*)

This also demonstrates the distinction between the law and the covenant with Abraham. They served two separate and distinct purposes. Granting to all nations the opportunity of salvation by the blood of Jesus Christ was one of the promises included in the covenant with Abraham. The law given through Moses, however, was not given for the purpose of granting man forgiveness. It was given to demonstrate man's sinfulness, but it had in itself no means to forgive those sins. As such, it helped prepare man to see their need for the gospel when it came.

3:23-25 – Before faith came, we were confined under the law, shut up to the faith that should be revealed. So the law became a tutor to bring us to Christ that we might be justified by faith. And now that faith has come, we are no longer under that tutor.

The law imprisoned men to sin.

All men sin (Romans 3:8-20), but sin placed all men under the curse of the law (Galatians 3:10). So, the effect of the law was to confine all under sin (verse 22). As a result, until the coming of the gospel system of faith, all were kept under guard by the law. They were "confined" (RSV) or "kept in custody" (NASB) like inhabitants of a besieged city. There was no escape by human means.

Other passages describe sinners as captives, slaves, or prisoners. See Romans 6:14-19; 11:32; 3:9; John 8:31-34; 2 Timothy 2:24-26.

The law, in effect, kept people in prison till the system of faith would be revealed, whereby they could escape. Why would God so arrange affairs? So that men could see how much they needed the sacrifice of Jesus, giving men reason to accept the gospel when it did come.

Had God simply sent Jesus soon after Adam and Eve sinned, without the period of subjection to the law, men would have believed they could save themselves by simply observing God's commands. They would have considered Adam's sin a random event: "But I would never do a thing like that." We always tend to see others' sins better than our own. By sending the law for 1400 years or so, God proved beyond doubt that no one will be saved by living a sinless life.

> "And the consciousness of a greater sickness, that they were found to be transgressors of the law itself, worked not to the ruin but to the good of those who believed, causing them to desire more fervently a doctor and to love him with more ardor." – Augustine (*Ancient Christian Commentary*)

The law was a preparation for the system of faith, but now that faith has come we are no longer under the law.

In that way, the law leads men to Christ. It prepared the way so that men would see their need for the law. This is compared to a "tutor" ("schoolmaster" – KJV; "guardian" – ESV). The tutor in Greek society was a slave responsible for the care of the children (see NKJV footnote; 1 Corinthians 4:15). The tutor guided and disciplined children and took them to their teachers. They were not so much instructors but supervisors and disciplinarians.

There came a time, however, when the child no longer needed the tutor. Likewise, having arrived at the system of faith, we no longer need the law as our tutor. The law's purpose was to prepare man for the system of forgiveness by obedient faith toward Jesus. In this system we have true forgiveness by Jesus' blood. God has proved His point that we will not save ourselves by a sinless life. So the Old Testament was no longer needed and was replaced by the New Testament. (See the further explanation of children, guardians, and inheritance in 4:1-7; compare to 3:23-29.)

To be "under" a law means to be subject to it or under obligation to obey it – note 4:4,21 (not just that we are condemned by it). (Compare 1 Corinthians 9:20,21; Matthew 8:9; Romans 3:19.) We are freed, not just from condemnation of the law, but from the law itself, which was the tutor. (Compare 3:16,19.)

Here is a clear statement that we are no longer under ("subject to") the tutor, which is the Old Testament law. It has been removed and replaced. This point disproves once and for all the viewpoint of those Judaizers whose teaching Paul was opposing because they claimed we are still subject to circumcision and the Mosaic system.

"The custodian guards another person's son and will depart from him when the lawful time of inheritance arrives." – Jerome (*Ancient Christian Commentary*)

"The custodian makes the child ridiculous when he keeps him close at hand even after the time has come for his departure." – Chrysostom (*Ancient Christian Commentary*)

Paul's evidence here likewise disproves the viewpoint of those today who appeal to the Old Testament to teach we must observe the seventh-day Sabbath, a special priesthood, special holy days, tithing, instrumental music, etc. We still have our modern Judaizers today, and Paul's arguments disprove their views just as effectively as they did the views of the first-century Judaizers. We are no longer under the tutor.

Passages that Show We Are No Longer Subject to the Old Law.

Hebrews 7:11,12 – Therefore, if perfection were through the Levitical priesthood (for under it the people received the law), what further need was there that another priest should rise according to the order of Melchizedek, and not be called according to the order of Aaron? For the priesthood being changed, of necessity there is also a change of the law.

Hebrews 8:6-13 – But now He has obtained a more excellent ministry, inasmuch as He is also Mediator of a better covenant, which was established on better promises. For if that first covenant had been faultless, then no place would have been sought for a second. Because finding fault with them, He says: "Behold, the days are coming, says the LORD, when I will make a new covenant with the house of Israel and with the house of Judah – not according to the covenant that I made with their fathers in the day when I took them by the hand to lead them out of the land of Egypt; because they did not continue in My covenant,

---

and I disregarded them, says the LORD. ... – For I will be merciful to their unrighteousness, and their sins and their lawless deeds I will remember no more." In that He says, "A new covenant," He has made the first obsolete. Now what is becoming obsolete and growing old is ready to vanish away.

Hebrews 10:1-10 – For the law, having a shadow of the good things to come, and not the very image of the things, can never with these same sacrifices, which they offer continually year by year, make those who approach perfect. For then would they not have ceased to be offered? For the worshipers, once purified, would have had no more consciousness of sins. But in those sacrifices there is a reminder of sins every year. For it is not possible that the blood of bulls and goats could take away sins. ... then He said, "Behold, I have come to do Your will, O God." He takes away the first that He may establish the second. By that will we have been sanctified through the offering of the body of Jesus Christ once for all.

Galatians 3:24.25 – Therefore the law was our tutor to bring us to Christ, that we might be justified by faith. But after faith has come, we are no longer under a tutor.

Galatians 5:1-6 – Stand fast therefore in the liberty by which Christ has made us free, and do not be entangled again with a yoke of bondage. Indeed I, Paul, say to you that if you become circumcised, Christ will profit you nothing. And I testify again to every man who becomes circumcised that he is a debtor to keep the whole law. You have become estranged from Christ, you who attempt to be justified by law; you have fallen from grace. For we through the Spirit eagerly wait for the hope of righteousness by faith. For in Christ Jesus neither circumcision nor uncircumcision avails anything, but faith working through love.

Romans 7:2-7– For the woman who has a husband is bound by the law to her husband as long as he lives. But if the husband dies, she is released from the law of her husband. So then if, while her husband lives, she marries another man, she will be called an adulteress; but if her husband dies, she is free from that law, so that she is no adulteress, though she has married another man. Therefore, my brethren, you also have become dead to the law through the body of Christ, that you may be married to another--to Him who was raised from the dead, that we should bear fruit to God. For when we were in the flesh, the sinful passions which were aroused by the law were at work in our members to bear fruit to death. But now we have been delivered from the law, having died to what we were held by, so that we should serve in the newness of the Spirit and not in the oldness of the letter. What shall we say then? Is the law sin? Certainly not! On the contrary, I would not have known sin except through the law. For I would not have known covetousness unless the law had said, "You shall not covet."

Ephesians 2:11-16 – Therefore remember that you, once Gentiles in the flesh--who are called Uncircumcision by what is called the Circumcision made in the flesh by hands – that at that time you were without Christ, being aliens from the commonwealth of Israel and strangers from the covenants of promise, having no hope and without God in the world. But now in Christ Jesus you who once were far off have been brought near by the blood of Christ. For He Himself is our peace, who has made both one, and has broken down the middle wall of separation, having abolished in His flesh the enmity, that is, the law of commandments contained in ordinances, so as to create in Himself one new man from the two, thus making peace, and that He might reconcile them both to God in one body through the cross, thereby putting to death the enmity.

Colossians 2:13-17 – And you, being dead in your trespasses and the uncircumcision of your flesh, He has made alive together with Him, having forgiven you all trespasses, having wiped out the handwriting of requirements that was against us, which was contrary to us. And He has taken it out of the way, having nailed it to the cross. ... So let no one judge you in food or in drink, or regarding a festival or a new moon or sabbaths, which are a shadow of things to come, but the substance is of Christ.

"Tutor" (παιδαγωγος) – "... the man, usu. a slave ... whose duty it was to conduct a boy or youth ... to and from school and to superintend his conduct gener.; he was not a 'teacher' ... When the young man became of age, the π. was no longer needed ... In our lit. one who has responsibility for someone who needs guidance, *guardian, leader, guide. ...*" – Bauer-Danker-Arndt-Gingrich.

3:26,27 – *You are all sons of God through faith in Christ Jesus. For as many of you as were baptized into Christ have put on Christ.*

Sons of God through faith

Having received in the gospel the system of faith in Jesus and His saving sacrifice (verses 24,25), we now have what the law could not provide. We have full fellowship with God as His sons. We are sons of Abraham, because we have faith as he did (verses 7,29). But far more, we are actually viewed as God's special children.

This was something Jews especially desired because, believing their birth made them God's special people, they thought they were children of God as Jews (John 8:31ff). But Paul is saying that a person is not a child of God simply on the basis of physical birth. Truly being a child of God requires a special relationship by means of forgiveness which can be provided only by the gospel system of obedient faith – something the Old Testament could never provide.

Many other New Testament passages speak of people becoming children of God. This occurs by the new birth. This birth is based on Jesus' death (John 1:12), but requires faith and obedience in baptism. See 4:5; John 3:1-7; 1 Peter 1:22-25; Romans 8:14; 6:3,5; 2 Corinthians 5:17.

Baptized into Christ

Here Paul specifies that one is a child of God by faith. He has been affirming this repeatedly. But now we learn another significant fact. The new birth requires baptism, exactly as taught in the passages above.

Note that everyone who is in Christ came into Him by baptism. The expression "into Christ" and "put on Christ" imply fellowship and right relationship with Him. We need this relationship because "in Christ" are numerous spiritual blessings nowhere found outside Him. These include salvation, eternal life, freedom from condemnation, etc. See John 15:1-10; Acts 4:12; Ephesians 1:3,7; 2:12-17; Romans 6:6,11; 8:1,39; 2 Corinthians 5:17; 2 Timothy 2:1,10; Galatians 5:4; 1 John 5:11,12.

How many are "in Christ"? As many as have been **baptized** into Him — no more and no less. But remember we are born again (new creations) only when we are in Christ. So how many are born again? As many as have been Scripturally baptized — no more and no less.

This connection is confirmed by verse – 26. Note the verb tenses:

"For you *are* all sons of God through faith in Christ Jesus. For as many of you as *were* baptized into Christ have put on Christ."

This		This
You *were* baptized into Christ	must come **before**	You *are* sons of God.

This must happen "by faith" because faith gives one the right or power to become a child of God (John 1:12). One who lacks faith has no right to be baptized (Mark. 16:15,16; Acts 8:35-39). But **after** faith has led to **baptism** — only then is one a child of God (born again).

Baptism is essential for anyone to come into Christ. See also Romans 6:3,4. Clearly, then, baptism is essential to salvation.

The conclusion is undeniable for any who seek the truth, and it clearly contradicts those who claim salvation by faith means by "faith alone" so baptism is not necessary. On the contrary, salvation by faith most definitely *includes* and requires baptism. And here – right in the very midst of one of Paul's major treatises on salvation by faith – is a clear statement of this fact!

Commentary on Galatians

What Is Required to be Born of God?

One must hear the gospel.

1 Peter 1:22-25 – We are "born again" by the incorruptible seed, which is God's word, the gospel that was preached. Birth is the product of **seed** that is planted, germinates, and produces a new organism. Spiritually, the seed by which we become children of God is God's word (compare Luke 8:11). This is planted in men's hearts when they hear the gospel. (Compare James 1:18; 1 Corinthians 4:15.)

John 1:13 – We can be born again only by following God's will, not man's will. It follows that the only way you or I can know we are born again is by knowing what the word of God says about it.

John 6:44,45 – You cannot come to Jesus without hearing, learning, and being taught God's word.

John 8:31,32,24 – To be made free from sin, you must know the truth and believe in Jesus.

Romans 1:16 – The gospel is the power of God to save those who believe.

One must believe the gospel.

John 1:12 – To have the power or right to become a child of God ("born again"), one must believe in Jesus. Note that the Scripture does not say that believing immediately makes one a child of God. It says that believing gives one **the right or power to become** a child of God.

Romans 10:17 – Faith comes by hearing God's word.

One must obey God's word.

1 Peter 1:22-25 – We are born again by God's word. But verse 22 adds that we must **obey the truth** in order to purify our souls.

Romans 6:17,18 – We are made free from sin as a result of **obeying** the doctrine delivered from God. (See our earlier notes about the need for obedience.)

One must be baptized in water.

2 Corinthians 5:17 – If anyone is **in Christ**, he is a new creation. "New creation" is another way of saying "born again."

Romans 6:3,4 – We are "**baptized into Christ**." As a result of being buried (immersed) in baptism and rising from it, we have "**newness of life**" (born again!).

Galatians 3:26,27 – "For you **are** all **sons of God** (born again) through faith in Christ Jesus. For as many of you as **were baptized** into Christ have put on Christ."

Mark 16:15,16 – To be saved, one must believe **and** be baptized.

Acts 2:38 – Everyone must repent and be baptized for the forgiveness of sins.

> Acts 22:16 – Saul (Paul) had already believed in Jesus, but was still in sin. He was told to be baptized and wash away his sins.
>
> John 3:3-7 – To enter the kingdom, one must be born of the water and of the Spirit. "Water" in John 3:5 must refer to water baptism, since baptism is the only command in the New Testament that **requires** the use of "water" (Acts 8:35-39; 10:47; John 3:23; Hebrews 10:22; etc.).

So Paul's discussions shows that, though we are no longer under the Old Testament law and are now justified by faith in Christ, this is not intended to exclude the need for obedience to divine commands in order to receive salvation. As we have discussed earlier, these works of obedience to the gospel are not meritorious works intended to earn salvation. Nevertheless, gifts can be and often are conditional.

In order to receive the salvation offered according to the promise given to Abraham and fulfilled in Christ, we must have obedient faith that includes baptism. And note furthermore that baptism, as described in verses 26,27, must be based on faith. It follows that baptism is not for babies since they have no faith. As shown in the Scriptures cited above, before one can be scripturally baptized, he must first hear the gospel, believe it, repent of sins, and confess Christ.

3:28,29 – There can be neither Jew nor Greek, neither bond nor free, neither male nor female, for you are all one in Christ Jesus. And if you belong to Christ, then you are the seed of Abraham, heirs according to the promise.

All one in Christ

Finally, Paul states the conclusion of his extended discussion about faith in Christ by the gospel, Abraham's promise, and the application of all this to Jews and Gentiles. He concludes that distinctions between Jew and Gentile do not matter "in Christ," just as distinctions between slave and free, male and female, do not matter. We are all one in Christ.

Remember that we get into Christ by faith at the point of baptism (verses 26,27). This is the blessing of the gospel that Paul has been describing throughout the discussion. So, this salvation in Christ is for everyone, regardless of nationality, gender, or social status. None of these factors influence in any way whether or not one can be saved in Christ. See also Romans 10:12.

The conclusion that would follow from Paul's statement is that the gospel is for all. All need to submit to the gospel terms of salvation to receive cleansing by the blood of Christ, and those who are converted then all become one in Jesus' church. This applies to all other social distinctions as well as those specifically mentioned here by Paul.

Note also the emphasis on "one." Paul's goal is to urge Jews, not just to accept Gentiles as being saved by the gospel, but to recognize the need for being united with them as spiritual equals. It is not enough to grudgingly accept them in the kingdom, while giving them second-class status as marginally worthy of membership. We are all one and should appreciate one another, seeking to bond together as members of the same body, the same family. Nor should there be warfare, bitterness, and animosity. All should love one another as brothers.

To have separate Jewish churches and Gentiles churches is not at all what Jesus died to accomplish. Likewise today people of all nationalities and social backgrounds should learn to overcome their differences and accept one another in Christ.

Furthermore, we should be just as concerned about the salvation of people of other nationalities, races, social statuses, and economic classes as we are concerned about the salvation of people who are like ourselves in these areas. The gospel must be spread to all. Jesus said to go into all the world and preach the gospel to every creature in every nation – Mark 16:15,16; Matthew 28:19; Luke 24:47. This must be our goal absolutely unlimited and unhindered by favoritism regarding those whom we teach.

Abraham's seed and heirs according to the promise

In particular, if all are in Christ (verses 26-28), then all belong to Christ and are spiritual descendants of Abraham, inheriting the blessing through Him (verse 29). This is clearly the blessing promised to all nations through Abraham's seed (see verses 8,16-18, compare Romans 8:17; Acts 13:39; etc.).

As shown earlier, this blessing is justification and true forgiveness through Jesus' death. This blessing is for "all nations." It comes to all under the gospel, Paul affirms, not through circumcision or the law. In fact, the law is now irrelevant because it is no longer even in effect.

Here is the grand conclusion of Paul's argument throughout the chapter: the blessing Jews were looking forward to as descendants of Abraham is now available to all men through Jesus' gospel system, not through the law. The force of this was to demonstrate conclusively that the Judaizers were wrong in seeking to bind circumcision and the law on Gentiles. This is not only unnecessary, it is wrong and sinful.

Elimination of distinctions in authority?

Note that verse 28 affirms that the classes listed there should have spiritual unity in Christ, but nothing here or elsewhere says these groups will cease to exist because of the gospel. We will still have Jew and Gentile, male and female. Likewise, Paul showed that slave and free will continue to exist. The gospel did not forbid these as inherently sinful.

It is a mistake to conclude, as some do, that passages like this mean there should be no authority distinctions between these groups. Feminists have tried to use this passage to claim that, if male and female are one in Christ, then men cannot have authority over women. This contradicts the numerous passages that show men do have authority both in the home and in church affairs. See Genesis 2:18; 3:16; Ephesians 5:22-33; Colossians 3:18; 1 Corinthians 11:3; 14:34,35; 1 Timothy 2:12-14; 3:4,12; Titus 2:4,5; 1 Peter 3:1-7.

Surely masters do not cease to have authority over slaves simply because one or both is converted. Paul made this clear in other passages, such as the book of Philemon; 1 Corinthians 7:17-24; Ephesians 6:5-9; Colossians 3:22-4:1; 1 Timothy 6:1,2; etc. Likewise, authority relations between men and women are not removed because one or both are Christians.

The oneness the passage emphasizes is clearly stated in verse 29 to be that all can be saved and receive the full blessing promised to Abraham as God's children, heirs of eternal life, etc. Paul emphasized the same concept also in Ephesians 2:11-21. (Compare 1 Peter 3:7; Philemon 16).

Galatians 4

4:1-20 - The Status of the Galatians

4:1-7 – The child as a slave: an illustration

4:1,2 – As long as an heir is still a child, he is no different from a servant even though he owns everything. He is under guardians and stewards until the time the father has appointed.

Paul here summarizes his points from chapter 3 and applies them specifically to the case of the Galatian Christians.

He first returns to the illustration of a child who is subject to a tutor (3:24,25). This person may be an heir, destined to inherit and become master of his father's entire estate. But that is simply a hope for the future. In his present state he is in essence like a slave. He is subject to guardians and stewards, who act on behalf of his father. These guardians are themselves servants, yet they have authority over the son, while he is still a minor! The future blessings awaiting the child do not change the fact he is still in a subservient stage as a minor.

This condition continues until the time appointed by the father. That is, the father sets a time and determines when the child will come to inherit the estate and become able to exercise his power as master over it.

These conditions are exactly what Paul had described in 3:19-25 regarding people who were subject to the law. They were subject to authority and held in bondage like slaves because they were guilty of sin and unable to do anything about it. So, the law guided and cared for them, like guardians and stewards. This continued until the Father determined to send the system of faith in Jesus. This Old Testament system, which amounted to the equivalent of slavery and bondage, is exactly what the Judaizers wanted Gentile Christians to accept instead of the freedom from sin provided by the gospel!

4:3-5 – Likewise, we were held in bondage under the rudiments of the world. When the fullness of time came, God sent His Son born of a woman, born under the law, so He might redeem those under the law and we might receive adoption as sons.

Bondage under the elements of the world

Paul makes application of the illustration to the Galatians (and to himself and to all people), saying they were in bondage like that child. They were in bondage to the elements of the world. This surely means sin and its consequences (compare Colossians 2:8,14-17,20-23). Those who commit sin are bondservants to it (see verses 19,22,23).

This was the condition even of Jews under the law till Jesus came and replaced it with the gospel. They were under the curse of sin (3:10-12), unable to remove that curse by any sacrifices the law provided. It was a yoke neither those in the first century nor their fathers were able to bear (Acts 15:10). Finally, becoming a curse for us by His own death, Jesus provided the sacrifice that could truly take away sins.

Willis reminds us that Paul is here speaking primarily to Gentiles (see verse 8). Jews were seeking to bring these people into subjection to the Old Testament. The Gentiles were surely in bondage to sin before they obeyed the gospel, so Paul's statements here included them (Romans 1:18-32; 1 Corinthians 1:21). They had been in bondage but had been redeemed and become adopted as sons by redemption through Christ.

But what the Jews did not realize is that they too were in bondage to sin until Jesus removed the law! All were in sin (see Romans 1-3). So if the Judaizers were to take Gentiles, who had been converted and set free, and put them back under the law, that would simply put them in bondage again!

God sent forth his Son to redeem those under the law that they might receive the adoption as sons.

To solve this problem, God sent His Son. Through Him we receive redemption from sin and adoption to become Sons of God (see 3:26-29). Note that, where other passages use the figure of a new birth, this one uses the figure of adoption. There is no conflict, since both are illustrations or comparisons. The point is that, where we were not children of God, by His mercy He made it possible for us to change spiritual families and become members of His saved people. See also Romans 8:15.

The Bible clearly states that redemption was accomplished by the blood or the death of Jesus – Ephesians 1:7. The context here in Galatians 4 refers to the fact that Jesus was born of a woman and that He was born under the law. And we know that He kept the law perfectly. Nevertheless, it was neither the birth of Jesus nor His sinless life – important as they were – that was the means of our redemption.

Redemption or forgiveness occurred through the sacrifice of Christ on Calvary.

Note that sending someone implies that they existed before they were sent. Jesus sent His apostles to preach the gospel, but they existed before they were sent. Yet this passage says that God sent forth His son when He was born of a woman. This implies that He existed before He was sent to this earth to be born of a woman. This clearly implies preexistence, confirming many other passages that show that Jesus existed in heaven with the Father before He was born as a human being (John 1:1-3,14; Philippians 2:6-8). This in turn implies the Deity of Jesus, since mere humans do not exist before their earthly lives.

Furthermore, note that Jesus redeemed those who were under the law. This point is also made in Hebrews 9:15,16. Paul has repeatedly stated here and elsewhere that those who lived under the law could not be forgiven or saved by that law. How then could they have hope of eternal life? The answer is that the death of Jesus provided redemption for those who lived under the law, if they faithfully obeyed the conditions of forgiveness, as well as for the salvation of those who live under the gospel.

The fullness of time

Jesus came "in the fullness of time." He came in the fullness of time (Ephesians 1:9,10), when the time was fulfilled (Mark 1:15,16; see also Titus 1:2,3).

This compares to the time the father set for the child to inherit (verse 2). The father had to determine the time. Until then, the children were still in bondage like slaves because of sin. Before Jesus came, Jews had the law and the promise to Abraham of blessing through his Seed, yet that blessing had not yet come. Jews were still in bondage, and the law itself did nothing to change this. Rather, the law was like the servant who had authority over the child.

"The fullness of time" shows that there was a specific time or set of circumstances God looked for before He determined to send the Son. We are not here told exactly what all these circumstances were. Surely they included the fact that many prophecies had been made regarding Jesus' life and death. The time had to be right for these to be fulfilled. See Luke 24:25-27,44-46; John 5:39,46; Acts 2:23-36; 3:18-24; 17:2,3; 10:43; 13:27-39; 26:22,23; 1 Corinthians 15:1-8; 2 Peter 1:19.

Some have pointed out the advantages the Roman Empire offered to the spread of the gospel. The authority of Rome controlled the entire area where the gospel needed to be spread in the first century. This gave a unity of law, conditions of peace, and good roads. The Greek language also gave a language that could be spoken throughout the empire.

Perhaps more specifically of importance to God's plan was the condition of the Jews and Gentiles that would lead the Jews to kill

Jesus, but then allow the gospel to be spread through the world as God wanted.

In any case, we can be sure that God sent Jesus at the best time, regardless of whether or not we understand why it was best.

Born of a woman

Jesus was "born of a woman." Note that He was not born of "man" or a male human father, for he did not have a human father (Matthew 1:18-25; etc.). He was born of woman, Mary. Nevertheless, this may not be a direct reference to the Virgin Birth, since any man would be born of a woman (compare Matthew 11:11).

Still, this harmonizes with the Virgin Birth since it emphasizes that Jesus was born of a woman, but no human father is mentioned. Had Jesus had a human father, one would expect His father to be mentioned in contexts such as this, especially because He and His apostles claimed He was heir to the throne of David. Establishing the right to the throne would normally emphasize who His father was. Yet no father is mentioned.

Furthermore, stating that Jesus was born of a woman would definitely confirm His humanity. He had existed as Deity before His birth, but being born of a woman means that He was a man or a human being when He came to earth.

This also may refer back to Genesis 3:15, where God promised that the serpent would bruise the heel of the woman's seed, but the seed of the woman would bruise the head of the serpent. This refers to Jesus, who was slain by the powers of Satan, yet He arose and gave Satan a death blow. All this required Him to be "born of a woman."

Born under the law

Jesus was also "born under the law." At the time He was born, the law was still in effect. He was subject to its commandments and requirements (see notes on 3:25 regarding the significance of being under the law). The law remained in effect till He died (Colossians 2:14). It is only after His death that we are no longer subject to the law (Hebrews 9:16,17).

This explains why, during His lifetime, Jesus kept the Sabbath day. Some have use this as evidence that we should keep the Sabbath day today. But Jesus kept the law because He lived under the law. It was removed when He died.

Jesus also was circumcised (Luke 2:21), had animals offered for him (Luke 2:22-24), taught others to offer animals (Matthew 8:4; Mark 1:44; Luke 2:22ff; compare Leviticus 14:1-32), observed Old Testament feast days (Luke 2:41f; Matthew 26:17ff), and showed great zeal for the physical temple (John 2:13-17). He taught others to observe all things taught by those who sat on Moses' seat (Matthew 23:2,3). Must we observe all these today?

Jesus kept the law because it was still in effect, and He was subject to it like other Jews. He was the only person who ever kept it without sin! He lived under it so that He might die and remove it, to free others from it. He was born under the law in order that He might redeem those who were under the law.

When that happened, then the heirs of the promise were able to receive the true benefits of their inheritance. But the blessing was to both Jews and Gentiles, so both received the inheritance. This was not received through the law but could only be achieved when the law was removed. Why then would anyone want to go back to the law?

4:6,7 – Because we are sons, God sent the Spirit of His Son into our hearts crying "Abba! Father!" So we are no longer slaves but sons, and if we are sons then we are heirs through God.

Here is the conclusion of the illustration of verses 1-7. Paul has compared those who are in bondage under sin, including those under the Old Testament, to those who are like minor children. Even though they have the promise that they will someday come into their inheritance so they may enjoy it all, yet in the meanwhile they are in bondage like bondservants. So the Jews had been promised the blessing of Abraham; but while they were still under the law, the blessing had not come.

Finally, through Jesus, the promised blessing came. God sent His Spirit, who taught us to cry out "Abba, Father!" Notice that God sent the Spirit (verse 6) even as he sent forth His Son (verse 4). The Spirit was sent to teach us the gospel through inspired men and to confirm that message by miracles (John 16:13; 1 Corinthians 2:9-13). This gospel message, revealed by the Spirit, moves us to cry "Abba, Father."

"Abba" is an Aramaic term of endearment for a father. It may be like our expression "Daddy." The point here is that, because Christ has come and fulfilled the promised blessing of salvation available to all, we are no longer like slaves but have now reached the status as sons, truly able to call God our Father. And we can do this with a sense of endearment because we love God, who has so shown His love for us. We ought to have a sense of a close personal relationship with Him because we realize how much He has loved and blessed us.

This understanding came through the Spirit who comes into our hearts, not by a personal indwelling, but through the message of the gospel (see 3:2,5; Ephesians 6:17). It is this message that teaches us about God's blessings for His children. When we respond obediently, we honor God as our Father. It is in this sense that the Spirit calls out "Abba, Father" through us.

Now through Christ the promised blessing has come! We are no longer in status like slaves. We have received the inheritance of sons (3:18,29; Romans 8:17)! We are like the heirs in Paul's illustration who have now reached the time of inheritance. We have received the promised blessing of forgiveness. This is true of both Jews and Gentiles, for all were promised the blessing when God spoke to Abraham.

Does it make sense then, having so received this promise, to go back to the Old Testament law, which did not have the actual forgiveness? Such would be returning to bondage to sin in a system that did not have lasting forgiveness!

We observe here that the "Spirit of His Son" is surely a reference to the Holy Spirit. The Holy Spirit is referred to in various Scriptures as the Spirit of God and the Spirit of Christ. This becomes another evidence of the Deity of Jesus. Surely the Holy Spirit would not be called the Spirit of one who was just a man or even one who was an angel. He is the Spirit of God; but if He is the Spirit of Christ, then Christ must possess deity.

4:8-11 – The Galatians' return to unacceptable practices

4:8,9 – At the time when they did not know God, they were enslaved to those who are not truly gods. But now that they had come to know God, or rather to be known by God, why would they turn back again to the weak and beggarly rudiments so as to be once again enslaved?

When they were serving false gods, the Gentiles did not know the true God.

"You" here clearly shows that Paul is addressing Gentiles. They did not know the true God but served those who were not true gods. This was when they were in bondage to the elements of the world (verse 3). So, the main group Paul was addressing consisted of Gentiles who had been idol worshippers but had later accepted the gospel. These were the ones on whom the Judaizers sought to bind circumcision and the Old Law.

In the past they had not known God. Typically, Gentiles had no concept of the true God (Ephesians 2:12; Acts 17:22,23: 1 Corinthians 1:21; 1 Thessalonians 4:5; 2 Thessalonians 1:8; Romans 1:18-32). They surely did not know Him in a true relationship. Under the gospel, however, they had come to know Him (1 John 2:3-6). Even greater, they were known by God (2 Timothy 2:19). It is one thing for a lowly, common person to have some knowledge of a great, important person. It is quite another to know him so well that you can say with confidence that he knows you!

I may say I know some famous man because I have met him once or twice and can recognize him when I see him. Yet he may meet so many people that he would have no recollection of who I am at all. It is quite another matter to say he knows me so well that he would recall me and have a personal relationship with me. This latter is what we have as God's children. It is especially amazing for Gentiles, since they had no relationship whatever with God before.

Instead of knowing the true God, the Gentiles had served those who by nature were not God.

Notice that God is God because of His nature, and idols and other false gods are not gods because of their nature. This is important, because we need to understand that God is not God because some men decided to invent Him or to make Him a God. He is God because by His very nature He deserves to be God. God is God because He is the Creator of all and therefore the ruler of all. He is eternal, all wise, all-powerful, and otherwise possessing all the characteristics of Deity.

On the other hand, idols do not truly become gods simply because men designate them to be gods. Men may claim that the sun and stars are gods, or that some statue they have made is a god, but that does not make these truly into gods. They cannot be gods because they do not have the characteristics of God. Anything that did not create the universe, is not eternal, is not all wise and all-powerful, and does not possess the other characteristics of God, cannot possibly be God because its very nature is not the nature of God.

Why would Gentiles want to submit to the law?

This status, in which the Gentiles knew God and He knew them, was accomplished by the gospel of Jesus, surely not by the Old Testament. Consider then, how foolish it would be, having achieved this status, to try to submit to the law. It is one thing for Jews to want to go back to it – it gave them favored status. But why, of all things, would Gentiles want to accept a system that gave them no blessings at all?

In doing so, they would be going back to weak and beggarly elements. The law itself was weak in that it could not forgive sins (Hebrews 7:18; Romans 8:3). I wonder, however, if Paul would call the law itself "beggarly," since it was given by God. Perhaps Paul refers, not just to the law alone, but to the whole consequence of submitting to the law as the Judaizers urged.

Another alternative, however, according to Hogg and Vine is that the word for "beggarly" simply refers to one like a beggar who is very poor. He has no inheritance and no hope of an inheritance. This meaning would fit those who sought to go back to the law. Serving the law would make people under it like beggars for the same reason that they the law is said to be weak: it could not give anyone the inheritance of eternal life. They would be truly poverty-stricken.

What the Gentiles were being pressured to accept was the Judaizers' position and its consequences. The Judaizers' view would bind the Gentiles to a system that had never been given to Gentiles and that had in fact been removed by God. Further, it had never been able to really remove guilt for anyone, not even Jews.

So, for Gentiles to go to that system, after it had even been removed and replaced by a better system, would bind the Gentiles in sin. Paul says they had been in bondage to their idols, but to go back to the law would be to simply put them in a different form of bondage. Rather than becoming free they would return to the bondage of sin, that is, to "weak and beggarly elements" (compare verse 3). It returned them to the sinful status they had before they knew and obeyed the gospel!

4:10,11 – They observed days, months, seasons, and years. Paul was afraid that he may have bestowed labor upon them in vain.

Paul then gives a specific example of the Galatian Christians' actions that concerned him. They were observing days, months, seasons, and years. "Observe," as used here, would surely refer to a religious observance. Why would Paul be concerned for secular or non-religious activities? His concern is that the Galatians were following a different gospel (1:8,9).

What days were they observing? Doubtless they had observed religious days in their worship of idols (verse 8), and Paul would object if they went back to such religious observances (see 1 Corinthians 8,10). Yet the whole context is discussing the fact the Judaizers were seeking to bind the Old Testament on the Gentiles, and Paul was concerned that the Gentiles were accepting these ideas (2:3,12,14,16,3:10,12; 4:21; 6:12; etc.).

So the context would imply that the Galatians were observing Old Testament holy days. Paul warned about the danger of binding these also in Colossians 2:14-17. These days involved daily, weekly, monthly, and annual observances, as well as special years. This would include the Passover, the Day of atonement, the seventh-day Sabbath, etc. (Compare Leviticus 23:24; Numbers 28:11; Psalm 81:3; Isaiah. 66:23; Leviticus 25:1-7; 25:8f; 1 Chronicles 23:30,31; 2 Chronicles 2:4; 8:13; 31:3; Nehemiah 10:33; Ezekiel 45:17; Hosea 2:11. Note that the Septuagint in 2 Chronicles 8:13 refers to the annual feasts using the same Greek word as is used here in Galatians 4:10.)

The seriousness of these activities is shown in that Paul feared that his labor in teaching the Galatians the saving gospel would be in vain. Clearly this meant they were in danger of being eternally lost because they were observing these days, though this was just one example of the errors he was concerned about. He had labored diligently to teach them the gospel. If they now turned from it to a different gospel, Paul's labor in teaching them would be in vain.

Paul did not object to circumcision as a personal custom or medical practice (Galatians 5:6; 1 Corinthians 7:19). He did object when it was being bound as a religious observance. Likewise, it is not likely that he was objecting to the Jewish holy days simply as customs celebrated by Jews as family times and national observances, like we observe July 4, Labor Day, etc. Doubtless there were many aspects of the days that could have been observed without religious significance. This appears to be what Romans 14:5 is saying is acceptable. What concerned Paul was that Jewish Christians were convincing Gentiles that these should be observed religiously.

Since Paul was concerned about their observance of these Jewish holy days, even to the point that he feared for their salvation, should we not likewise oppose the observance of such days today? Proper application of this context would mean that people are teaching and following a different gospel today when they bind observance of the seventh-day Sabbath as necessary to pleasing God.

And if Paul objected to these Jewish holy days, which had once been authorized as God's will for His people, how much more should we object to religious observance of holy days such as Christmas and Easter, etc. These never had God's authority behind them. They are primarily pagan in origin, having been adopted by apostate Catholicism. While these may yet have some secular, traditional, family aspects that Christians could observe without religious significance, yet to keep them religiously would surely violate the same principles Paul is discussing.

Have we really left the errors of false religion, or are we, like the Galatians, returning to the weak and beggarly elements of the world? If so, would not that also make our past obedience to truth vain?

4:12-20 – Paul's former relations with and present hope for the Galatians

4:12-14 – Paul urged them to become as he was for he was like they were. They had not wronged him but because of an infirmity in the flesh he had preached the gospel to them the first time. They did not despise that which was a temptation to them in his flesh, but received him even as an angel, as Christ Jesus.

Paul next discussed about his past contacts with the Galatians and what he hoped they would do in the future.

He desired they would become like he was since he had become like them.

Compare 1 Corinthians 11:1. He does not name specifically the ways he wanted them to become like him, so we can only draw conclusions from the context.

He has been disproving the Jewish doctrine that all people, including Gentiles, must be circumcised and keep the Old Law to be saved, so the gospel alone is not enough to save. Paul himself had preached, instead, that the gospel alone would save, that the Old Law never could save people, and that it had in fact been removed. I conclude that he here is calling on the Galatians to become as he is regarding this doctrine. He is wanted them to identify with his teaching in this matter, even as they had in the past.

He mentioned how he had become like them. This might mean several things. Among Gentiles, he adopted Gentile customs as much as he could while still obeying God (in contrast to the Judaizers and Peter, who would not even eat with Gentiles – 2:11-14). Specifically, when among them, he did not keep the Old Law, but acted like Gentiles who did not have to keep the law (1 Corinthians 9:19-23). He had taught them the truth that led to their salvation, but he never acted like one who had to also keep the Old Law.

So he here asked them to again become like he was: act like people who were saved by Christ but did not have to keep the Old Law.

He then described how they had personally treated him when he had been among them.

Note that this shows he definitely had been among them and had taught them the gospel (see introduction and 3:1).

He said that he had suffered no wrong among them. This is past tense (in contrast to the way the Judaizers wanted them to treat him now). The context of verses 13,14 implies he is talking about how they received him when he first went there. They might have tempted to do him harm, but instead they had received him kindly.

In particular, he had originally come to them and preached there because of a physical infirmity. They could have despised, rejected, ridiculed, or even sought to harm him because of this infirmity. Sometimes handicapped people are treated this way. Some physical infirmities are disgusting and repulsive. Apparently, Paul's was such that people could have turned from him, but the Galatians had not.

We are not told here exactly what this infirmity was. It is described simply as a physical infirmity, a trial in Paul's flesh. The description is so like that of 2 Corinthians 12:7-10 that I assume it is the same, yet I still do not know what it was. Some claim it was blindness, because Paul said they would have plucked out their own eyes (verse 15) and he wrote with large letters (6:11). However, this is speculation, surely not conclusive.

Some claim it was a lingering effect of the blindness placed on him on the Damascus road. But if anything, that convinces me Paul was **not** blind. Miracles were always complete and lasting cures. A partial cure is no miracle. Ailment caused by a later, unrelated source might occur, but it was surely not from that event.

Nor is it clear how this infirmity caused Paul to originally go to them, but he said the Galatians knew. Whatever the cause, something about it apparently changed Paul's travel plans so he either went to Galatia when he had not intended to, or perhaps he stayed there when he had not intended to. In any case, the infirmity was the occasion of his being among them, and he took the opportunity to teach them.

Whatever the ailment was, instead of mistreating Paul because of it, the Galatians were kind to the point Paul says they received him as an angel of God, even as Christ Jesus. They treated him as they would have treated Jesus among them. This, of course, is the kind of love we ought to have for one another. Jesus said that the way we treat one another is the way we treat Him (Matthew 25:31-46). But for these Gentiles to be so kind to a Jew is quite impressive.

Surely Paul's point here is to remind them of their kind treatment of him before, so why had they become so willing to believe the worst of him, as claimed by the Judaizers?

4:15,16 – Paul asked what happened to the blessing they had enjoyed. He testified that, if possible, they would have plucked out their eyes and given them to him. So had he become their enemy by telling them the truth?

So what had happened to the blessing they had enjoyed?

Paul reminded the Galatians that they considered his first visit(s) among them to be a great blessing. The idea seems to be that they gave thanks for the fact he had come, though he had not intended to. He does not name the blessing, but surely it pertained to the hearing of the message he preached and the salvation they received as a result.

But if the Judaizers were correct, where was the blessing to the Galatians? The Judaizers claimed Paul was teaching error, so the Galatians were not saved at all through Paul's preaching. In fact, they would be saved only if they were circumcised and kept the law, none of which Paul had taught them to do. So where was the blessing in Paul's visit(s) to them?

They had been so grateful and appreciative for Paul's presence among them that they would have plucked out their eyes and given them to him, if possible. As we noted on verse 13 above, some claim this proves the infirmity Paul had was blindness, but this is speculation.

Paul is simply using an expression showing their extreme care for him. It is like our saying, "He would give you the shirt off his back." We may not need a shirt, or may not have any real need at all. This is simply an expression for people's kindness and generosity. Paul's expression is similarly showing how caring the Galatians had been toward him.

The point clearly is to remind them of their past concern for him so as to make them consider why they had changed. They had formerly considered his coming to be a blessing, they were grateful and extremely kind. Why had they now changed to the point they treated him like an enemy? What had changed them?

Did telling them the truth make him an enemy?

Finally, having reminded them of their past treatment, he offers the real reason for the change – it was his doctrine that the Judaizers objected to and had convinced them he was not telling them the truth. But the Galatians had accepted it as truth when he had been there, and he was still preaching the same as he had then. He was now telling the same truth again and opposing the errors of those who taught differently. Did this make him their enemy?

Of course, telling someone the truth of God's word, especially when they are in error, is an act of love and kindness, not the act of an enemy. But many people do not view it that way. They resent being told they are wrong, so they turn against the preacher instead of changing their lives to harmonize with truth. See Revelation 3:19; Galatians 6:1,2; James 5:19,20; 1 Thessalonians 5:14; Ephesians 5:11; 2 Timothy 4:2-4; Matthew 5:23,24; 13:13-15; 18:15-17; Proverbs 15:31,32; 13:18; 18:13; 10:17; 29:1; 19:20; 1 Peter 3:15; John 3:19-21; 7:7.

It is this attitude of resentment toward truth that leads to persecution of faithful preachers. Jews had expressed it repeatedly toward Christians, especially toward Paul. Paul is questioning the Galatians whether they too were developing that attitude. Matthew 5:10-12; 13:21; John 15:20; 16:33; Acts 14:22; Romans 5:3; 8:17-39; 2 Corinthians 1:4-10; 4:17; 7:4; 2 Timothy 3:12; Hebrews 10:32-36; 1 Peter 2:19-23; 3:14-18; 4:1,15-19; 5:10.

Surely this is an excellent question to ask people whenever they resent the truth we teach. Remember, if it is truth, then people do us a favor to teach it to us, because it gives us the opportunity to change and become right. That is why telling it is an act of love, not hatred.

4:17,18 – They eagerly sought the Gentiles but not for a good purpose. They desired to exclude them so they would seek them. But it is good to be zealous in a good matter all the time, not just when Paul was present.

The Galatians' attitude had changed because someone (obviously the Judaizers) had been zealously courting them.

This is an interesting expression for the influence teachers seek to have. They are like a young man wooing a young lady to gain her favor. So the Judaizers had gone out of their way to impress the Galatians and gain their favor.

Though they seemed to be interested in the Galatians, they were not acting toward a good end. They may have thought it a good end, but it was not really. It was not good for Paul, but more important it was not good for the Galatians or for their service to God.

What the Judaizers really wanted was to gain the Galatians' favor so the Galatians would be zealous toward them – i.e., toward the Judaizers. But the effect would be to exclude the Galatians. Exclude them from what? Surely they would be excluded from Paul and from all the blessings of the message of the truth that he taught. In short, they

Commentary on Galatians

would be causing a separation or breech of fellowship which caused the Galatians to go into error.

Note they were leading people to be zealous for **them** (the Judaizers), not for truth. There is a difference between being zealous for truth and being zealous to please people. Being zealous for what is good, Paul said, was good to do. He supported that and encouraged it. The implication, of course, is that this was not a good zeal.

Paul's closing expression is that being zealous for good is a good thing to do, and not just when he was present among them.

This seems to be refer back again to the zeal they had for him and his message when he had been there – that was a good zeal. He is comparing how they had treated him when present, compared to how they had treated him after he had left. They had been very zealous for him and his message when he had been there (verses 12-17). But they had become estranged from him since he left.

The zeal they had for his message when he had been present with them was good, and it would have been good to continue it after he left. Instead, they had allowed Judaizers' to change their zeal from that directed toward Paul's message to that directed toward the Judaizers.

Note that some Christian still have the same problem today. When we are in the presence of strong and faithful teachers of God's word, we accept the truth and follow it. But when we are not around such people, we may be easily swayed by those who teach error. So we are unstable or fickle. We are not really standing for truth but are too easily influenced by people.

4:19,20 – Paul viewed himself as being in travail again until Christ was formed in the Galatians. He wished to be present with them and change his tone, for he was perplexed about them.

Paul concludes his description of the Galatians' treatment of him by recalling how he had labored for their conversion, like a mother in travail for the birth of a child. This is a process of pain and hard work for the mother, yet it leads to great joy when the child is born. This is indeed how the teaching process often is. The teacher labors hard, often suffering mental torment whether the students will really accept the truth or not. Compare the new birth of 3:26,27.

Having so labored when he had been among them before, Paul was now laboring in birth pains for them again, though they were already like his children (spiritually, since he had taught and converted them – compare 1 Corinthians 4:14,15). Now this new travail concerned whether or not Christ would be formed in them.

This is the experience of a parent with the child. First there is the pain of childbirth. But that is just the beginning of pain and labor. Following that comes the labor and pain of working to see a mature, useful, upright person form from that baby. In some ways this is more mentally painful than the physical birth.

This is also the common experience of the faithful teacher. It is not enough for people to be converted. They must go on to perfection, growing to maturity in Christ. This process is here described as Christ being formed in them. What a beautiful picture! The goal of a disciple is to be like his Master – to have the character of the Master develop in the disciple's life. Until that happens, the disciple is not mature. See notes on Galatians 2:20.

Notice that the goal is not just for a person to be baptized, receive forgiveness of his past sins, and become part of the church. The purpose of the gospel – which ought to be the purpose of our teaching – goes far beyond that. The goal is for Christ to be formed in the lives of every Christian. Their conduct, speech, and attitudes should be such that they model and imitate Christ Jesus Himself. Until that point is reached, we still have much to do.

This growth to Christ-like-ness does not always happen in the disciple, and it is painful for the teacher to labor and watch for it. So Paul expressively compares it to the birth pains all over again.

If "once saved, always saved" is true, one wonders why Paul would experience such pain. If the first birth pains had led to true conversion, according to Calvinistic doctrine, the person is saved and cannot be lost. So why be so concerned about whether they would or would not develop Christ's character? They would be saved in any case.

Paul then expressed his doubts, just like the parent of a rebellious, delinquent child. He would like to have reassurance about their future commitment to truth, but at the moment he was in doubt. They had treated him well and received him when he had been there before, so he would like to be among them again. Perhaps they would again accept his message, instead of rejecting it, and he could change his tone toward them so he would not have to rebuke them as he was doing.

4:21-31 - An Allegory of the Two Covenants

4:21-23 – Paul then appealed to events in the law as a way of teaching those who desire to be under the law. Abraham had two sons, one the son of the handmaid born after the flesh, but the other the son of the freewoman born according to promise.

Those who desire to be under the law

Paul now concludes his evidence by giving an extended illustration of his conclusion. He says he is saying this to those who desire to be under the law. Note that here is the issue under consideration. Some people wanted to be under the law. They bound circumcision and other aspects of the Mosaic Code as though all people must keep them. This is the doctrine Paul is refuting.

Notice that there are still people today who desire to be under the law. The meaning of being under the law clearly refers to being subject to his teaching – that is, being required to submit to its requirements. Surely it does not mean, as some would claim in other places, simply being subject to the penalty of the law. Surely the people did not desire that!

Since these people claimed such respect for the law, Paul used teaching from the law to help illustrate his point. This is an effective teaching method, to appeal to the consequences or teaching of that which people profess to accept.

The son of the bondwoman and the son of the freewoman

Paul proceeds to talk to them about something that is taught in the law. It is based on two of Abraham's sons (he had more than two, but the illustration concerns just the two better known ones).

The first son was born to him by a bondwoman. This obviously refers to Ishmael who was born to Abraham by Hagar (Genesis 16:1-4,15). The second son was born by a freewoman. This obviously refers to Isaac who was born to Sarah (Genesis 21:2). Note that neither Paul nor the Genesis account denied that Hagar was married to Abraham: Ishmael was not born from adultery. Hagar was a concubine, who was a bondwoman, in contrast to Sarah who was a freewoman. But Abraham was married to both of them, which was permissible at that time.

The son of the bondwoman (Ishmael) was born simply of the **flesh**. He was simply the result of the physical union of Abraham and Hagar. There was no special significance other than that to his birth (compare Romans 9:7,8). In particular, God had made no special promise regarding him nor had He offered any special blessing to Ishmael. Ishmael's birth was entirely the result of human planning and human conduct – it was not the result of a promise or instruction from God.

The second son was the son of **promise**. God had promised repeatedly to give this son to Abraham and Sarah, and God had made many important promises about this son (Genesis 17:15-19; 18:10; 21:1; Hebrews 11:11). In fact, the promises about which Paul has been talking throughout the book of Galatians were promises made to come true through Isaac.

The distinction between flesh and promise

This point is absolutely critical to the understanding of the illustration! We might expect Jews and Judaizers to conclude, in this illustration, that they should be classed with Isaac, since they were descendants of Isaac. But Paul's whole point is the distinction between **physical fleshly ancestry** on the one hand and **inheritance according to promise** on the other hand.

Jews and Judaizers thought they should receive the fullness of God's special blessings simply because they were physical descendants of Abraham. But Paul's point is that Ishmael was a physical descendant of Abraham too. Did he receive the blessings of the promise? No! Did Jews believe he should have received the blessings? No! Why then should they think physical ancestry is all that was needed to receive the blessings?

Clearly something else is involved. What else was lacking in the case of Ishmael? God had made no **promise**! But remember that Paul has just spent 1½ whole chapters discussing the promise that God did make, showing that the blessing of the promise was fulfilled in Jesus and granted to those who have obedient faith in Him, whether they are Jews or Gentiles. The promise stated that a blessing would be made available to all nations – not just to Jews. The one who came to bring that blessing would be a descendant of Abraham through Isaac and Jacob, but the blessing of the promise came only to those who met the conditions. See 3:14,26,27,29.

The clear lesson will be that merely being physical descendants of Abraham would grant no special blessing to Jews, any more than it would to Ishmael and his descendants, apart from the promise that God made to Abraham. The blessing came through the promise and through meeting the conditions of the promise, not simply by being descendants of Abraham.

> "...the one not born according to the flesh was in greater honor than the one who was. Do not, then, be dismayed that you were not born according to the flesh, for your not being born according to the flesh makes you all the more kin to him. For conception that is not according to natural processes is more remarkable and more spiritual." – Chrysostom (*Ancient Christian Commentary*)

4:24,25 – An allegory can be based on these events. The two women represent two covenants. The one given at Mount Sinai was similar to Hagar whose children were in bondage. This is similar to the present Jerusalem.

Paul then states that there is symbolism in this story.

Some people seem to think they have the right to teach just any allegorical meaning they think some Scripture might have, despite the fact they cannot prove the Scripture means that. This makes nonsense of the Bible, because people could assume all kinds of ideas, but no one could ever prove any of them. We must remember that Paul gave this allegory by Divine inspiration.

Some conclusions that Paul draws should be obvious from the Old Testament events that he discusses. However, not all of Paul's observations would necessarily be obvious to everyone who reads the Old Testament story without further proof. His point is simply that there are similarities between these events and the point Paul is making.

So, the events discussed here may constitute ***proof*** of some aspects of Paul's point, but other aspects simply help ***illustrate*** or explain his point. The proof is not always in the illustration itself, but in the fact that he, as an apostle, taught this by Divine inspiration. The similarities have some evidential value, but in some ways they simply should help Jews understand how the conclusion makes sense.

Note that we do similar things today in our teaching based on Scripture. Sometimes we use a Bible event to illustrate a point of similarity to some current situation. However, the similarity we see may not of itself prove our point to be true. To prove it to be true we must find Scriptural proof that our conclusion is valid. The parallel we draw may simply illustrate our point without conclusively proving the point.

For example, suppose someone accuses me of having done wrong, when in fact they are the one who did wrong. I may point out the similarity between this and the fact that Potiphar's wife accused Joseph of wrong when she herself was the one who had done wrong. This may illustrate my point, but of itself it does not prove that I am in the right and the person who is accusing me is in the wrong. In order to prove they are wrong, I must demonstrate their conduct violates Scripture.

Note that Paul is not saying that the record in the book of Genesis is simply an allegory. That is, he is not denying the historical reality of the events. He is simply using them as illustrations of the lesson he intends to teach here.

> "...the apostle does not deny the history or pick apart the events of the distant past, but he has stated them as they happened at the time, while using for his own purpose the

interpretation of these events." – Theodore of Mopsuestia (*Ancient Christian Commentary*)

Paul says these two sons of Abraham illustrate two covenants.

The first covenant is the one given at Mount Sinai. Paul says, in his comparison, this corresponds to Hagar! Hagar illustrates the law given at Mt. Sinai and to the current Jerusalem. Jerusalem was the current capitol of Judaism, and Mt. Sinai was where the Jewish law was given. Clearly Paul is saying that the Judaistic system is compared to Hagar! This is the opposite of what Jews would have expected. They would have assumed that the Judaistic system should be associated with Isaac, since they were descendants of Isaac.

What reasons does Paul give why, in the comparison, Judaism should be compared to Hagar? (1) Because Hagar's son was simply the result of fleshly relationship, having no special place in God's promised blessing. And (2) because Hagar and her son were slaves. Ishmael was a slave because he was the son of a slave.

But this is exactly parallel to Judaism. Jews were claiming special privileges based simply on a physical relationship with Abraham. But Ishmael could claim that much! The promises regarding Israel had all been fulfilled. They no longer had grounds to claim special privileges. The last promise to be fulfilled was that a blessing would come on all men through Christ's death. But that had been fulfilled and left no greater blessing for Jews than Gentiles. Paul had proved at length that Gentiles would receive this blessing same as Jews. God just used the Jews *through* whom to bring Christ's blessing to the world.

Further, the law given at Sinai brought its adherents into bondage. Paul had proved that at length – 2:4,16; 3:10-13,22,23; 4:1-7,9; 5:1; Acts 15:10; etc. They were in bondage to sin because the law condemned them for sin but could not remove it. Furthermore, the fact that the Judaizers claimed to be Christians would indicate that they realized that they needed forgiveness beyond what the law would provide. So the bondage to sin under the law made them like Ishmael in the allegory, not like Isaac who was free.

So, Jews who sought to bind the law were not like Isaac but like Ishmael! They were slaves claiming a spiritual blessing (justification) on the mere basis of fleshly ancestry! Clearly this claim is neither valid nor convincing. Yet it is the only basis the Jews had left to use.

Note: The references to Mt. Sinai "in Arabia" might refer to another similarity in that Mt. Sinai, where the law was given, was located in the territory of the descendants of Ishmael. This, of course, is not an issue of doctrinal force.

Commentary on Galatians

4:26,27 – The Jerusalem from above is our mother. It is written, rejoice you who does not bear and does not travail. For the children of the desolate are more than the children of the one who has a husband. The Jerusalem above is the mother of us all.

But Paul had referred to **two** covenants in verse 24. The first was the one given from Mt. Sinai (verse 24). What about the second one? It is not directly named, but clearly refers to the gospel of Christ, since this is what Paul has contrasted to the law throughout the book.

This covenant is compared by Paul, not to the Jerusalem on earth, but to the Jerusalem above, the mother of us all (i.e., of all Christians). This Jerusalem **above** is spiritual, not earthly. It is based on spiritual promises and blessings, not mere earthly, physical ones.

Clearly this refers to the covenant in which we are blessed on the basis of spiritual relationship according to promises, not mere fleshly relationship. Also we will see that it gives true freedom, not bondage. This must refer to the gospel.

Spiritual Jerusalem is elsewhere used to refer to the church (Hebrews 12:22,23; compare Revelation 3:12; 21:2,10; Philippians 3:20). It is the "mother" of us all in that, as Ishmael was a slave because his mother was a slave, so we are free because our spiritual covenant makes us free.

The barren woman will have more children than the married woman.

Verse 27 seems to be the most difficult part of the comparison to understand. It is a quotation from Isaiah 54:1, saying that a barren woman who does not bear or have labor pains, should yet rejoice because the barren one will have more children than the married woman.

This is confusing especially in light of the comparison to Hagar and Sarah. If Sarah is the married woman, then this means Hagar (the Old Testament and the Jews) should rejoice more than Christians under the gospel. Surely that is not the point. In fact, it was Sarah who was barren and had no child, whereas Hagar had a child.

Willis explains that Isaiah 54:1 is discussing Israel's future. They had been married (spiritually) to God, but because of sins would be cast off by being sent into Babylonian captivity. This is the barrenness or desolation to which Isaiah refers. But they would return and God would eventually send the suffering servant described in chapter 53. When that happened, the desolate woman would have more children than they had when they were married to God.

I.e., though Israel had been rejected by God, when Jesus came they would have more spiritual children then they had before God cast them off. This could mean more saved people or greater spiritual blessings, but either way the point is similar. Because of the blessing through Christ, they would be blessed more greatly after they had been cast off than they had been before. (Another possibility is that the Gentiles, who had not been married to God under the Old Testament, would have more spiritual children than the Jews when the gospel came.) (See Isaiah 54.)

If this is the proper explanation, then Paul's application of it is that here is an Old Testament passage proving that even Jews would receive God's blessings through Christ according to the gospel, not through the law on the basis of mere physical ancestry.

4:28,29 – *So we are children of promise like Isaac. And just as the one who was born after the flesh persecuted the one born after the Spirit, so it was in the first century.*

Now the conclusion of the comparison is stated directly in verses 28-31. First, Paul completes the comparison to Isaac. As Isaac was the child of promise, not just a fleshly descendant (verse 23), so we brethren (Christians) are children of promise. We receive the spiritual inheritance promised to true children.

That promised blessing has been described throughout the context and must refer to justification and all the privileges of spiritual childhood (3:14,26,17,29). Compare 4:26. We are children who inherit according to the promise. But Jews, who are only physical descendants of Abraham, have no basis to claim inheritance.

Paul then raised a further point of comparison. The one who had mere fleshly relationship (Ishmael) persecuted the one born according to the Spirit – i.e., the one who received the promise through the Spirit (verse 23). This, of course, refers to the time when Isaac was weaned and Ishmael mocked him (Genesis 21:9). Ishmael at that time was at least 15 years old (Genesis 16:16).

Ishmael's mockery of his infant brother doubtless was quite a serious thing. First, it was entirely improper for one who was old enough to know better to ridicule a little child. Second, it was wrong for a slave to ridicule the child born to a free woman. Third, one who was born with no special blessing should not be ridiculing one who was born by a promised blessing from God.

As some commentators explain, it is possible even that Ishmael mistreated Isaac because he knew Isaac would inherit the promises from Abraham, whereas Ishmael would not. It may have been an expression of jealousy, which would fit the definition of persecution. The fact that Sarah reacted by determining to send Ishmael and Hagar away demonstrates that what Ishmael did was not simply a childish argument between siblings. It was serious enough that it resulted in Ishmael and his mother being sent away. Even so, the persecution of the descendants of Ishmael against the descendants of Isaac has continued throughout the ages, even till today.

Commentary on Galatians

Here then is another parallel in which the Jews were like Ishmael. Ishmael persecuted Isaac, not the other way around. So Jews and Judaizers were persecuting Paul and other Christians, not Christians persecuting Jews. This confirms our point on 3:4 that Christians were being persecuted at the hands of Jews. Compare 5:11; 6:12.

Paul has brought up the subject of persecution to show the Christians that they should not feel guilty because the Judaizers were ridiculing and pressuring them for their refusal to obey the old law. Nor should they feel inferior because they were not physical descendants of Abraham. The fact that Ishmael persecuted Isaac did not mean that Isaac was wrong or that he had no special promise from God. And the fact that Ishmael was bigger and stronger physically and was a descendant of Abraham did not make him right.

4:30,31 – So the Scripture said that the handmaid and her son should be cast out and would not inherit with the son of the freewoman. So we as brethren are not children of the handmaid, but of the freewoman.

Cast out the bondwoman and her son, for the son of the bondwoman will not inherit with the son of the freewoman.

So what did Genesis say regarding the incident in which Ishmael persecuted Isaac? It said that the bondwoman (Hagar) and her son (Ishmael) were to be "cast out," so they would not inherit with the son (Isaac) of the freewoman (Sarah).

Here is a conclusive proof that mere physical lineage is not an adequate basis to claim inheritance! Ishmael was a fleshly descendant but was disinherited. Not only did he not receive the **promised** blessing, but he was entirely cast out! He had to leave home and was no longer part of the family with the promised son.

Now what is the consequence to Jews with their cherished law? The law was not the basis of inheritance but the basis of bondage. **So the children (Jews) and their mother (the law at Sinai) were both cast out!** This means that the law is no longer in effect at all – see notes on 3:24,25. And furthermore, those who adhere to it will not receive the inheritance (see verses 26,28). Like Ishmael, despite their physical lineage, they will be treated as though they are not even part of the family!

What a blow to the mindset of the Judaizers! They were arguing that one had to become like a Jew to be part of God's spiritual family and receive His blessings. Paul has proved that this is not necessary. That is bad enough, but now Paul goes further. Even if one tries to be a Christian but binds the Old Testament, he is still enslaved and will be cast out! He is disinherited like Ishmael!

What a shameful consequence to affirm to a Jew. To be compared to an Ishmaelite was a supreme insult! The Ishmaelites were outcasts who did not inherit. But Jews were the chosen ones (in their mind). Paul has affirmed the Jews too will be cast out, if they rely on their physical lineage and bind the Old Testament.

Who then will inherit the blessing? The brethren who are children of the freewoman will inherit (verses 26,28). Christians who follow the gospel will receive the promised inheritance, as stated throughout the discussion. We are not children of slavery but of freedom.

Note the application regarding the religion of Islam.

Muslims claim that Muhammed restored the ancient worship practiced by Abraham and that the promises God made to Abraham were actually passed down through Ishmael. However, Paul here claims that Ishmael was cast out and would not inherit the promises with Isaac. Furthermore, this is exactly what the Old Testament itself said about it.

Paul is saying that physical Jews were the ones through whom the promise God made to Abraham would come true. But even they will not inherit the promised blessing unless they accept Christ and let go of the law. Clearly if no one can be justified on the basis of Israelite religion, then no one can be justified on the basis of Ishmaelite religion!

God never had any special place for Ishmael or Ishmael's descendants in His plan for man's salvation. God's promises were to come true through Isaac and his descendants. But those promises to Israel as a nation or physical descendants of Abraham have all been fulfilled. All of God's special blessings today are for those who obey the gospel, whether those people are descendants of Israel, descendants of Ishmael, or Gentiles in the flesh.

To claim any special promise today for the descendants of Ishmael is to completely misuse God's plan.

Commentary on Galatians

Galatians 5

Chapter 5,6 – Applications of the Gospel

5:1-15 - Consequences of Heeding False Teachers

5:1,2 – Christ set us free so we could be free, so stand fast and do not again be entangled in a yoke of bondage. If we receive circumcision, Christ will profit us nothing.

Paul has concluded his efforts to explain and prove the teaching that we are saved by the gospel of Christ with the blood of Jesus, not by the Law of Moses. Beginning with this verse he begins to state the conclusions, consequences, and applications that follow.

Stand fast in the liberty by which Christ had made us free.

What is this liberty? Clearly it is contrasted to the bondage later in the verse.

Christ set us free from the law: Galatians 2:4; 3:22,23; 4:3,9; 5:13; Acts 15:10; 13:39 (see the notes on those verses).

Christ set us free from sin: James 1:25; 2 Corinthians 11:20; Romans 8:15; John 8:32,36; 2 Corinthians 3:17; 2 Peter 2:19.

The first group of verses above show that the law was a burden which put men in bondage, but Christ sets us free from that bondage. The second group shows that sin is enslavement or bondage, from which Christ sets us free. These may be viewed as two different things from which Christ sets us free: sin and the law. However, they are closely related in Paul's argument because, as discussed in these passages (especially 3:22,23; 4:3,9), the bondage of the law *is* the bondage of sin!

> "He shows first that it is the utmost foolishness, having become free instead of slaves, to desire slavery again instead of freedom. Second, he reveals them to be unmindful of and

ungrateful to their benefactor, despising the one who frees them and preferring that which enslaves them." – Chrysostom (*Ancient Christian Commentary*)

(Note that the Jews should understand the concept of bondage and should strongly oppose it because their ancestors had been in bondage in Egypt and later in Babylon. And they themselves were subject to Rome at this very time.)

The reason the law was an unbearable yoke was that it proved to people that they were guilty of sin, but then it gave them no means to remove the sin. So, the bondage of the law was the bondage of sin. Jesus removed this bondage by giving us a way to be truly and permanently forgiven of sin. To do this, He had to remove the Old Testament, which could not give forgiveness, and give us instead the New Testament with its true forgiveness through His death.

Paul then commands the Galatians (and us) not to go back to that yoke of bondage (the law), but to stand fast for the freedom we have in Christ. Here is the conclusion of Paul's lengthy argument. Note that subjection to the Old Testament is not required of a Christian. What is more, it is not even an option. That law was removed because it could not save. We are now *forbidden* by Scripture to go back and practice or bind that system again as religious rite. To do so is to fail to stand fast in Christ and His freedom. (Compare this to the error of the people of Israel in Numbers 13 and other places who wanted to go back to the slavery of Egypt.)

This does not mean that all practices of the Old Testament are sinful, but as such they are not law for us today. Some are repeated in various forms in the New Testament and are therefore binding, not because they were in the Old Testament, but because they are in the New Testament. Other practices (including even circumcision) may be fine as health measures or civil or family customs (see verse 6). But they must not be practiced as religious rites, especially not if they are taught as necessary in order to please God.

Note further that the "freedom" Paul describes that we have in Christ is clearly defined in the context and other passages. It is not absolute freedom to do as we please (see verse 13). It is not freedom from all law. We are subject to Divine law, but many New Testament commands are different from those of the Old Testament, and especially the system we have now includes a means of forgiveness by trusting Jesus' sacrifice.

Passages that Show We Are Under Law to Christ

Galatians 6:2 – Bear one another's burdens, and so fulfill the law of Christ.

Romans 3:27 – Where is boasting then? It is excluded. By what law? Of works? No, but by the law of faith.

> Romans 8:2 – For the law of the Spirit of life in Christ Jesus has made me free from the law of sin and death.
>
> Romans 8:7 – Because the carnal mind is enmity against God; for it is not subject to the law of God, nor indeed can be.
>
> James 1:25 – But he who looks into the perfect law of liberty and continues in it, and is not a forgetful hearer but a doer of the work, this one will be blessed in what he does.
>
> James 2:12 – So speak and so do as those who will be judged by the law of liberty.
>
> James 2:8 – If you really fulfill the royal law according to the Scripture, "You shall love your neighbor as yourself," you do well;

Specific passages that teach Christians are required to be obedient according to the gospel of Christ: Matthew 7:21-27; 22:36-39; John 14:15,21-24; Acts 10:34,35; Romans 2:6-10; 6:17,18; Hebrews 5:9; 10:39; 11:8,30; Galatians 5:6; 2 Thessalonians 1:8,9; James 2:14-26; 1 Peter 1:22,23; 1 John 5:3; 2:3-6.

If anyone accepts circumcision, Christ profits that man nothing!

"... To 'receive' circumcision is to acknowledge it to be of Divine authority and of Christian obligation, and in like manner to acknowledge all that for which it stood in the mind of the Jews." – Hogg and Vine.

Becoming circumcised here is used to stand for the law and its obligations. This is so because circumcision was the symbol of being a Jew. As such it was the defining act which expressed whether or not one considered himself to be subject to the law. This is why it was a test case regarding Titus (see 2:3,4) and became the focus of controversy as to whether or not the law was binding (see 5:3,6,11; Acts 15:1,5). Again, Paul is not forbidding circumcision for personal reasons (verse 6), but he is showing that it is not necessary.

But consider the force of this conclusion. He says that, to receive circumcision as religious ritual is to receive no profit from Christ. But Christ is the Savior. To believe, as did the Judaizers, that one must also be circumcised and keep the law, is to cut oneself off from Christ's salvation (verse 4). It is to deny the saving power of Jesus' sacrifice, claiming we must also have submission to another law. The people Paul was speaking to and about were Christians (3:26,27). But even so, if they bound the Old Testament, Christ would be of no profit to them.

The law is not an option. It is not an appendage to the gospel nor the gospel to it. One cannot take both the law and gospel. It is one or the other. And if one takes the law, he cannot claim salvation through Christ. That leaves him only the law, which cursed all who were subject to it because of sin (3:10-12).

Since these were Christians being addressed, what is the conclusion regarding the doctrine of "once saved, always saved"? How can one be saved if Christ profits him nothing? Clearly these would be saved people who ceased to be saved. Calvinism is simply false teaching.

5:3,4 – *Everyone who receives circumcision becomes a debtor to do the whole law. Those who would be justified by the law are severed from Christ and fallen away from grace.*

Debtor to keep the whole law

Here Paul enlarges on the message of verses 1,2, stating clearly that "every man" who accepts circumcision (religiously) is a debtor to keep the whole law. Note that this applies to every one – Jew or Gentile. It is not just Gentiles that are not obligated to keep the law. Jews are not either.

The law is a "whole": a complete unit. One cannot accept part of it (circumcision) and skip other parts. If a person views any part of the old law to be required today, he is required to submit to all of it: circumcision, animal sacrifices, dietary laws, holy days, the Levitical priesthood, Tabernacle ceremonies, etc.

> "The law is not to be conceived of as a bundle of separate strands, whereof if one be broken the rest may still remain intact, but rather as a sheet of glass which, if it be broken in any part, is broken as a whole." – Hogg and Vine.

What is said of circumcision is logically just as true of any other part. To keep part is to subject yourself to the whole. Even the Judaizers did not keep it all (6:13). But violation of any one part brings condemnation (see James 2:10,11; Galatians 3:10; Matthew 5:17,18). Either it is all in effect or none in effect. Doubtless the Galatians – and probably even the Judaizers – had not considered this consequence.

Yet people today want to do just as these Judaizers did. They pick parts they say are in effect, such as the Sabbath, the priesthood, tithing, incense, or instrumental music. But then they reject other parts as not binding. They even argue that the law consisted of moral parts (still binding) and ceremonial parts (removed). Paul denies it. It is a "whole." All is in effect or none is in effect. But he has already shown, and will show further, that to view any as being in effect is to put oneself in bondage to sin and cut oneself off from Christ. See also Hebrews 10:1-10; 7:11-14; 8:6-13; 9:1-4; 2 Corinthians 3:6-11; Galatians 3:24,25; 5:1-6; Romans 7:1-7; Ephesians 2:11-16; Colossians 2:13-17.

Estranged from Christ

Again, Paul repeats and strengthens the conclusion. He had said that those who bound the law were not standing fast in Christ's freedom, were entangled in a yoke of bondage, and Christ would profit

Commentary on Galatians

them nothing. Now he goes further and says they are estranged or severed from Christ. Imagine being estranged or cut off from the Savior! That is how much this issue matters!

Here Paul speaks of the folks he is referring to as seeking to be "justified" by the law. But keep this in context! Paul is simply talking to and about those who sought to be "under" the law (4:21). He is speaking to Christians who knew Christ had died for them. They claimed to believe they were obligated to obey the gospel. So they did not seek to be justified by the law in the sense that they thought the law could give them forgiveness of sins without Christ and the gospel. They were trying to keep the gospel and still bind the law as a condition essential to stand right before God in **addition** to the gospel. This is what they thought was needed to be "right" (justified) before God.

So, if a person claims he can be saved by the gospel of Christ and still binds the law, that person is seeking to be justified by the law in the sense that Paul is here using the term. See 2:16; 3:10-12; Acts 13:39. And this did not mean binding all the law, for the Judaizers did not do that (6:13). So, anyone today who seeks to bind any part of the law (instrumental music, Sabbath, etc.) is seeking to be "justified by the law" in the sense that Paul is rebuking.

Fallen from grace

What then is the condition of such people? They are fallen from grace! They have denied the power of the only means whereby God's grace can really save them. So, they have fallen from grace. How then can they be saved, since we are saved by grace (Ephesians 2:8,9; etc.)? Clearly this is likewise the condition of anyone today who tries to use the Old Testament to bind religious practices.

Again, these were Christians being addressed (3:26,27). They had been in grace, since one cannot fall from someplace where he has not been. Yet they could fall from grace. How then can the doctrine of "once saved, always saved" be true?

Summarizing, those who sought to be under the law had failed to stand fast in the liberty in Christ (verse 1), had become entangled in a yoke of bondage (verse 1), Christ profits them nothing (verse 2), they are debtors to keep the whole law (verse 3), they are severed from Christ (verse 4), and fallen from grace (verse 4).

Other verses show that it is possible to receive the grace of God in vain (2 Corinthians 6:1), do despite to the Spirit of grace (Hebrews 10:29), or fall short of the grace of God (Hebrews 12:15) in contrast to continuing in the grace of God (Acts 13:43) or standing in grace (Romans 5:2).

Other Passages Showing that a Child of God Can Fall Away and Be Lost

---

John 15:2-6 – Every branch in Me that does not bear fruit He takes away; and every branch that bears fruit He prunes, that it may bear more fruit. You are already clean because of the word which I have spoken to you. Abide in Me, and I in you. As the branch cannot bear fruit of itself, unless it abides in the vine, neither can you, unless you abide in Me. I am the vine, you are the branches. He who abides in Me, and I in him, bears much fruit; for without Me you can do nothing. If anyone does not abide in Me, he is cast out as a branch and is withered; and they gather them and throw them into the fire, and they are burned.

Acts 8:12,13,18-23 – But when they believed Philip as he preached the things concerning the kingdom of God and the name of Jesus Christ, both men and women were baptized. Then Simon himself also believed; and when he was baptized he continued with Philip, and was amazed, seeing the miracles and signs which were done. ... And when Simon saw that through the laying on of the apostles' hands the Holy Spirit was given, he offered them money, – saying, "Give me this power also, that anyone on whom I lay hands may receive the Holy Spirit." But Peter said to him, "Your money perish with you, because you thought that the gift of God could be purchased with money! You have neither part nor portion in this matter, for your heart is not right in the sight of God. Repent therefore of this your wickedness, and pray God if perhaps the thought of your heart may be forgiven you. For I see that you are poisoned by bitterness and bound by iniquity."

Romans 6:12-18 – Therefore do not let sin reign in your mortal body, that you should obey it in its lusts. And do not present your members as instruments of unrighteousness to sin, but present yourselves to God as being alive from the dead, and your members as instruments of righteousness to God. For sin shall not have dominion over you, for you are not under law but under grace. What then? Shall we sin because we are not under law but under grace? Certainly not! Do you not know that to whom you present yourselves slaves to obey, you are that one's slaves whom you obey, whether of sin leading to death, or of obedience leading to righteousness? But God be thanked that though you were slaves of sin, yet you obeyed from the heart that form of doctrine to which you were delivered. And having been set free from sin, you became slaves of righteousness.

Romans 8:12-17 – Therefore, brethren, we are debtors--not to the flesh, to live according to the flesh. For if you live according to the flesh you will die; but if by the Spirit you put to death the deeds of the body, you will live. For as many as are led by the Spirit of God, these are sons of God. For you did not receive the spirit of bondage again to fear, but you received the Spirit of adoption by whom we cry out, "Abba, Father." The Spirit Himself bears witness with our spirit that we are children of God, and if children, then heirs – heirs of God and joint heirs with Christ, if indeed we suffer with Him, that we may also be glorified together.

1 Corinthians 9:27-10:1-12 – But I discipline my body and bring it into subjection, lest, when I have preached to others, I myself should become disqualified. Moreover, brethren, I do not want you to be unaware that all our fathers were under the cloud, all passed through the sea, all were baptized into Moses in the cloud and in the sea, ... But with most of them God was not well pleased, for their bodies were scattered in the wilderness. Now these things became our examples, to the intent that we should not lust after evil things as they also lusted. And do not become idolaters as were some of them. As it is written, "The people sat down to eat and drink, and rose up to play." Nor let us commit sexual immorality, as some of them did, and in one day twenty-three thousand fell; ... Now all these things happened to them as examples, and they were written for our admonition, upon whom the ends of the ages have come. Therefore let him who thinks he stands take heed lest he fall.

2 Timothy 2:17,18 – And their message will spread like cancer. Hymenaeus and Philetus are of this sort, who have strayed concerning the truth, saying that the resurrection is already past; and they overthrow the faith of some.

Hebrews 3:11-14 – So I swore in My wrath, "They shall not enter My rest." Beware, brethren, lest there be in any of you an evil heart of unbelief in departing from the living God; but exhort one another daily, while it is called "Today," lest any of you be hardened through the deceitfulness of sin. For we have become partakers of Christ if we hold the beginning of our confidence steadfast to the end,

Hebrews 6:4-8 – For it is impossible for those who were once enlightened, and have tasted the heavenly gift, and have become partakers of the Holy Spirit, and have tasted the good word of God and the powers of the age to come, if they fall away, to renew them again to repentance, since they crucify again for themselves the Son of God, and put Him to an open shame. For the earth which drinks in the rain that often comes upon it, and bears herbs useful for those by whom it is cultivated, receives blessing from God; but if it bears thorns and briars, it is rejected and near to being cursed, whose end is to be burned.

Hebrews 10:26-31 – For if we sin willfully after we have received the knowledge of the truth, there no longer remains a sacrifice for sins, but a certain fearful expectation of judgment, and fiery indignation which will devour the adversaries. Anyone who has rejected Moses' law dies without mercy on the testimony of two or three witnesses. Of how much worse punishment, do you suppose, will he be thought worthy who has trampled the Son of God underfoot, counted the blood of the covenant by which he was sanctified a common thing, and insulted the Spirit of grace? For we know Him who said, "Vengeance is Mine, I will repay," says the Lord. And again, "The LORD will judge His people." It is a fearful thing to fall into the hands of the living God.

2 Peter 2:20-22 – For if, after they have escaped the pollutions of the world through the knowledge of the Lord and Savior Jesus Christ, they are again entangled in them and overcome, the latter end is worse for them than the beginning. For it would have been better for them not to have known the way of righteousness, than having known it, to turn from the holy commandment delivered to them. But it has happened to them according to the true proverb: "A dog returns to his own vomit," and, "a sow, having washed, to her wallowing in the mire."

5:5,6 – Through the Spirit by faith we wait for the hope of righteousness. For in Christ neither circumcision avails anything nor uncircumcision, but faith working through love.

The hope of righteousness by faith

"You" who would be justified by the law are fallen from grace. But "we" eagerly wait for the hope of righteousness by faith. The law could not lead to true righteousness since everyone under it disobeyed it, and it could not then give a lasting cleansing from sin. But "through the Spirit" (according to the teaching of the Holy Spirit in the gospel) we can be righteous by faith – i.e., by the gospel system of justification by obedient faith. We have therefore the hope that can be received only by those who are truly righteous on the basis of faith. Clearly this is the hope of eternal life.

Those under the law had no hope as part of that system. Their only hope was the coming of a better system. We now have that system and with it true justification. This gives us a greater future hope, and we can eagerly await the results.

In Christ we have true forgiveness (3:13,14,24-29). So in Him circumcision does not matter or avail anything either way. But wait! He just said if you receive circumcision Christ profits you nothing (verse 2); now he says it does not matter. Clearly he is referring to it in a different sense.

Verse 2 referred to those who received circumcision as a religious ritual necessary to please God (verses 1-4). Now he simply means you can be a Jew (circumcised) or a Gentile (uncircumcised) and please God either way (compare 3:28). You may be circumcised as a matter of national tradition and not be condemned. But if you are uncircumcised you will still not be condemned.

The Judaizers said that even in Christ circumcision matters: it is essential to salvation. But the true gospel says that circumcision does not matter either way, so one must not bind it as essential to salvation. (See notes on 6:15.)

"For just as when one is choosing athletes, it matters nothing in this trial whether they be hook-nosed or snub-nosed, dark or fair, but all that need be looked for is that they be strong and skillful. So when a person is to be enrolled in the new covenant, the lack of these bodily trappings does no harm, just as they do no good if they be present." – Chrysostom (*Ancient Christian Commentary*)

Faith working through love

What then does matter? Faith working through love! This is a basic statement of the elements of **man's** responsibility under the gospel.

Contrary to the Judaizers, we are not saved by works of the law such as circumcision. Faith in Christ is needed.

On the other hand, contrary to the Calvinists and other Protestants, neither are we saved by "faith only" – i.e., faith without obedience.

Both faith and works are required, and both must act according to love. While this "avails" in Christ to receive His blessings, none of it earns salvation, for that would be impossible. See also James 2:14-26; Hebrews 11.

Faith refers to our conviction and trust in Christ and His word. We must realize that we have sinned against God and therefore will never earn salvation. We need forgiveness by Jesus' blood in accordance with His revealed will. See Hebrews 10:39; 11:1,4-8,17,30; Romans 1:16; 4:19-21; 5:1,2; 10:9,10,13-17; Galatians 5:6; 2 Corinthians 5:7; James 2:14-26; John 1:12; 3:15-18; 8:24; 20:30,31; Mark 16:15,16.

Working involves doing what God says in His word. However, again this does not earn salvation. It is simply meeting the conditions He has stated so we can be forgiven and remain in His favor. Matthew 7:21-27; 22:36-39; John 14:15,21-24; Acts 10:34,35; Romans 2:6-10; 6:17,18; Hebrews 5:9; 10:39; 11:8,30; Galatians 5:6; 2 Thessalonians 1:8,9; James 2:14-26; 1 Peter 1:22,23; 1 John 5:3; 2:3-6

Note: Some may argue that the verse means our "faith" is what is "working" for our salvation, but **we** are not working. This seems silly since faith can work only through those who possess it. It is not something disembodied that can act of itself apart from a person. But even if the concept were true, the verse says faith is working by **love**. And love requires obedience – see verses under love below. So, faith works by love only when we obey God's commands.

Some commentators, in an effort to salvage their doctrine of salvation by faith alone, claim that Paul is not saying that a faith that works by love is essential in order to come into union with Christ, but only avails in manifesting or making known that one is in Christ. However, the context is clearly discussing what is essential to be saved and have eternal life.

The Judaizers were teaching that one must be circumcised in order to be saved. Paul denies that by saying that neither circumcision nor uncircumcision avails – that is, neither is essential to salvation – but what is essential to salvation is faith that works by love. Furthermore, this concept has been stated elsewhere in the book and numerous places throughout the New Testament (see our notes on 3:26,27).

Note the parallel to 1 Corinthians 7:19 – Circumcision is nothing and uncircumcision is nothing, but keeping the commandments of God is what matters. Contrary to the Judaizers, circumcision is not necessary to salvation. But what is necessary is obedience to divine commands. But other Scriptures show that obedience must be based on faith and motivated by love, hence faith working by love.

Love is our commitment to act in such a way as to express our good will toward God. It is the attitude that leads us to show concern for His will and to be pleasing to Him. Just as faith without obedience is not a true and saving faith, so love without obedience is not a true and acceptable love. Those who claim to love God must obey him, and without obedience we do not have true love. See Matthew 22:37-40; Luke 6:27,28,31-33; 10:25-37; 1 Corinthians 13:1-8,13; John 14:15,21-24,31; Romans 13:8-10; Galatians 5:6; Hebrews 10:24; 1 John 2:3-6,15-17; 5:2,3; 2 John 5,6; Revelation 3:19.

> "Faith" (πιστις) – "...faith; i.e. 1. conviction of the truth of anything, belief ...; in the N.T. of a conviction or belief respecting man's relationship to God and divine things, generally with the included idea of trust and holy fervor born of faith and conjoined with it...a. when it relates to God [it] is the conviction that God exists and is the creator and ruler of all things, the provider and bestower of eternal salvation through Christ ... b. in reference to Christ, it denotes a strong and welcome conviction or belief that Jesus is the Messiah, through whom we obtain eternal salvation in the kingdom of God ... c. univ. the religious belief of Christians; ... subjectively: ... in the sense of a mere acknowledgment of divine things and of the claims of Christianity ... objectively, the substance of Christian faith or what is believed by Christians ... d. with the predominant idea of trust (or confidence) whether in God or in Christ, springing from faith in the same .. 2. fidelity, faithfulness, i.e. the character of one who can be relied on ..." – Grimm-Wilke-Thayer. [Compare the verb "believe"]

> "Working" (ενεργεω) – "1 intr. to put one's capabilities into operation, *work, be at work, be active, operate, be effective* ... 2 trans. to bring someth. about through use of capability, *work, produce, effect...*" – Bauer-Danker-Arndt-Gingrich.

> "Love" (Gk. αγαπη) – "...In signification it follows the verb αγαπαω, consequently it denotes 1. affection good-will, love,

Commentary on Galatians

benevolence ... Of the love of men to men; esp. of that love of Christians towards Christians which is enjoined and prompted by their religion ... Of the love of men towards God ... God towards men ... God towards Christ ... Christ towards men..." – Grimm-Wilke-Thayer.

5:7,8 – *You were running well. Who hindered you so you would not obey the truth? This persuasion did not come from Him who called you.*

Paul here begins to make even more direct application to the Galatians. He said they had been running well, but someone hindered them. This uses one of Paul's common illustrations: a runner in a race. They were doing well in the race, headed for victory, but someone hindered them. As a result of their conversion and commitment to Christ, they had been serving effectively. They had much reason to hope for their salvation, but someone threw a stumbling block in their path. Who was it?

Clearly the answer is the Judaizers: those who taught this doctrine Paul is refuting. He knew that, and they got the picture from context and his rhetorical question.

The result of this influence was that they were hindered in obeying the truth. Note that truth must be obeyed, not just understood or believed. If obedience to the truth did not matter, why would Paul be concerned? It follows that hindering people from obeying the truth is a serious error because it causes them to be lost. To accuse someone of this is a serious accusation. Paul was not taking this matter lightly. His view was not the ecumenical view of compromise: you believe it your way and I'll believe it mine.

Note that it is possible to have an influence for good or evil in the salvation of others. The gospel often emphasizes our need to be an influence for good, but it also warns of the danger of being an influence for evil. We should seek above all else to be saved eternally and to help others to be saved. To hinder anyone's salvation is tragic. 1 Timothy 4:12; Matthew 5:13-16; 18:6,7; Titus 2:7,8; 1 Peter 2:11,12; 2 Corinthians 6:3; 8:20,21; 1 Corinthians 8:9-13; 10:23-33; 15:33; 1 Thessalonians 1:6-8; Proverbs 13:20.

The persuasion that was influencing the Galatians, therefore, most surely did not come from the One who called them. God calls us through the gospel (note verse 13; 2 Thessalonians 2:13,14). Surely He would not then hinder those who obey Him. God did not do it, so those who did it were not acting according to God's will. They were teaching a different gospel, not according to the gospel from God (1:8-12).

5:9,10 – A little leaven leavens the whole lump. Paul had confidence in them in the Lord that they would not accept another view. But the one who was causing the trouble would bear his judgment.

Here Paul uses another illustration common in Scripture, that of leaven in a lump of dough. See 1 Corinthians 5:6; Matthew 13:33; 16:6,12; Luke 13:21. The reference is to influence (see verses 7,8 above). Just a little bit of yeast in a lump of dough will cause the whole thing to rise. It is not necessary to deliberately place yeast in each part of the lump. Place it anywhere in the lump and it will spread to the rest.

This is the way sin is. It has an influence for evil that spreads and grows. It does not remain isolated or insignificant. Sometimes people think sin is not a big problem in a congregation. They see only a few people involved or only a seemingly insignificant error, so they think it can be ignored. Or perhaps they may say something about it occasionally, but they see no need for firmer measures. Paul is saying sin cannot be ignored. It must be cast out (see the context of 1 Corinthians 5).

Error spreads numerically in that it gradually leads astray greater and greater numbers of people. Only a few may accept it at first, but if it is not dealt with, it will engulf more and more. Willis states that the same principle applies to the progressive nature of sin. It starts out with just a seemingly small departure from truth – not very different. But then it grows to greater and greater errors till those who are involved are far from truth (Hebrews 12:15). This is illustrated repeatedly in many Bible examples and in more recent history of the Lord's church.

The conclusion must be that the Galatians should not tolerate the error but deal with it. Doctrinal error that leads people into sin must not be ignored in a congregation. Unity is required. It is hard to avoid the conclusion that Paul is here requiring them to take necessary disciplinary steps toward the Judaizers, even as he meant in 1 Corinthians 5. For other passages regarding chastising erring members, see 2 Thessalonians 3:6,14,15; Matthew 18:15-17; Titus 3:10,11; Romans 16:17; 1 Timothy 1:3-11,19,20; 2 Corinthians 2:6-11; 2 John 9-11.

Paul then expressed confidence that they would recognize the error and accept the truth. They would not, in the long run, be led astray by the error but would stand for truth. We are not to be divided in mind but have the same mind in Christ.

But whatever the outcome was, Paul was sure that those who were causing the trouble among the Galatians would eventually receive the judgment they deserved. All must bear the judgment without partiality for departing from the truth: "whoever he is." We can always know this will be the case. Sometimes people are punished for sin in this life, as by governing authorities, by the church, etc. In other cases, they may appear to get away with sin in this life, but they will surely be punished by God at the judgment. In any case, they will bear their judgment.

Finally note that those who teach and advocate error are responsible for troubling a congregation, causing confusion and disturbance. Sometimes people who expose and oppose error are called trouble makers. Paul put the responsibility where it really belonged. Those who teach or practice error are the real trouble makers (1 Kings 18:17,18).

5:11,12 – If Paul was still preaching circumcision, why was he being persecuted? The stumbling block of the cross would have been abolished. He wished that those who were causing the trouble would cut themselves off.

Was Paul preaching circumcision?

Paul then asked why he was being persecuted if he was still preaching circumcision. For a Jew to deny the need for circumcision would bring on the wrath and persecution of Jews. See 3:4; 4:29; 6:12. Paul had been persecuted by Jews nearly everywhere he went. Surely this proved that he was not preaching circumcision as necessary for salvation. If he believed it was necessary, he would not have suffered as he did.

This was, in his view, the "offense" which the cross caused. Jews were upset with the preaching of the gospel because it said the cross removed the law and granted salvation to all men (Jews and Gentiles) through Christ without circumcision or the law. Jews did not like that at all, and many Jewish Christians had the same problem. They were prepared to accept Christ as the Savior, yet still wanted circumcision and the law to be viewed as necessary.

It appears that some were saying that Paul was still preaching the need for circumcision. One wonders, in light of all the other accusations against him, why they would make this one. Perhaps it was because he had Timothy circumcised. That was done so Timothy could teach Jews effectively, not as a religious act necessary to please God (see 2:3). Perhaps some claimed this was an inconsistency on Paul's part, as though sometimes he taught circumcision and other times he did not. Compare 1 Corinthians 9:19ff.

He wished the false teachers would cut themselves off.

He then makes the difficult statement that he wished those who were teaching this troubling doctrine (compare verses 7,10) would actually cut themselves off. This seems difficult to understand. The NKJV footnote says "mutilate themselves." This agrees with the NASB and RSV. The meaning seems to be that, rather than just circumcising the foreskin, Paul hoped they would go all the way and cut off their entire organ, castrating themselves!

Why would Paul hope such a thing as that? Surely he was not so vindictive as to wish for a physical mutilation, just so he could get even with them. Willis states that the Galatians had in their society a heathen cult that mutilated themselves in this way. Yet under the law such mutilation would separate one from the assembly of Israel (Deuteronomy 23:1).

So, if these Judaizers would go beyond circumcision and mutilate themselves, they would be seen by all to be in extreme error. Their error could be identified as easily as was the error of this heathen cult, so they would clearly not be worthy of fellowship with any Christian. Paul was not hoping for something vindictive so much as he was hoping that their error would become obvious so that no Christian would be misled by it. By cutting off their physical organ, they would cut themselves off from the other Christians.

So Paul's reference to cutting themselves off might have a double meaning. If they believed so much in circumcision, he wished that they would cut themselves off in the sense of isolating themselves from the body of members. This would make their error obvious and prevent their influence on faithful brethren.

5:13-15 *–You, brethren, were called for freedom, but do not use freedom as an occasion to the flesh; instead serve one another through love. For the whole law is fulfilled in the statement, "You shall love your neighbor as yourself." If you bite and devour one another, take care lest you consume one another.*

Liberty is not license to serve the flesh but should lead us to serve one another through love.

Having dealt very forcefully with the Judaizers who were influencing the Galatians, Paul then turned to deal with other related dangers. While they were not subject to the Old Testament law, neither should they conclude that freedom was license.

This may have been a concern for two reasons. Some may conclude that, if we are not subject to the law, then we do not need to obey divine commands at all. This concern is often raised today when we teach people that we are not subject to the Old Testament law. They ask if that means we are free to commit adultery, murder, stealing, etc.

The same concern was raised in Acts 15 after the apostles and elders concluded by the guidance of the Holy Spirit that circumcision and the Old Testament law was not necessary to salvation. Nevertheless, they were careful to remind Gentiles that there were things that were forbidden by the law which are still forbidden today. This may be Paul's point here as well.

A second reason for the need to warn the Gentile converts about the danger of living to the flesh would be the heathen influences among them. See 1 Peter 2:15,16. Like the Corinthians, the Galatians had come from a background of heathen idol worship (see 4:8). This idolatry involved indulging every form of evil and immorality, including drunken orgies, sexual immorality of all kinds, etc.

So, having warned the Galatians not to follow the Old Testament law, Paul immediately warns them this freedom did not mean they were free to live however they pleased. They were not to live in the lusts of the flesh (see verses 16-21 below), but they should serve one another according to God's will.

They had been called (verse 8) to liberty (see 5:1). This was freedom from the law and from the guilt and consequences of sin. But it was not license to live in sin (compare Romans 6). We still have responsibilities to God we must serve in order to be saved, and we have obligations to one another.

Many people, even in the church, have a misconception of the concept of liberty. Because the gospel emphasizes the freedom we have in Christ, people often think this means they are free to do as they please and can be saved eternally despite obvious disobedience to God. This is not the proper view of gospel liberty. Christ made us free from the law and from the guilt of sin, but no one is completely free. All of us are servants to someone. We must make sure that our service leads us to obey God in love.

Jesus himself set the example of serving because of love. Throughout His life He served the Father (John 14:31; Philippians 2:8). He also served His disciples (John 13:1). He loved us all to the point that He gave His life for our salvation (Matthew 20:28; Ephesians 5:25).

See 1 Peter 2:16; 2 Peter 2:19; Jude 4; Romans 6; 1 Corinthians 8:9.

Love is the fulfillment of the law.

Why would Paul argue at such length that the law was removed and they should not keep it, then immediately say they would fulfill the law if they had love? Jesus had similarly said that the whole law hung on the *two* greatest commands: loving God and loving one's neighbor. Yet surely Paul is not saying they must now keep circumcision and animal sacrifices and all these rules from which he has just shown they had been set free.

The conclusion is that the command to love is yet in effect today because it is part of the New Testament. Therefore, if one will keep it, he will keep all of God's law which has been revealed for us today. This includes parts of the Old Testament law that have been renewed as part of the New Testament as well as other instructions in the new that were not a part of the old. Love is the focus of the commands God has given. Specifically it will motivate us and guide us to treat our brothers right, which is the point Paul is making in context.

See Matthew 22:36-40; Romans 13:8-10; James 2:8ff; Leviticus 19:18; Luke 10:25ff; James 3:13-18; 1 Timothy 6:3-5.

The danger of biting and devouring one another.

Paul introduces the discussion of proper love vs. license by considering our obligations to one another, showing that the Gentile converts must not allow their conflicts to lead them to become divided, fighting and spiritually devouring one another. Rather they were to continue to serve one another and love their neighbor as themselves.

Paul specifically warns these Galatian brethren not to bite and devour one another lest they consume one another. It is not clear to me what was the cause of their conflicts unless it be the issue about whether or not to keep the Old Testament law. But evidently there was strife and conflict among the brethren. This is a common problem even today among those who profess to be disciples of Jesus, and we must be warned to stand on guard even as Paul warned the Galatians.

It is true that other passages instruct us to contend for the true faith and to strive against error, even as Paul was here contending and striving against those who sought to require obedience to the Old Testament law (see Jude 3). However, conflict between brethren is often the result, not of standing for the truth of God's word, but of demanding our own way. And even when standing for the truth, we must take care lest we show ungodly attitudes.

We must always remember that the purpose of contending must be so that we and all around us are encouraged to stand for the truth and to serve God faithfully, not simply so we can win an argument, achieve our own personal agenda, or exalt ourselves at the expense of others.

It follows that the solution to ungodly quarreling, uncontrolled anger, vicious insults, and vengeful speech is love. Love is what motivates us to speak for the good of others, not for their harm nor simply to exalt ourselves. As admonished here, we must remember that biting and devouring one another may lead us all to be consumed.

See Proverbs 6:16-19; 3:30; 17:1; 17:14; 18:19; 19:13; 20:3; 26:21; 1:29,32; 13:13; 1 Corinthians 3:3,4; Galatians 5:15,20,21; 1 Timothy 1:4; James 3:16-18; 4:1,2; 3 John 9,10; Ephesians 4:29; 1 Corinthians 13:5; 1 Timothy 6:3-5; 2 Timothy 2:14; 2 Timothy 2:23-25; Titus 3:9; 2 Corinthians 12:20.

Commentary on Galatians

5:16-26 - Works of the Flesh vs. Fruits of the Spirit

5:16-18 – Walk by the Spirit and you will not fulfill the lust of the flesh. The desires of the flesh are against the Spirit, and the desires of the Spirit are against the flesh. These oppose one another so you may not do the things that you please. But if you are led by the Spirit, you are not under the Law.

Paul here begins an extended comparison between flesh and Spirit.

He states basic principles of walking in the Spirit as compared to fulfilling the lust of the flesh, then he describes specific works that the flesh leads people to do and then other qualities that the Spirit leads people to develop.

Paul must be discussing these ideas because he is convinced the Galatians needed them. Willis suggests that some Judaizers were saying that the law was needed in order to keep people from practicing immorality, and Paul is answering that charge. As we have seen, there are those today who claim that, if the law has been done away, then people can murder, steal, commit adultery, etc. Paul's answer here is the answer to their view.

However, it may also be that Paul wants to make sure the Galatians understand that, simply because they are free from the law, that does not give them liberty to return to their old heathen immorality. Liberty in Christ is not license to sin (see verse 13 above). The Corinthians had serious problems with immorality of all kinds because of their heathen backgrounds (see 1 Corinthians 5,6,10, etc.). Perhaps the Galatians did also, or at least Paul wanted to make sure they realized that nothing he was saying would justify them in so returning.

Walking in the Spirit

The Spirit here must refer to the Holy Spirit, and walking in the Spirit refers to abiding by or following the teachings the Holy Spirit has revealed. See Romans 8. It is the same as being led by the Spirit – note verses 18,25. The term "walking" is often used in the New Testament to refer to our manner of conduct.

The Holy Spirit revealed the message of the gospel through inspired men. See 1 Corinthians 14:37; 2:10-13; Ephesians 3:3-5; John 14:26; 16:13; Matthew 10:19,20; Galatians 1:8-12; 2 Peter 1:20,21; 1 Thessalonians 2:13; 2 Timothy 3:16,17; Luke 10:16. So, the word is the sword of the Spirit – Ephesians 6:17. It is the means the Spirit uses to instruct and motivate people to obedience.

Nothing Paul says here refers to any direct guidance of the Spirit apart from the word in the life of Christians today, as some claim. Men in the first century did have the direct guidance of the Holy Spirit that enabled them to infallibly speak God's direct message. No one today has that power because spiritual gifts have ceased (see 1 Corinthians 13). We need no such guidance because we now have the written word to supply us to all good works (2 Timothy 3:16,17).

The Scriptures know nothing of the modern idea of a vague "leading of the Spirit" which causes people to think God wants them to do something or leads them to try to interpret signs in the events surrounding them to determine the Spirit's leading. See also Romans 8:5-16; 6:12; 13:14.

Even less does walking in the Spirit refer to some mysterious inward power given Christians by the Holy Spirit to enable – and in some people's view even to compel – us to live a life pleasing to God. The power that God gives us is given through the Scriptures and through the various blessings that are provided through the Scriptures (Romans 1:16; Ephesians 6:17). But this power never in any way violates the free will power of each individual to choose whether or not he will serve God.

Those who are led by the Spirit will not fulfill the lusts of the flesh.

"Flesh" is used here as in verse 13 above. It refers to the natural desires of the body which influence men to sin. These desires are not inherently evil, but neither are they inherently good. The problem is that, since the desires of the flesh do not know the difference between right and wrong, if they are left unrestrained by the gospel, they will eventually and inevitably lead people to do what is sinful.

See Titus 3:3; Mark 14:38; Romans 6:13; 8:1ff; John 6:63.

For example, consider the sexual desire. This is clearly a basic desire of the body. It is not inherently evil but was created by God. It has a proper fulfillment in marriage (Hebrews 13:4; 1 Corinthians 7:2-5). But these natural desires, of themselves, will make no distinction between the woman to which one is married as distinguished from any other woman. The body reacts naturally to whatever stimulation it receives, without recognizing the boundary of marriage.

If the body is not controlled by a mind led by the teachings of Gods' word, these natural desires will inevitably lead to fornication, adultery, etc., even as occurred among the Gentiles. See verses 19-21 for other examples of sins to which the flesh leads. See also 1 John 2:15-17; Ephesians 2:3; Romans 13:14.

So in that sense, the flesh and the Spirit are opposed to one another. The flesh, if unrestrained, will surely lead one to sin. The Spirit teaches the restraints we must place on our natural desires, so the Spirit and flesh conflict. Frequently we experience natural desires which would, if we let them, lead us to disobey the Spirit's teachings.

The conclusion is that, because of the Spirit, we learn not to do the things we would naturally desire to do.

Another aspect of the flesh which relates to the context is that the Judaizers, by emphasizing circumcision, were emphasizing a physical, outward relationship as necessary to salvation. Circumcision was not only an outward physical act, but it was the symbol of being a descendant of Abraham. To insist that one be circumcised to be saved is to require acceptance of a fleshly relationship as symbolized by a fleshly ritual (see 3:1-5).

The effect of this physical or fleshly emphasis was to deemphasize our spiritual relationship to God as taught under the gospel. The New Testament requires no particular nationality or birth. It requires simply a spiritual new birth, as discussed in 3:26-28. Obedience to the gospel by faith makes us spiritual children of Abraham, not fleshly children. By emphasizing circumcision and the Old Law, the Judaizers were removing the gospel emphasis on spiritual things and emphasizing instead fleshly things. Perhaps Paul's reference to the flesh shows that, rather than discouraging immoral conduct by emphasizing the law, the Judaizers were unintentionally encouraging it.

If we are led by the Spirit, we are not under the law.

Despite the teachings of the Judaizers, those who are led by the Spirit will also understand that we are not subject to the Old Testament law. Compare 3:1-5,24,25; Romans 8:3-16. The Spirit does not allow us to walk in fleshly lusts, but neither does He teach us to follow the Old Law. On the contrary, He teaches us, as Paul has taught at length, that we are no longer subject to the Old Law. The Judaizers were not right in binding the Old Testament, but neither would it be right to conclude we can live as we please. Both views are contrary to the Spirit.

Context requires us to recognize that "law" in this verse refers to the Old Testament law. It does not mean we are free from all law, as some would falsely teach. Paul has already shown that our faith must "work" in order to avail in Christ (5:6), and in particular we must be baptized to come into Christ (3:27). He is about to list a whole group of commands which, if we disobey, we cannot inherit the kingdom of God (5:19-21). To say we are under no law at all is nonsense and contradicts whole hosts of Scriptures. We are subject to God's new system, which includes many commands to be obeyed. The law to which we are not subject, according to the teaching of the Holy Spirit, is the Old Testament law.

> "Flesh" (σαρξ) – 1 the material that covers the bones of a human or animal body, *flesh* ... 2 the physical body as functioning entity, *body, physical body* ... In Paul's thought esp., all parts of the body constitute a totality known as σ. or *flesh*, which is dominated by sin to such a degree that wherever flesh is, all forms of sin are likew. present, and no good thing can live in

the σάρξ ... 3 one who is or becomes a physical being, *living being with flesh* ... 4 human/ancestral connection, *human/mortal nature, earthly descent* ... 5 the outward side of life as determined by normal perspectives or standards..." – Bauer-Danker-Arndt-Gingrich.

"...4. σαρξ, when either expressly or tacitly opposed to [the Spirit (of God)], has an ethical sense and denotes mere human nature, the earthly nature of man apart from divine influence, and therefore prone to sin and opposed to God; accordingly it includes whatever in the soul is weak, low, debased, tending to ungodliness and vice..." – Grimm-Wilke-Thayer.

5:19-21 – The works of the flesh

The works of the flesh are: fornication, uncleanness, lasciviousness, idolatry, sorcery, enmities, strife, jealousies, wraths, factions, divisions, parties, envyings, drunkenness, revellings, and such like. Paul warned them, as he had warned them before, that those who practice such things will not inherit the kingdom of God.

Having warned about the dangers of the flesh, and how its desires must be controlled by the leading of the Spirit (verses 16-18), Paul proceeds to list a number of specific works which the flesh leads many people to commit. These are "evident" perhaps in the sense that we see them everywhere around us. They are clearly desires of the flesh. All of them were common in the lives of idol worshipers, and therefore the Galatians lived in an environment characterized by these works of the flesh, and they themselves had come from such a background. Yet the Spirit teaches us we must avoid them because, if we practice them, we cannot inherit God's kingdom.

Consider them individually and their application.

Adultery (found in KJV and NKJV but not the ASV, etc.)

"Adultery" is sexual intercourse involving people at least one of whom is married to someone else (Hebrews 13:4). It is based on selfishness and harms everyone involved including both those who commit the act themselves and their spouses. It is unfaithfulness to one's marriage companion, it damages the marriage relationship, and it is a sin against God.

It is of such a nature that it gives the companion the only Scriptural grounds for divorce (Matthew 19:9). However, when one divorces for other causes and then remarries, he is guilty of adultery in his remarriage (Matthew 19:9; Romans 7:2,3). Therefore adultery is a very unloving thing to do. One who loves his neighbor will avoid it at all costs (Romans 13:8-10).

For passages on adultery and fornication see 1 Corinthians 6:9-11,18-20; 7:2-4,9; Romans 7:2,3; Revelation 21:8; 22:14,15; Exodus

Commentary on Galatians

20:14; Hebrews 13:4; Ephesians 5:1-11; Colossians 3:5-7; 1 Thessalonians 4:3-8; Proverbs 2:16-18; 5:1-23; 6:23-7:27; 9:13-16; Mark 7:20-23; Matthew 5:28; 19:9; 2 Samuel 11&12.

"Adultery" (μοιχεια) – "adultery" – Grimm-Wilke-Thayer

The related verb μοιχαω is defined: "to have unlawful intercourse with another's wife, to commit adultery with... Matthew 19:9..." – Grimm-Wilke-Thayer.

Fornication

Fornication is a general term for sexual relations outside of scriptural marriage. It includes all kinds of illicit sexual relations, including adultery. But when distinguished from adultery, it includes other forms of illicit sexual intercourse, such as premarital sex, homosexuality, etc.

Our society has become so corrupt that most people think little or nothing about premarital sexual relationships or living together without marriage, and few people seem to object even to homosexual relationships. Nevertheless, all are forbidden in Scripture, and all are forbidden for the same basic reason: they are violations of God's marriage law.

From the beginning, when God created man and woman, He instituted marriage to be a lifetime commitment between one man and one woman – Genesis 2:18-24; Romans 7:2-5. Jesus Himself reaffirmed this in His discussion about divorce in Matthew 19:3-9. The apostle Paul again reaffirmed it in his instructions about the relationship between a man and his wife – Ephesians 5:22-31.

The sexual union is a beautiful expression of marital affection and devotion when it is restricted to one's Scriptural spouse. When practiced within marriage as God intended, it also assures that any child who is conceived from the sexual relationship will have a family with a mother and father to love and care for him or her.

However, when practiced outside of a Scriptural marriage, the sexual union leads to Divine judgment – 1 Corinthians 7:2-5; Hebrews 13:4. This includes any form of sexual union outside marriage, including homosexuality (Jude 7).

Civil law may attempt to define relations outside of marriage as acceptable, society may justify and defend it, and people may practice it without remorse, yet in the end the will of God will prevail. The passage says those who practice such will not inherit the kingdom of God.

The word is here translated "fornication" (KJV, NKJV, ASV, RSV) or immorality (NASB).

See "adultery" above for other passages.

"Fornication" (πορνεια) – "...1 unlawful sexual intercourse, *prostitution, unchastity, fornication* 2 participation in prohibited degrees of marriage, *fornication* ..." – Bauer-Danker-Arndt-Gingrich.

Uncleanness

This is translated "uncleanness" (NKJV, ASV, KJV) or "impurity" (NASB, RSV).

It is a general word for that which is unclean, here clearly in a moral sense. The sexual significance of all the words around it implies that it here has the sense of sexual impurity in general. It would apparently cover any kind of sexual immorality.

This would surely include the fornication and adultery that have already been mentioned in the list. In Romans 1:24 it especially refers to homosexuality. It would include, not just homosexuality, but also other forms of sexual perversion. Modern pornography includes incredible forms of sexual abuse, filth, and obscenity. The modern entertainment industry in general, especially movies and television, appear to delight in finding every possible way they can to promote sexual immorality. All such would be included in this term.

Once again our society may wink at such sins, and many people become filthy rich by trafficking in such uncleanness. Yet the passage clearly shows that those who practice it – whether those who sell it or those who participate in it – will not inherit the kingdom of God.

"Uncleanness" (ακαθαρσια) – "1 lit. any substance that is filthy or dirty, *refuse* ... 2 fig. a state of moral corruption ... *immorality, vileness* esp. of sexual sins ... Of unnatural vices: ... *give over to vileness* Romans 1:24..." – Bauer-Danker-Arndt-Gingrich.

Lewdness

This word is translated "lewdness" (NKJV), "lasciviousness" (ASV), KJV), "sensuality" (NASB), "licentiousness" (RSV).

These English words are in turn defined as follows (from www.collinsdictionary.com)

"Lewd – characterized by or intended to excite crude sexual desire; obscene"

"Lascivious – lustful; lecherous; exciting sexual desire"

"Licentious – sexually unrestrained or promiscuous"

This word refers to anything that causes or tends to arouse sexual excitement, desire, or lust between people not married to one another. The previous word in this list forbids unlawful sexual intercourse, but this word goes further and forbids enjoying thinking about or suggestively talking about or doing things that would encourage sexual immorality.

This would include indecent clothing, modern mixed dancing of people not married to one another, mixed swimming in modern swimwear, suggestive jokes and speech, petting, and other forms of sexual suggestiveness. Even if no actual sexual intercourse occurs, it is still sinful to enjoy thinking about doing it with someone not your lawful spouse, or to want to see or touch that which is intimate or private. Anything that encourages the desire to do these is forbidden by this term.

See also Matthew 5:27,28; Proverbs 6:25; Philippians 4:8; Mark 7:20-23; Romans 13:13,14; 1 Peter 4:1-4

"Lasciviousness" (ασελγεια) – "...unbridled lust, excess, licentiousness, lasciviousness, wantonness, outrageousness, shamelessness, insolence ... 'wanton (acts or) manners, as filthy words, indecent bodily movements, unchaste handling of males and females, etc.' (Fritzsche) ..." – Grimm-Wilke-Thayer.

"...denotes 'excess, licentiousness, absence of restraint, indecency, wantonness;' 'lasciviousness' ... in 2 Peter 2:7, RV, 'lascivious (life),' AV 'filthy (conversation),' of the people of Sodom and Gomorrah ... The prominent idea is shameless conduct. ..." – Vine.

Idolatry

All translations here translate it as "idolatry."

Idolatry is worship of false gods. This is what the Galatians had been guilty of before conversion (4:8). It was the besetting sin of Israel in the Old Testament, for which God frequently rebuked them. The prophets repeatedly warned Israel of the sin of idolatry, yet their continued practice of it led God to eventually send them into captivity.

This same practice is still common in such religions as Hinduism and Buddhism. Some would tell us that we should accept those who participate in such idolatry as being pleasing to God. Yet the Scriptures say those who do so will not inherit the kingdom of heaven. But even those who claim to be Christian often use images in their worship before which they bow and offer prayer and worship. In addition, many bow and offer forms of obeisance to their religious leaders. They may deny that it is idolatry, yet it is expressly forbidden in Scripture.

In Acts 10:25,26, when Cornelius bowed before him to give him honor as a religious leader, Peter raised Cornelius up saying, "Stand up; I myself am also a man." The fact one is a man is, of itself, reason enough to conclude that men have no right to bow in religious reverence or as a form of religious respect. The same is true when done toward angels or any created thing (Revelation 22:8,9; Romans 1:25). Only God the Creator can rightly be worshiped (Matthew 4:10).

See also Deuteronomy 4:19; 5:7-9; 17:2-5; 2 Kings 21:1-6; 23:4,5; 1 Corinthians 6:9-11; 10:7,14; 2 Corinthians 6:16-18; Galatians 5:19-21; 1 John 5:21.

"Idolatry" (ειδωλατρια) – "...*image-worship, idolatry...*" – Bauer-Danker-Arndt-Gingrich.

"Idol" (ειδωλον) – "...an image, likeness, i.e. whatever represents the form of an object, either real or imaginary ... 1. the image of a heathen god ... 2. a false god ..." – Grimm-Wilke-Thayer.

Sorcery

This is translated "sorcery" (NKJV, ASV, NASB, RSV), "witchcraft" (KJV). The term refers to the practice of the occult, sorcery, witchcraft, etc.

At least two sorcerers played significant roles in the book of Acts: Simon in Acts 8:9-13 and Elymas in 13:4-12. Both cases show that sorcery is contrary to God's will and that it does not have the power that the Spirit gave to those who did true miracles from God. Likewise the Old Testament contains numerous examples of those who practiced witchcraft contrary to God's will.

Sorcery is wrong essentially because it is a form of idolatry. Note that it here follows idolatry. It is an attempt to obtain supernatural power or supernatural knowledge from spirit beings or sources other than God. These may be demons, dead people, or unknown sources, but they are not from God, therefore they are forbidden.

The occult has always been forbidden by God in all its aspects. As with God's people in the Old Testament, so in the New Testament we are commanded not to consult, believe in, or in any way have fellowship in any aspect of the occult. See especially Deuteronomy 18:9-14 which lists all aspects of the occult and forbids them all. See also Leviticus 19:31: 20:6,27; Exodus 7:11,22; 8:7,18,19; Isaiah 8:19,20; Daniel 1:20; 2:1-13,27,28; Galatians 5:19-21; Revelation 21:8; 22:15; Acts 8:9-13; 19:18-20; 13:4-12.

> "Sorcery" (φαρμακια) – "...primarily signified 'the use of medicine, drugs, spells;' then, 'poisoning;' then, 'sorcery,' ... In 'sorcery,' the use of drugs, whether simple or potent, was generally accompanied by incantations and appeals to occult powers, with the provision of various charms, amulets, etc., professedly designed to keep the applicant or patient from the attention and power of demons, but actually to impress the applicant with the mysterious resources and powers of the sorcerer" – Vine.

Hatred

This is translated "hatred" (NKJV, KJV) or "enmities" or "enmity" (ASV, NASB, RSV).

The word involves hostile feelings and actions so that one acts like an enemy toward someone else. In that sense hatred or enmity is the opposite of love. Love involves good will which leads us to do what is best for others. Hatred instead involves ill will which leads us to seek harm to someone else.

Every passage in the Scriptures that discusses the importance of love would serve as the antidote to enmity.

"Hatred" or "enmity" (εχθρα) "...is rendered 'enmity' in Luke 23:12; Romans 8:7; Ephesians 2:15,16; James 4:4; 'enmities,' Galatians 5:20, RV, for AV, 'hatred.' It is the opposite of agape, 'love.'" – Vine.

Contentions

This is translated "contentions" (NKJV), "variance" (KJV), "strife" (ASV, NASB, RSV).

Note the connection here to "enmity" or hatred and to jealousy, wrath, selfish ambition, etc.

Christians should seek to live peaceably whenever possible (Romans 12:18). We should never compromise truth to have peace, but neither should we cause strife and quarreling because of our own selfish desires or uncontrolled tempers.

Our English words for contending or striving can properly be used to refer to contending or striving for the truth of God's word against error – Jude 3. In that sense, Jesus and His apostles and faithful servants of God in all ages have been known to contend or strive. But that is not the significance of the word is used here.

Some folks, even in the church, are obnoxious and contentious. They frequently quarrel with others or stir up conflict. Some folks press their opinions instead of being peaceable in matters of personal conscience (Romans 14). They bind their personal views, even when they cannot really prove their position by Scriptures. Others attempt to get their own way regardless of the impact on others. They cannot get along with their family, their co-workers, their neighbors, or other followers of Christ.

See also Romans 1:29; 13:13; 1 Corinthians 1:11; 3:3; 2 Corinthians 12:20; Galatians 5:20; Philippians 1:15; 1 Timothy 6:4; Titus 3:9.

"Contention" (ερις) – "...Engagement in rivalry, esp. w. ref. to positions taken in a matter, *strife, discord, contention...*" – Bauer-Danker-Arndt-Gingrich.

Jealousies

This is translated "jealousy" (NKJV, ASV, NASB, RSV – some have it plural), "emulations" (KJV).

This word can be used in the good sense of zeal for God and His will. Obviously the word is used here in the bad sense of jealousy. It is good to be burning with fervor over God's will. But it is wrong to burn with fervor for our own will and personal desires even to the point of harming others or resenting good that comes to them.

This forbids that feeling of displeasure that resents when good things happen to others, thinking instead that we ought to receive the good. This is also a violation of love and shows a selfish spirit.

Jealousy can occur over any advantage that we perceive someone else has but we resent the fact they have it to a greater extent than we wish they had. This may include resentment over wealth and possessions, position and power, physical beauty, athletic ability, popularity and fame, success and achievements, business or job promotions, favorable family relationships, etc. even those who profess to be disciples of Jesus can develop an attitude of rivalry and resentment at the success of other people in service to God, including preachers, elders, teachers, song leaders, etc.

Other similar passages include: 1 Peter 2:1; Romans 1:29,32; Matthew 27:18; Titus 3:3; James 3:14-17; 1 Timothy 6:4; 1 Corinthians 13:4; 3:3; Galatians 5:19-26; Romans 13:13; 2 Corinthians 12:20.

"Jealousy" (ζηλος) – "...excitement of mind, ardor, fervor of spirit; 1. zeal, ardor in embracing, pursuing, defending anything ... 2. an envious and contentious rivalry, jealousy..." – Thayer.

"...1 intense positive interest in someth., *zeal, ardor,* marked by a sense of dedication ... 2 intense negative feelings over another's achievements or success, *jealousy, envy...*" – Bauer-Danker-Arndt-Gingrich.

Outbursts of wrath

This is translated: "outbursts of wrath" (NKJV), "wraths" (ASV), "outbursts of anger" (NASB), "anger" (RSV), "wrath" (KJV).

Often associated with hatred, jealousy, and contention is uncontrolled anger in various forms. Anger is not inherently sinful (Ephesians 4:26), but often leads to sin (James 1:19,20).

This word seems to emphasize the anger that flares up, leads to improper words or deeds, then calms down again, in contrast to the settled anger that plots vengeance. Either kind of anger can lead to sin, and is often associated with the other works of the flesh listed here, so we must guard against it.

The Christian must learn, as with all emotions, that he must control his anger or temper. It is good and proper to be angry against sin. The Bible frequently speaks about the wrath of God against the evils of men. But far too often our anger flares simply because other people do not do what we wish they would do or they somehow irritate us or cause us personal inconvenience. This is a selfish anger. All of us have feelings of anger but must learn to control them.

Many passages warn about the dangers of anger. See Ephesians 4:26,31; James 1:19,20; Psalm 7:11; Proverbs 14:17,29; 29:11,22; 16:32; 22:24,25; 15:1,18; 19:11,19; 25:28; Mark 3:5; Genesis 4:5-7; Leviticus 19:17,18.

"Wrath" (θυμος) – "1 intense expression of the inner self, freq. expressed as strong desire, *passion, passionate longing* ... 2 a state of intense displeasure, *anger, wrath, rage, indignation...*" – Bauer-Danker-Arndt-Gingrich.

"(1) Thumos, "wrath" (not translated "anger"), is to be distinguished from orge, in this respect, that thumos indicates a

Commentary on Galatians

more agitated condition of the feelings, an outburst of wrath from inward indignation, while orge suggests a more settled or abiding condition of mind, frequently with a view to taking revenge. Orge is less sudden in its rise than thumos, but more lasting in its nature. Thumos expresses more the inward feeling, orge the more active emotion. Thumos may issue in revenge, though it does not necessarily include it. It is characteristic that it quickly blazes up and quickly subsides, though that is not necessarily implied in each case." – Vine on "anger"

Selfish ambitions

Translated "selfish ambitions" (NKJV), "factions" (ASV), "disputes" (NASB), "strife" (KJV), "rivalries" (ESV).

This word also relates to strife and division (see "contention" and other words in the list). But the emphasis here is on the motive of personal gain, usually the idea of getting one's own way or gaining power and a following.

Some people just are determined to have their way. They want notoriety, attention, a following. Children who want attention will sometimes misbehave to obtain it. They would rather have attention for bad behavior than to have no attention at all. Of course, this often leads to denial, even to oneself, that the conduct was really wrong. Similar things happen to adults. They must have a following, must be the focus of attention, must have their own way, even if they must cause strife and division to get it.

Other people simply have never learned to give in for the good of the group. They want their way and will do whatever it takes to get it. They cannot admit they are wrong or that other views are as good as their own. They love preeminence or the praises of men more than truth.

> "Strife" or "Self-seeking" (ερɩθεɩα) – "...in the N.T. a courting distinction, a desire to put one's self forward, a partisan and factions spirit which does not disdain low arts; partisanship, factiousness..." – Grimm-Wilke-Thayer.

> "denotes 'ambition, self-seeking, rivalry,' self-will being an underlying idea in the word; hence it denotes 'party-making.' ... hence the meaning of 'seeking to win followers,' 'factions,' ... rivalries, or base ambitions..." – Vine.

Dissensions

Translated "dissensions" (NKJV, NASB, ESV), "divisions" (ASV), "seditions" (KJV). This word is also associated with "contention," "jealousy," "selfish ambitions," etc. It seems to emphasize the separation or parting of the ways that comes from strife and contention.

God wants His people to be united on the truth of His word. Yet error often leads to separation among God's people; and just as commonly, if not more commonly, people are separated because of the personal ambitions, jealousies, and self-will of those who will not, for the good of the group, give up their pet projects and ideas.

"Dissension" (Gk. διχοστασια) – "...dissension, division ... Romans 16:17; I Corinthians 3:3; Galatians 5:20...*" – Grimm-Wilke-Thayer.

"...the state of being in factious opposition, *dissension..." – Bauer-Danker-Arndt-Gingrich.*

Heresies

Translated "heresies" (NKJV, KJV), "parties" (ASV), "factions" (NASB), "divisions" (ESV), "party spirit" (RSV).

This word also is associated with the contentions, jealousy, selfish ambitions, and dissensions of the context. The emphasis here again is on the faction or division that results, but also on cases in which the alienation is the result of false teaching or personal opinions that differ from God's word yet are bound to the point of division. In other words, this is not just self-will or personal ambition that leads to division, but false ideas that are held as truth and pressed to the point of division. (This may not always be the emphasis of the word, but this seems to me to be what distinguishes it from other words listed here.)

(Willis says the distinction is more that the prior words referred to divisions in the process of occurring, while this one emphasizes the complete or final result of division.)

Note Titus 3:10,11; 1 Corinthians 11:19.

"Heresy" (Gk. αιρεσις) – "1. ... act of taking, capture ... 2. ... choosing, choice ... 3. that which is chosen, a chosen course of thought and action; hence one's chosen opinion, tenet; acc. to the context, an opinion varying from the true exposition of the Christian faith (heresy) ... 4. a body of men separating themselves from others and following their own tenets [a sect or party] ... 5. dissensions arising from diversity of opinions and aims ... " – Grimm-Wilke-Thayer.

"...denotes (a) 'a choosing, choice' ...; then, 'that which is chosen,' and hence, 'an opinion,' especially a self-willed opinion, which is substituted for submission to the power of truth, and leads to division and the formation of sects, Galatians 5:20 (marg., "parties"); such erroneous opinions are frequently the outcome of personal preference or the prospect of advantage; ..." – Vine.

"...1 a group that holds tenets distinctive to it, *sect, party, school, faction* ... c w. negative connotation, *dissension, a faction*

... 2 that which distinguishes a group's thinking, *opinion, dogma...*" – *Bauer-Danker-Arndt-Gingrich.*

Envy

This is translated "envy" (or some form of that word) in all the standard translations.

"Jealousy" is already in the list. What is the difference? As quoted below, Vine says, "The distinction lies in this, that 'envy' desires to deprive another of what he has, 'jealousy' desires to have the same or the same sort of thing for itself."

In any case, the terms are closely related. Neither are based on love, but on selfishness. And both lead to strife and bitterness. Neither is characteristic of Christ, and both are works of the flesh.

> "Envy" – (φθονος) "'envy,' is the feeling of displeasure produced by witnessing or hearing of the advantage or prosperity of others; this evil sense always attaches to this word ... Note: Zelos, 'zeal or jealousy,' ... is to be distinguished from phthonos ... The distinction lies in this, that 'envy' desires to deprive another of what he has, 'jealousy' desires to have the same or the same sort of thing for itself." – Vine.

Murders

(Absent from ASV and similar translations in Galatians 5).

This refers to taking the life of another human being. People are in God's image, therefore killing a man (male or female, regardless of age or physical condition) is sinful whereas killing a plant or animal is not (Genesis 9:2-6). This would forbid the modern practice of abortion, since the unborn is considered by God to be a child or baby just the same as those who have been born.

Others have as much right to live as we do. So, killing another is not doing good, but is unloving (Romans 13:8-10). We would not want others to do it to us, so we ought not do it to anyone else. Here is another command that love teaches us to obey.

"Murder" (φονος) – "is used (a) of a special act ... (b) in the plural, of "murders" in general ... (c) in the sense of 'slaughter'..." – Vine.

Drunkenness

The word is so translated in virtually every major translation (NKJV, KJV, ASV, NASB, RSV). The idea is that of intoxication. This sin was widely tolerated among heathen idol worshipers of that day and is likewise widely tolerated by many in our day. Modern advertisements and entertainment present drinking of alcoholic beverages as fundamental to a good time and social relationships. And drunkenness is presented as simply humorous while ignoring the tragic consequences.

Yet God's word, especially in the New Testament, plainly forbids intoxication. And it should be remembered that one is intoxicated, by definition, when he has impaired the ability of his mind to recognize right from wrong and exercise the self-restraint or inhibition to do right instead of wrong. Intoxication does not necessarily require slurred speech, stumbling, or other similar effects that may be obvious to others.

Bible "wines" were not necessarily alcoholic: Isaiah 16:10; 65:8; Jeremiah 48:33; Genesis 40:9-11; Revelation 19:15; 14:10. The Bible term for wine is similar to our word for cider: it may or may not be fermented.

Furthermore, with the typical alcoholic drinks of antiquity, one had to drink far more in order to reach intoxication than is the case with our drinks today for several reasons. Distilled liquors (whiskey) were unknown in Bible times – there were not invented till later. Wines in Bible times were naturally less alcoholic than ours, and even then they were generally diluted with water. Drinking undiluted wines led to intoxication (drunkenness) in the fundamental meaning of that term.

One is intoxicated in the sense of having impaired his sobriety – his ability to distinguish right from wrong – by just one or two of today's typical drinks. One can or bottle of beer contains as much alcohol as a shot of whiskey. So, one need not be obviously drunk or a gutter drunk or alcoholic to be intoxicated or drunk. Typical modern "social drinking" leads to intoxication in the fundamental meaning of that term.

To have a fuller understanding of the Bible teaching about the use of alcoholic beverages, one must consider not only passages about drunkenness or intoxication, but also passages about the danger of drinking in general and the need for sobriety. The Bible not only instructs us to avoid intoxication it also urges us to be sober.

In a society such as ours in which drinking of alcohol is such a serious problem and creates tragic consequences in so many lives, surely every Christian should oppose the practice and set an example of complete abstinence.

Study such passages as the following: Romans 13:12-14; Galatians 5:19-21; 1 Corinthians 6:9-11; 5:11; Proverbs 23:31,32,20; 20:1; 1 Peter 4:3; 5:8; 1:13-17; 1 Thessalonians 4:4-8; 1 Corinthians 9:25-27; Proverbs 4:23. Consider also the importance of good influence.

The Greek word here is μεθη. See related words below.

"Drunk" (μεθυω) – "signifies 'to be drunk with wine' ..." – Vine.

(μεθυσκω) – "signifies 'to make drunk, or to grow drunk' (an inceptive verb, marking the process or the state expressed in No. 1), 'to become intoxicated,' ...– Vine.

(μεθη) – "'strong drink' ... denotes 'drunkenness, habitual intoxication,' ..." – Vine.

Revelries

This word is translated "revelries" (NKJV) "revellings" (ASV, KJV), "carousing" (NASB, RSV).

This is what we would call a "wild party" with drinking (or drugs) and sexual looseness (dancing, immodesty, etc.). It would condemn nearly all modern dancing and drinking parties, which are typically associated with lewdness (lasciviousness), indecent clothing, and drinking.

The drinking here does not necessarily involve apparent or obvious drunkenness (note "*half*-drunk" in Thayer's definition), but just drinking associated with a circumstance encouraging lack of restraint. The world views this as the high point of life, the ideal good time. Some defend it, yet the Bible still condemns it.

Christians should avoid such circumstances because they are sinful of themselves, because of other problems to which they can lead (verse 14), and because of the evil influence and reputation the Christian would have on others if he participated.

> "Revelry" (κωμος) – "a revel, carousel, i.e., in the Grk. writ. prop. a nocturnal and riotous procession of half-drunken and frolicsome fellows who after supper parade through the streets with torches and music in honor of Bacchus or some other deity, and sing and play before the houses of ... friends; hence, used generally of feasts and drinking parties that are protracted till late at night and indulge in revelry ... Romans 13:13; Galatians 5:21; I Peter 4:3...*" – Grimm-Wilke-Thayer.

"...excessive feasting, ... carousing, revelry" – Bauer-Danker-Arndt-Gingrich.

and the like

Various translations express this idea as "the like" or "such like" or "things like these." The point is that Paul has not listed all the works of the flesh, but just enough to give us the idea. There are many other things that are similar in nature to these and that also displease God.

This should lead us to take care that we do not practice even that which is close to the items he has listed. Rather than seeing how close we can get without anyone being able to prove absolutely that we have sinned, we should rather seek to make sure we stay away from such activities and don't get close. Even "such like" will condemn us in God's eyes.

Those who practice such as these, Paul warns, will not inherit the kingdom of God (compare 1 Corinthians 6:9-11). He had warned them of this before, and he warns them again. Clearly they (and we) need repeated warning about such dangers. Again, these practices would have been common in their Gentile background, so that there was special danger to them.

Note that some people today may justify some or all of these activities, but that does not change God's view of them. Those who practice them **will not** inherit the kingdom of God. And since these instructions were plainly addressed to Christians, it follows that we have here further evidence that a child of God can so sin as to be lost.

Note also that teaching the same things repeatedly is not wrong or shameful. On the contrary it is often needed. People who have been told things "in times past" yet need to be reminded. It is important to remember and not drift into evil habits.

5:22,23 – The fruits of the Spirit

The fruit of the Spirit is love, joy, peace, longsuffering, kindness, goodness, faithfulness, meekness, self-control; against such there is no law.

In verses 16-18 Paul had explained that the Spirit was contrary to the flesh in that the flesh tends to lead us into practices that contradict the teaching of the Spirit. To illustrate, he listed several works of the flesh in verses 19-21. Here he begins to list those opposite fruits which come from following the Holy Spirit.

These are all "fruits" of the Spirit in that, if we allow God's word to work in our lives, it will instruct and motivate us to develop these qualities. So, they are "fruits" of the Spirit like fruit produced by a tree (compare John 15:1ff). Nothing here or elsewhere says that the Holy Spirit produces these results in our lives apart from the word or by any direct action based on some personal indwelling of the Holy Spirit. Rather, these fruits are produced when we study and learn the teaching of the Spirit and obey.

All of these are qualities against which there is no law. Obviously this is a way of emphasizing that they are good and should be developed in our lives as Christians.

Love

Translated "love" in all the standard translations.
Love is concern for the wellbeing of others.
1 John 4:8-11 (Ephesians 5:25,28,29) – God demonstrated His love in the sacrifice of Christ. New Testament teaching about love is ultimately based on the example of the sacrifice of Jesus. He loved us so much He gave His life so we could be saved. This teaches us the meaning of the love we should have for others. Love requires us always to do what is best for others. (1 John 3:16; John 13:34; 15:12; Ephesians 5:2; Matthew 5:44,45)
1 Corinthians 13:5 – Love is not selfish.
Romans 13:10 – Love works no harm to its neighbor.
Love is a choice of the will.
Biblical love is not fundamentally a feeling or emotion. It is a choice. Feelings or emotions may follow, but love begins with an act of

the will. Some think love just happens: you "fall in love" or out of love, but this view makes us victims of circumstances, so we are not in control.

Matthew 22:37-39 – Love for God and for others are the greatest commands. Love can be commanded because it is a matter of the **will**. We can choose whether or not to love, just like we choose whether or not to obey any other command.

Romans 5:6-8 – Christ loved us while we were yet sinners, not because we were so lovable that He couldn't help Himself. He **chose** to do what we needed done. Just as Christ initiated love toward us when we were not acting lovingly, so **it is our responsibility to initiate love.**

Luke 6:27,28 – We are commanded to love our enemies. How do you love an enemy? Not by falling uncontrollably into love, but by **choosing** to do what is best for them.

Love must be expressed in words and in deed.

Ephesians 4:15 – We must **speak** the truth in **love**. We must be sure we always speak for the good of all concerned. And we should reassure one another that we really do care about one another. Do not wait for an overwhelming "feeling" to move you. Since love is a choice of the will, we can choose at any time to state that love. And our speech must always be guided by love.

1 John 5:2,3 – Love for others requires us to love God and keep His commands. Keeping God's commands is loving God.

1 John 3:18 – We must love, not just in words, but in deed and in truth. This is a vital principle in every relationship. We ought to say loving things, but that alone is not enough. We must act in love. Whatever we do and say must be directed by God's will, motivated by love.

In particular, love requires obedience. Those who do not obey, have not yet learned to love as they should. It follows, in this context, that the gospel which saves us does require obedience. See John 14:15,21-24,31; Romans 13:8-10; Galatians 5:6; Hebrews 10:24; 1 John 2:3-6,15-17; 5:2,3; 2 John 5,6; Revelation 3:19.

(Luke 10:25-37; 6:27,28; John 14:15,21-24,31; Romans 13:8-10; Galatians 5:6; Hebrews 10:24; 1 John 2:3-6,15-17; 5:2,3; 2 John 5,6; Revelation 3:19)

Love requires giving and self-sacrifice.

Ephesians 5:25 – Jesus loved the church and **gave** Himself for it.

John 3:16 – God so loved the world that He **gave** His only-begotten Son.

1 John 3:14-18 – If you see your brother in need and don't **give** what is needed, you don't have love. Surely this applies in the home or the church. If I see my spouse, child, or brother in need and don't give

what is needed, I do not have love. (Notice that says "need," not "want.")

Romans 12:20 – Even loving your enemy requires **giving** food and drink when needed.

This attitude is what motivates all proper service to God. Without it, we will not likely do what God requires; but even if we did do it, God would be displeased because of our improper motives! Love leads to faithful service. If we are not serving faithfully, we do not truly love. Matthew 22:37-40; Luke 6:27,28,31-33; 10:25-37; 1 Corinthians 13:1-8,13.

"Love" (Gk. αγαπη) – "...In signification it follows the verb αγαπαω, consequently it denotes 1. affection good-will, love, benevolence ... Of the love of men to men; esp. of that love of Christians towards Christians which is enjoined and prompted by their religion ... Of the love of men towards God ... God towards men ... God towards Christ ... Christ towards men..." – Grimm-Wilke-Thayer.

"Love" (αγαπαω) "...Love can be known only from the actions it prompts. God's love is seen in the gift of His Son, 1 John 4:9,10 ... it was not drawn out by any excellency in its objects, Romans 5:8. It was an exercise of the Divine will in deliberate choice, made without assignable cause save that which lies in the nature of God Himself ... Christian love has God for its primary object, and expresses itself first of all in implicit obedience to His commandments ... Christian love ... is not an impulse from the feelings, it does not always run with the natural inclinations, nor does it spend itself only upon those for whom some affinity is discovered. Love seeks the welfare of all ... and works no ill to any ..." – Vine.

Joy

This is translated "joy" in all the standard translations.

The gospel of Christ gives Christians great cause for joy.

Philippians 4:4 – Rejoice in the Lord always. Again I will say, rejoice!

Romans 14:17 – The kingdom of God is not food and drink, but righteousness and peace and joy in the Holy Spirit.

But some people mistakenly think joy means Christians should constantly be on an emotional high. In some "Christian" novels you can supposedly tell just by looking at people that they are "Christians," because they are always so happy. They speak as if Christians should always smile and bubble over with excitement. But notice:

Ecclesiastes 3:4 – There is a time to weep, and a time to laugh.

Romans 12:15 – Rejoice with those who rejoice, and weep with those who weep.

Jesus wept at Lazarus' death (John 11:35).

He underwent great suffering in the Garden (Matthew 26:36ff).

Jesus and His disciples often sorrowed or wept. It is true that Christians should always have the joy of the gospel, but this does not mean we always enjoy an emotional high.

Joy in the gospel is basically an inner attitude of appreciation for God's goodness based on our relationship with Him. It is not determined by outward circumstances. Bible characters had joy in their service to God even while they sorrowed over their difficult circumstances. Consider, for example, Paul in the Roman jail. He wrote an epistle emphasizing joy to the Philippians (see below) despite his hardships.

So, joy is not necessarily a constant emotional high, nor should we seek to artificially drum up such feelings in order to say we have "joy." Nor should we use "joy" as an excuse to avoid unpleasant responsibilities because they will ruin our "joy." Rather, we should remember our spiritual blessings in Christ, despite our hardships and duties. This will give us inner joy, not an artificial appearance of joy. Joy in Christ involves the following"

Forgiveness of sins

Psalms 35:9 — My soul shall be joyful in the Lord; It shall rejoice in His salvation.

Psalm 51:1-3,8-12 — David's guilt over his sin with Bathsheeba destroyed his **joy**. Note that **guilt destroys joy.** David asked for forgiveness that the **joy** may be restored.

Acts 8:39 — The eunuch, after baptism, went on his way rejoicing.

Acts 16:34 — After baptism, the jailer **rejoiced greatly,** having believed in God.

When we are guilty of sin, we may experience emotional highs from other enjoyments in life; but we will not have the real joy described in the Bible. We can have joy, if we are forgiven by Christ according to the gospel.

Faithful service to God

Proverbs 21:15 — It is a joy for the just to do justice. Those who love God will obey Him and will find joy in doing so.

Deuteronomy 10:12,13 — God gives commands for our **good**. One reason we may lack joy in serving God is that we don't see His commands as **good** for us. We think they take the fun out of life. When we trust God, we know that we are better off serving Him. Appreciating this will give joy when we serve.

Daily Bible study

Psalms 19:8 — The statutes of the Lord are right, rejoicing the heart. When people find no joy in Bible study, the problem is that they don't realize that God's word is "**right**." When we appreciate the fact that the Bible is **true** and describes the best way to live, then we find joy in studying so we can have the blessings and avoid the consequences.

Psalm 119:162-165 — When we love God's word, appreciate it, and praise God for the fact it guides us to eternal life, then we find *joy* in studying and knowing it.

Concern for others

True joy comes, not from pleasing self, but from serving others.

Acts 20:35 — The person who seeks to **give** rather than **receive**, this is the one who is truly blessed (joyful).

Luke 15:7,10,22-24 — The lost sheep, coin, and son, all teach the *joy* that comes when a lost soul is saved. What does it mean to you when a soul is converted? Does this give you *joy*?

Appreciation for blessings

Philippians 4:4-8 — Paul said to rejoice (verse 4), then said to not be anxious but to let our needs be known to God "with thanksgiving."

Luke 6:22,23 — When we are persecuted, hated, and mocked we should **rejoice** and **leap for joy**. Christians have joy despite problems, because we have a great **reward in heaven**. What gives real joy is our final destiny, not our circumstances on earth.

Hebrews 12:1-3 — Jesus on the cross is an example of joy; we are told to imitate Him. Did Jesus' joy mean He had no problems? He was in great agony. He **despised** the shame. His **joy** came by looking at what was **set before him**. He kept His eye on the final result. We have joy in the same way.

John 16:22 — If we serve God faithfully, we have joy no man can take away.

Many try to find joy in doing their own thing, serving pleasure, accumulating possessions, etc. These things are temporary, fleeting, and give no lasting joy. You may never obtain what you want; and if you obtain it, you may easily lose it. Then your joy turns to sorrow.

Joy from serving God is the only lasting joy. Joy in Christ is the only kind of joy really worth having. Everyone can have it. And no one else can keep you from having it. Do you have true joy?

See also Matthew 13:44; 25:21,23; Luke 6:23; 10:20; Acts 5:41; 8:39; 13:52; 16:34; Romans 15:13; Philippians 2:17; 3:1; 4:4; Colossians 1:24; 1 Thessalonians 5:16; 1 Peter 1:6,8; 4:13.

"Joy" ($\chi\alpha\rho\alpha$) – "... 1 the experience of gladness ... 2 a pers. or thing that causes joy, *joy*..." – Bauer-Danker-Arndt-Gingrich.

Peace

This is translated "peace" in all the standard translations.

"Peace" refers to a harmonious relationship between persons, freedom from strife or enmity. It also includes the state of calm, safety, or security that results from this harmony.

1 Peter 3:10,11 — One who wants to see good days should seek **peace** and pursue it.

Peace with God

The Bible describes different kinds of peace or peace between different groups of people. But the most basic and important peace of all is peace we need with God.

Isaiah 57:20,21 – God says there is no peace for the wicked. They are like a troubled sea that cannot rest. Guilt alienates men from God, destroys peace of mind, and gives fear of judgment and eternal torment. We are tossed about by torment like a sea in a hurricane. When sin is forgiven, the troubled sea is calmed like Jesus calmed the storm on the Sea of Galilee.

John 14:27; 16:33 – Jesus gives peace, not like the world gives. In the world we have tribulation, but Jesus overcame the world so we could have peace. The result is that our hearts do not need to be troubled or afraid. Note that the world cannot give true peace. No government agency can give it – not the Congress, the President, or the UN – no psychiatrist or self-improvement book, no college course, no friend or family member can give it. It comes only from Jesus.

Romans 5:1 – This peace comes from being justified and can be obtained only through Jesus Christ.

Colossians 1:19-23 – Alienation between us and God comes when we violate God's word – "wicked works." This makes us enemies of God, not because He wants enmity, but because He cannot have fellowship with people in sin. So when we sin, we become alienated as enemies of God. The process of making peace with God is called "reconciliation." When our sins are forgiven, the cause of alienation is removed, so we are presented holy and blameless before God.

Philippians 4:6,7 – When sins are forgiven, we have the privilege of prayer so we need not be anxious but can have the peace the passes understanding. Peace with God gives peace within.

Peace with God is the most important peace, but it can always be achieved. We may not always be able to achieve peace with other people, depending on their attitudes. But peace with God is always achievable, because He is always willing to forgive. It depends entirely on our willingness to repent and meet the terms of forgiveness. We must be willing to turn from sin and dedicate our life to serving God.

Peace between children of God.

Mark 9:50 – Have peace with one another. If I have peace with God and you have peace with God, then we should have peace with one another. The best way to have peace with another person is if we both have peace with God.

Ephesians 4:3-6 – Endeavor to keep the unity of the Spirit in the bond of peace. Peace and unity go together and are based on God's plan for oneness of each item listed. Unfortunately, God's people sometimes have strife because some fail to maintain the truth in one or more of these areas. God gives the platform for peace and unity, but He requires us to work to "endeavor to keep" that unity and peace.

2 Timothy 2:22 – Pursue peace with those who call on the Lord out of a pure heart. Peace does not happen by chance. We must "pursue" it. Diligent effort is required.

Sometimes peace is broken by doctrinal differences. But often it results from a conflict of personalities or personal opinions. One wants things done one way, another wants them done another way. One may have a personality trait that is not really wrong but just rubs another brother the wrong way. God expects those who serve Him to bear with one another and have peace despite such differences. But this takes effort. We must "pursue" that peace.

A true peacemaker must be firmly committed to peace among God's people. If others go into error, he seeks their restoration. He works for peace on the basis of God's word, and never wants his own will or opinions to be the cause of strife.

Peace with all other people.

Hebrews 12:14 – Pursue peace with **all** men, not just with Christians.

Romans 12:18 – As much as depends on you, live peaceably with **all** men. With some people peace may not be possible, but we should always seek peace. And we should not cause alienation by our improper attitudes or motives.

Proverbs 20:3 — It is honorable for a man to stop striving, since any fool can start a quarrel. Anybody can cause trouble All you have to do is to start arguing about something. What takes wisdom and self-control is learning how to **solve** conflicts in harmony with God's word. Jesus' disciples must seek peace and be willing to follow God's word to achieve it with all around us.

Truth and righteousness more important than peace

John 16:33 – Jesus gives peace, but the world gives tribulation. Worldly people may oppose us despite the fact we do right and sometimes **because** we do right. In such cases, we are not responsible for the conflict, and we should not compromise truth just to have peace.

Matthew 10:34-37 – Jesus came to bring strife and conflict instead of peace! He came to set close family members against one another, so one's enemies may be people in his own household. Sometimes our dearest loved ones will oppose our stand for the gospel. When this happens, we must not compromise Jesus' will. Whoever loves father or mother more than Jesus is not worthy of Him.

James 3:16-18 – The wisdom from God leads us to be peaceable and willing to yield. The fruit of righteousness is sown in peace by those who make peace. But we must be first pure, then peaceable. Important as peace is, truth is more important.

Commentary on Galatians

Peace is a major goal. Some seem to think it is the only true goal, and we should compromise anything to achieve it. But we must not sacrifice our stand for God's will in order to have peace. Nevertheless, it must not be our improper conduct or attitudes that cause the problems.

See also Matthew 5:9; Romans 14:19; Genesis 13:8; Proverbs 20:3; Psalm 133:1; 1 Thessalonians 5:13; 2 Corinthians 13:11; Mark 9:50; Hebrews 12:11; 14:19.

> "Peace" (ειρηνη) – "...peace, i.e. 1. a state of national tranquility; exemption from the rage and havoc of war ... 2. peace between individuals, i.e. harmony, concord ... 3. ... security, safety, prosperity, felicity ... 4. spec. the Messiah's peace ... 5. acc. to a conception distinctly peculiar to Christianity, the tranquil state of a soul assured of its salvation through Christ, and so fearing nothing from God and content with its earthly lot, of whatsoever sort that is ... 6. of the blessed state of devout and upright men after death ..." – Grimm-Wilke-Thayer.

Longsuffering

This is translated "longsuffering" (NKJV, ASV, KJV), "patience" (NASB, ESV).

Note that this term refers especially to being "patient in bearing the offenses and injuries of others ... slow to anger, slow to punish...."

We need patience in enduring hardship.

2 Timothy 2:9-12 – Paul suffered hardship: he was in prison and about to die for preaching the gospel. He endured so the elect may obtain salvation in Christ. Suffering tends to cause us to quit. Patience leads us to endure.

Hebrews 10:32-38 – When suffering, we need patience to hold fast our confidence and receive the reward. God is not pleased if we shrink back.

Hebrews 12:1-4 – We should imitate Jesus' example of suffering. He endured (was patient) despite the cross and the sinners who spoke against Him. We must do the same.

1 Peter 2:19-23 – God is pleased if we patiently suffer mistreatment, even though we have done good. We must follow Jesus' example of not retaliating to harm those who harm us.

We need patience in teaching others.

2 Timothy 4:2 – Preach in season and out with longsuffering. Teaching requires longsuffering for many reasons. One reason is that we tend to get discouraged and quit. Preaching "in season and out" requires that we teach whether or not we want to and whether or not other people want us to.

2 Timothy 2:24-26 – Servants of God should not quarrel, but be patient, in meekness correcting those who are in error.

Some people think that patience equals tolerance, so we should never rebuke people for sin. If we do, especially if we do so firmly, they think we have lost patience and are unkind. On the contrary, we must correct those who oppose the truth and try to bring them to know the truth and repent. We seek to snatch them from the power of the devil.

However, we must not argue for the sake of pride or ego, to win an argument, or simply to get our own way. And we must continue acting for the good of others, if they do not accept the truth and even if they become nasty and hateful. If quarreling results and people are losing control of their tempers, we may need to discontinue the discussion. But it does not justify failing to act for the good of all involved.

1 Thessalonians 5:14 – Be longsuffering toward all, including the disorderly, the fainthearted, and the weak. Note again that patience does not mean we neglect to admonish people for sin, but it does affect how we approach them.

When a person is in error, some people will push them to change immediately. They talk for hours to the person, interrupt them, insist on doing all the talking, bring the subject up every time they see him, insist on having the last say, and generally insist that people immediately admit their error. Such pressure fails to give people time to digest the evidence. If people are to reach their own conclusions, not just accept our word for it, they must think things through for themselves.

All of us have been in error at times. And most of us were not convinced we were wrong by just one conversation, and certainly not if people used the methods described above. We need to approach people as we need to be approached, then give them time to study the evidence for themselves.

We need patience in doing good.

Luke 8:15 – In the parable of the sower, the good soil represents those who bear fruit with patience. Fruit represents good works. Some of the other soils began to grow crops, but they quit. The stony soil represents those who fell away in temptation. The thorny soil represents those whose service was choked by cares, riches, and pleasures of this life. The result was they brought no fruit to perfection.

To please God, we must patiently continue resisting temptation. We must not be turned aside by the desires to gather wealth, or to pursue the pleasures of life, or to please self or friends and loved ones.

James 1:12 – Blessed is the man who endures temptation. He receives the crown of life, when he has been proved. Temptation leads us into error. To endure requires patience, especially when we face temptation after temptation.

Ephesians 4:2,3 – Patience is needed to bear with other members of the church. Some people are just hard to get along with. Some must have their own way, even in matters of personal preference. Some cannot work out their differences in love according to God's word. They make false accusations, slander the reputation of others, and revile them.

Patience is required to bear with such people without committing sin. We want to retaliate against those who hurt us. Or we just give up and quit or become members of some false group. Patience is needed to continue to face temptation without giving in. Are you patient in the face of temptation, or have you given in?

See also Hebrews 6:15; James 5:8; Luke 18:7; 2 Corinthians 6:6; Colossians 3:12; 2 Peter 3:15.

"Patience" (Gk. μακροθυμεια) – "...1. patience, endurance, constancy, steadfastness, perseverance; esp. as shown in bearing troubles and ills ... 2. patience, forbearance, long-suffering, slowness in avenging wrongs ..." – Grimm-Wilke-Thayer.

Kindness

This is translated: "kindness" (NKJV, ASV, NASB, ESV), "gentleness" (KJV).

This is a very difficult word to define. It is very close in meaning to the following term "goodness."

Ephesians 4:31,32 uses a related word: Put away bitterness, wrath, anger, clamor, evil speaking, malice, and be kind, tender-hearted and forgiving to one another. Kindness is clearly opposed to malice and is the solution to the malicious conduct described in verse 31.

God is said to be rich in goodness, which was demonstrated in giving the sacrifice of His Son (Romans 2:4; Ephesians 2:7; Titus 3:4).

Perhaps the best definition of "kind" would involve something like "concerned for helping others." It is a form of consideration in which, instead of seeking to hurt others or even to justify self, we seek foremost to be helpful in all aspects of our conduct.

In the home, on the job, in the church, some people criticize others repeatedly with sharp, sarcastic, angry outbursts. If they don't get their way, they nag and gripe. They seem to think if they make life miserable long enough, others will get tired of hearing it and give in. This is unkind and unloving. It destroys the happiness of many homes, congregations, and relationships.

Kind, loving people need to be grateful and express appreciation for good done for them. Paul often expressed appreciation and offered praise to people who had helped Him (Romans 16). Some people expect others to do good deeds for them, but then they say little or nothing to thank them. This is unkind and unloving.

Kindness must be defined in harmony with God's word, not by human opinions. Some people object to church discipline, rebuke of sin, and forceful opposition to error as "unkind." But the Bible often shows we are commanded at times to do all these things. Sincere helpfulness may lead us to confront others for sin, but it will not be done maliciously. It will be done to help them be better people, for their good.

See also 2 Corinthians 6:6; Colossians 3:12.

"Kindness" (χρηστος) is defined: "manageable ... mild, pleasant (opposite to harsh, hard, sharp, bitter)" – GWT.

Goodness

Translated "goodness" in all standard translations.

That which is "good" is that which God's word instructs us to do, for it provides us to "every good work" (2 Timothy 3:17). So, as we study the Spirit's word and obey it, it produces "goodness" in us.

Romans 15:14 – Now I myself am confident concerning you, my brethren, that you also are full of goodness, filled with all knowledge, able also to admonish one another.

In order to admonish others as we should, we need a knowledge of God's word. Otherwise, we may admonish them to do that which is sinful. Also, we need goodness that enables us to set a good example and that leads us to want to give the instruction that is needed.

Christians should seek to be "good" to be like God, because God is good. This is similar in meaning to "righteous." We seek to do good that we might stand right before God. Sin is the opposite of "good." It makes us "evil" and unrighteous.

"Goodness" (αγαθοσυνη) – "...positive moral quality characterized esp. by interest in the welfare of others..." – Bauer-Danker-Arndt-Gingrich.

"Goodness" here is the noun form of the adjective defined as follows:

> "Good" (αγαθος) "describes that which, being 'good' in its character or constitution, is beneficial in its effect; it is used ... (b) in a moral sense, frequently of persons and things. God is essentially, absolutely and consummately 'good'... To certain persons the word is applied ...

> "The neuter of the adjective with the definite article signifies that which is 'good,' lit., 'the good,' as being morally honorable, pleasing to God, and therefore beneficial. Christians are to prove it, ... to cleave to it, ... to do it, ...to work it, ... to follow after it, ... to be zealous of it, ... to imitate it, ... to overcome evil with it ..." – Vine

Faithfulness

This is translated "faithfulness" (NKJV, ASV, NASB, RSV), "faith" (KJV).

This is the normal word for "faith." Faith is trust or belief in God and in His word. This comes by hearing the word of the Spirit (Romans 10:17), so faith is a fruit of the Spirit. As we practice that faith consistently, we become "faithful" or full of faith, which in turn leads us to be trustworthy. This shows in that we live a life such that we can be relied on or trusted to do right.

In 2 Peter 1:5-8 Peter describes faith as the basis on which we build godly character. It is the root and trunk of the tree, from which all the other qualities branch off. People must have faith to become Christians, but that faith must grow by adding virtue, knowledge, patience, etc.

Faith requires us to believe in God (Hebrews 11:6), in Jesus as God's Son (John 8:24; Galatians 2:20; Acts 20:21; 8:37; John 3:16; 20:30,31; 6:28,29), and in the Bible as the word of God (Mark 1:14,15; 16:15,16; Acts 8:12; John 5:46,47; 3:12; 6:45-47,43,44; Romans 10:14-17; 1:16; 2 Thessalonians 2:10-12; 1:10; Luke 6:46; 24:25).

In the Bible, faith refers to different things in different contexts. Faith is clearly essential to salvation, yet there is faith that can save (Hebrews 10:39; 11:1) and faith that cannot (James 2:14-26). Faith involves three elements, all of which a person must possess in order to be saved by faith:

(1) Acceptance of certain facts as true (James 2:19; John 12:42,43; Hebrews 11:3).

(2) Trust or willingness to depend on God and commit one's life into His hands as Lord and Savior (2 Timothy 1:12; Galatians 2:20; Matthew 12:21; 1 Timothy 4:10; 2 Corinthians 1:9).

(3) Obedience, requiring a surrender to submit to His will for our lives (Hebrews 3:18,19; 11:6; examples in chapter 11; Galatians 5:6; James 2:14-26; John 6:28,29).

One who is faithful, when given a responsibility, can be trusted to get the job done. God needs to be able to rely on His people to do as He says.

See verse 6 for definitions.

Gentleness

Translated "gentleness" (NKJV, NASB, ESV), "meekness" (ASV, KJV).

This is a difficult word to translate into English. It is sometimes translated "gentleness," but to many people, the English words "meekness" and "gentleness" imply weakness. But weakness is no part of the significance of this word. A meek person is inherently a strong person.

The best way to know the meaning of a word is to study passages where it is used.

Numbers 12:3 — Moses was very meek, above all men on earth. Was he weak and spineless?

Matthew 11:29,30 — Jesus said, "I am meek and lowly in heart." Was He weak in character? (2 Corinthians 10:1; Matthew 21:5)

Moses and Jesus were both powerful and influential, but they are especially held up as examples meekness. Their character will help us understand what meekness means.

(Galatians 6:1; Ephesians 4:2,3; Colossians 3:12,13; 2 Timothy 2:24-26; Titus 3:2; James 3:13-18; 1:21-25; 1 Peter 3:1-6)

One who is meek will submit to God's commands.

James 1:21-25 — Meekness toward God's word requires putting away filth and wickedness. Be doers of the word, not just hearers.

The selfish person says "I want this, I want that...." The meek person says, "What does **God** want? Is this really **best** according to **God's** way?" God's ways are so much better than ours that the meek person carefully considers **God's will first**, then his own will last.

We tend to want to please ourselves; so we may conclude an act doesn't matter to God, even when it really **does** matter to Him. True meekness will lead us to examine every act, word, and thought to see what effect it will have on our service to God. Then we do only what we are sure pleases Him.

One who is meek will accept difficult circumstances of life without rebelling against God.

As shown in the book of Job, meekness teaches us that God is in charge – He knows what He is doing, even when He chooses to allow us to suffer (Job 1:21).

Numbers 12:1-3 — Moses' meekness was described in context of a complaint against his leadership. People constantly complained against him, even though he was just doing what God said. How many of us would have stood for it? No wonder he was called the meekest man on earth!

Matthew 26:39 — Knowing what was coming, Christ prayed in the garden to avoid the suffering of the cross. Yet He said, "Not as I will, but as You will." That is meekness.

We want to control our own lives. I have had panic attacks facing problems I could not remove. But hardships, that we cannot solve alone, may teach us to be humble and depend on God. Of course, we should try to eliminate our problems. But if He chooses to allow the problem to continue, instead of blaming Him, we should look for the lessons such problems can teach us.

The truly meek person realizes that God can use hardships for our good, so he will submit without rebelling.

One who is meek will urge others to turn from their sins.

Some people think a meek person will not speak out against error. If he does, some people think he is intolerant, egotistical, self-willed, pushy, and motivated by "hate." But this is a misunderstanding.

Exodus 32:19,20,26-28,30 — When Israel made the golden calf, Moses became angry, plainly told them they had sinned, and called for disciplinary action. Yet he was the meekest man on earth!

Matthew 15:3-9,12-14 — When Jesus rebuked the sins of the Pharisees, His disciples told Him He had offended the Pharisees. What did Jesus do: Back off? Apologize? No, he proceeded to call them blind guides and told the disciples not to follow them. But remember, He was "meek and lowly in heart."

Galatians 6:1 — If a man is overtaken in a fault, those who are spiritual should restore him in a spirit of **meekness** ("gentleness" - NKJV). Meekness does not prevent us from showing others they are wrong.

2 Timothy 2:24-26 — In **meekness** ("humility" - NKJV) correct those who oppose themselves so they can recover themselves from the snare of the Devil. Rather than hindering godly people from telling people to turn from sin, meekness **leads** us to do that very thing!

When people are sincere but ignorant, meekness may involve speaking quietly. And surely meekness will teach us to be patient. But when people ought to know better, as in the examples of the golden calf and the Pharisees, meekness may lead to forceful rebukes. And in no case are we doing anyone a favor when we let them stay in sin without warning them!

So we may conclude that meekness is an attitude or quality of heart (1 Peter 3:4) whereby *a person does not act primarily from his own self-interest, but submits his will and sacrifices his desires in order to accomplish what is best for others.*

Meekness is the opposite of self-will, self-interest, and self-assertiveness. A meek person, instead of exalting himself, his ways, ideas, and wishes, chooses to put himself in second place to achieve what is good for others. This is a sign, not of weakness of character, but of strength.

The word is used secularly to describe a tame animal that submits to its master's will instead of doing as it pleases. So a meek (tame) horse will respond to the reins. Does this mean the horse is weak? Surely not, but it is willing to follow its master's will.

See also Matthew 5:5; Ephesians 4:2,3; Colossians 3:12,13; 2 Timothy 2:24-26; Titus 3:2; James 3:13-18; 1:21-25; 1 Peter 3:1-6.

"Meekness" (πραυτης) — "...the quality of not being overly impressed by a sense of one's self-importance, *gentleness, humility, courtesy, considerateness, meekness* in the older favorable sense..." – Bauer-Danker-Arndt-Gingrich.

> "Meekness ... is an inwrought grace of the soul; and the exercises of it are first and chiefly towards God. It is that temper of spirit in which we accept His dealings with us as good, and therefore without disputing or resisting; ... it is only the humble heart which is also the meek, and which, as such, does not fight against God and more or less struggle and contend with Him.

This meekness, however, being first of all a meekness before God, is also such in the face of men...' (Trench, Syn. xlii)."

"...It must be clearly understood, therefore, that the meekness manifested by the Lord and commended to the believer is the fruit of power. The common assumption is that when a man is meek it is because he cannot help himself; but the Lord was 'meek' because he had the infinite resources of God at His command. Described negatively, meekness is the opposite to self-assertiveness and self-interest; it is equanimity of spirit that is neither elated nor cast down, simply because it is not occupied with self at all. ..." – Vine.

Self-control

This is translated "self-control" (NKJV, ASV, NASB, ESV), "temperance" (KJV).

The word emphasizes self-control and self-restraint, the ability to master one's mind and body so as to participate (or not participate) in an activity to the extent most useful in accomplishing God's will. It is self-government, continency, "will power." The original meaning of the Greek word was "to hold one's self in."

"Temperance" may have been an adequate translation many years ago, but that word has come to mean either abstinence from alcohol or moderation. Both these concepts are included in the word used here, but much more is also included.

1 Corinthians 7:9 – If the unmarried cannot "*contain*," they should marry.

1 Corinthians 9:24-27 – An athlete is "*temperate*" in all things, so Paul kept his body in subjection.

Self-control will lead one to:

Control his temper (Ephesians 4:26; James 1:19,20)

Control his tongue (James 3:1-12; Ephesians 4:25,29; 5:4; 1 Corinthians 6:10)

Control his thoughts (Matthew 15:19; 5:27; 1 Corinthians 6:10; Galatians 5:21)

Control his conduct to set a good example (Romans 14:20,21; 1 Corinthians 8:12,13; 10:23,24,31-33; 9:19-23).

Self-control should be exercised in all things, but the amount done of each thing depends on the nature of the act and the circumstances. Consider the application in different areas of life:

In things that are **sinful** or that hinder our usefulness in God's service, proper self-control will lead us to completely **abstain**: Romans 8:13; 1 Peter 2:11; 1 Thessalonians 5:22.

In other matters, self-control will lead to **moderation**. Some things should be done to some extent but not overdone, such as eating, exercise, and obtaining material possessions. In these and some other areas, a moderate, middle-ground course should be pursued.

In other matters, self-control will lead to a diligent effort to **_fully participate_** in good works that God requires of us, such as worship (Acts 2:42; Hebrews 10:25; 1 Thessalonians 5:17), teaching others (Acts 8:4; Hebrews 5:11ff), Bible study, etc.

This self-control comes from studying God's word to know what we ought to do and to see examples of people who did God's will. It comes from practice (Hebrews 5:14) and exercise in self-discipline.

Other similar related passages are 1 Corinthians 6:19,20; Romans 12:1,2; 2 Corinthians 10:5; Matthew 16:24; Romans 8:13; Proverbs 16:32; Genesis 4:7.

"Self-control" (εγκρατεια) – "...self-control ... (the virtue of one who masters his desires and passions, especially his sensual appetites)..." – Grimm-Wilke-Thayer.

"...the various powers bestowed by God upon man are capable of abuse; the right use demands the controlling power of the will under the operation of the Spirit of God..." – Vine.

"restraint of one's emotions, impulses, or desires, _self-control_" – Bauer-Danker-Arndt-Gingrich.

5:24-26 – _Those who belong to Christ have crucified the flesh with its passions and lusts. If we live by the Spirit, then let us walk by the Spirit. We should not become boastful, provoking and envying one another._

Verses 16-18 said that the flesh contradicts the will of the Holy Spirit, leading us to do works of the flesh, such as are listed in verses 19-21. The Holy Spirit, however, leads us to develop good qualities such as the fruit of the Spirit in verses 22-24.

Crucifying the flesh with its passions and desires

Christians belong to Christ. See 1 Corinthians 6:19,20; 3:23; 2 Corinthians 10:7. If we belong to Christ we will crucify the flesh with its passions and desires. This happens according to the power of the Holy Spirit through the gospel. See notes on 2:20. This does not mean we no longer have natural desires; it means we no longer let them control us. Like a dead body is powerless to act, so the power of natural lusts does not dominate us because we are dominated instead by the Spirit.

If we live in the Spirit, we should walk in the Spirit. The Spirit gives us life through the word. As we obey the gospel of the Spirit, we are forgiven of sins, made alive in Christ, and given the hope of eternal life. But living in the Spirit requires us to crucify the flesh with its passions and desires. Something must live and something must die. To live in the Spirit, the flesh must die. And this is not just any death but an absolute and conclusive death such as can be described as a crucifixion.

Life in the Bible often refers to being united with something, whereas death refers to being separated from it. Physical death involves the separation of the spirit from the body (James 2:26). So spiritual death is separation of man from God (see Ephesians 2). Spiritual life is union with God. When we are guilty of sin, sin separates us from God. The only way to be united with God and have life is by forgiveness through Jesus' blood (Romans 6:23). We are taught to do this by the Spirit through the word. So we live in the Spirit.

If so, then we ought to walk according to the teachings of the Spirit. If we seek life by the Spirit's teaching, then we must act according to His teachings. It is foolish to seek union with God by having our sins forgiven, but then think we can go back to live in sin. See Romans 6.

Do not be conceited, provoking and envying one another.

Finally, walking by the Spirit teaches us not to be conceited, provoking and envying one another. Conceit is the opposite of the meekness that the Spirit produces in us (verses 22-24). It is surely not kind or loving. So, we must not exalt self over others.

Nor may we envy others. This too is a work of the flesh (see verse 21).

Envy and conceit, along with other works of the flesh (verse 20), lead us to do that which provokes others. It is possible to provoke others to do good (Hebrews 10:24), but here Paul clearly refers to provoking others to that which is spiritually harmful.

Some were provoking the Galatians to turn from truth (5:7-9). Those who emphasized the law as essential to salvation often became conceited in their own accomplishments as though somehow they deserved God's blessings. They would then look down on others. See the example in Luke 18:10,11. This conceited self-righteousness often led to biting and devouring others. Such is not the fruit of the Spirit. We must stand for truth and oppose error, but this must be done in a spirit of love, not from selfish motives.

Paul has now made clear to the Galatians that the gospel is what can save them, not the law. But following the gospel does not justify improper conduct. Rather it motivates pure lives and sincere concern for others.

Commentary on Galatians

Galatians 6

6:1-10 - Reaping What We Sow

6:1,2 – If a man is overtaken in a trespass, those who are
spiritual should restore such a one in a spirit of
meekness, considering themselves lest they also be
tempted. We should bear one another's burdens and so
fulfill the law of Christ.

Paul's admonitions regarding the issue of circumcision and the
Old Testament appear to have been generally completed at this point,
with the exception of a few comments in verses 12-15. The remaining
comments appear to be general thoughts of admonition and
encouragement. They may have been based on Paul's knowledge of the
needs of the Galatians.

Restoring those overtaken in a trespass

He first exhorts them to restore one who is overtaken in a trespass
(or "fault" – KJV; "transgression" – ESV). "Trespass" refers to "offense,
wrongdoing, sin..." – Bauer-Danker-Arndt-Gingrich. See Romans 5:15-
18; Ephesians 1:7; 2:1,5.

Many passages warn about the danger of error. But why should we
be concerned if, as some teach, one cannot thereby lose eternal life (see
notes on 5:4)? Yet Paul says such a person should not be ignored but
must be restored. Telling someone that they are guilty and need to
repent of sin is not an act of ill-will. Properly done it is an act of love,
because it gives the person opportunity to correct his life.

This restoring should be done by those who are spiritual. See 1
Corinthians 2:15; 3:1; 14:37; Romans 8:4-11. The context would tie to
Galatians 5:16-26. A spiritual person is one who is led by the Spirit and
develops in his life the fruits of the Spirit. He is spiritually minded,
emphasizing spiritual concerns in his life, rather than emphasizing
material or earthly concerns. "... men in Christ who walk so as to please
God are said to be 'spiritual'" (Hogg and Vine). This ought, of course, to
include all Christians. We ought all, therefore, to be concerned about
restoring the erring.

If we are spiritually minded and led by the Spirit, we will see the
need to restore the erring, because the Spirit tells us to do so. We will

be concerned about the spiritual well-being of a brother and will want to see him restored. Those who neglect this work show that they are not truly spiritually minded.

On the other hand, it follows that those who are not spiritually minded – those who are spiritually indifferent, negligent, or living in sin – cannot be effective in such work. They will not be likely to attempt to do much of it; and if they do try, they may approach it poorly, and will find their own example hinders their work. Truly this is a work for those who emphasize spiritual concerns.

Other passages regarding rebuking sin: Revelation 3:19; Matthew 5:23,24; 18:15-17; Luke 17:3,4; James 5:19,20; 1 Thessalonians 5:14; Ephesians 5:11; 2 Timothy 4:2-4; 1 Timothy 5:20; Titus 1:10-13; Proverbs 28:4.

"Trespass" (παραπτωμα) – "...in imagery of one making a false step so as to lose footing: a violation of moral standards, *offense, wrongdoing, sin...*" – Bauer-Danker-Arndt-Gingrich.

"Spiritual" (πνευνατικος) – "...In the great majority of cases in ref. to the divine πνεῦμα ... having to do with the (divine) spirit, *caused by* or *filled with the (divine) spirit, pert./corresponding to the (divine) spirit...*" – Bauer-Danker-Arndt-Gingrich.

"Restore" (καταρτιζω) – "... 1. to cause to be in a condition to function well, *put in order, restore. a. restore to a former condition, put to rights* ... b. *put into proper condition ... adjust, complete, make complete...*" – Bauer-Danker-Arndt-Gingrich.

A "spirit of gentleness" or "meekness" is needed.

See on 5:23 for a definition of this term and a list of passages. Meekness is especially needed in teaching – see 2 Timothy 2:24-26; Ephesians 4:2; compare 2 Timothy 4:2-4.

Meekness is a willingness to submit to the will of others, rather than insisting on our own will. Specifically and above all, we must submit to the will of God. God tells us to restore the erring, so in order to submit to His will, we must do so. We speak, not primarily because we are personally upset or hurt by the sins of the erring, but because we care about his soul, the souls of those he may influence, and about God's will.

Meekness is also a willingness to submit to others. This is needed in teaching the erring so that we do not enter the discussion determined to win a personal victory. The issue is not that the person has criticized us, blamed us, or left our "party," so now we must get vengeance by attacking and harming him personally. We must control our temper, not becoming enraged because he is stubborn or refuses to submit to our instruction. Rather the issue must rest on the fact he is alienating himself from God and losing his hope of eternal life. We love God and our brother's soul too much to let that happen without attempting to restore him.

This spirit of meekness will then show itself in how we approach a person. Rather than being quarrelsome, bossy, and easily angered, we will be patient, willing to listen, and will base our statements on the real facts of the case, sincerely attempting to reason based on the evidence of he Scriptures.

Considering yourself, lest you also be tempted.

This shows that there is real danger to the teacher that he might fall into sin. Why might this be so? All sin can influence us (see 5:9 on "leaven"). We may be tempted to commit the same sin as our erring brother. This is one of the many reasons why sin must be opposed, not ignored.

Yet teachers also face many other temptations. One danger is the temptation to compromise truth. It is so hard to tell others they are in sin and must repent. It is so much easier to overlook their sin or find a way to justify it. Sinners will likely make arguments to excuse or rationalize their conduct. It is so easy to accept these rationalizations rather than continue to speak for truth.

Other temptations include the temptation to lose one's temper or become quarrelsome, as discussed above. Another temptation is to show favoritism in teaching, standing against the sins of those who are poor or uninfluential, while keeping quiet about the errors of those who are wealthy, powerful, family members or special friends.

Another temptation is the desire to take vengeance on the sinner, embarrass him, or otherwise harm him for what he did, rather than seeking in sincere spiritual concern to help save his soul. Still another is the temptation to become discouraged and quit teaching because some refuse to listen. We must speak out of concern for the souls of others, but we must guard also for the sake of our own souls.

Sinners face many temptations, but so do teachers. Those who have fallen into sin often tell sad tales about the problems they face that led to their downfall. Yet in many cases they fail to realize that their own conduct is creating serious problems for other people.

Perhaps in this context Paul is also reminding the one doing the restoring that he too has been guilty of sin. He ought to have a spirit of meekness because he knows that he too has been in sin, just as surely as is the one he is seeking to restore.

Bear one another's burdens, and so fulfill the law of Christ.

Christians must be concerned about the needs of others. This is fundamental to love and service to others. Brethren have many burdens that we should try to help them bear.

This does not mean we should take upon ourselves the duties that others should fulfill so they become lazy and irresponsible toward their own duties. On the contrary, they should also learn to help other people bear their burdens. Yet there are many things we can do to help one another fulfill responsibilities or deal with problems without relieving people of their responsibilities.

One burden we can help with is the burden of sin, as discussed in verse 1. Talking to a brother about his sins is not a hateful, egotistical thing to do, but is an attempt to help him deal with the burden of his own guilt.

Other burdens with which we may need to help people are listed in verses such as Matthew 25:31-46. People may need food, clothing, etc. They may face sickness, loss of loved ones, imprisonment. They may be persecuted for righteousness' sake. They may face loneliness, discouragement, temptation. They may need help in teaching the gospel to others, training their children, having a good home life, etc.

In helping others we are fulfilling the law of Christ. The law of love for God and love for neighbor leads to fulfilling all God's will (1 John 5:2,3; Matthew 22:26-40; Romans 13:8-10; see on 5:14).

This verse is important in understanding Paul's overall teaching about law. He has repeatedly said that we are not justified by the law, meaning the law of Moses and the principle of justification by sinlessly observing any law. Instead, we need faith in Jesus' sacrifice that can save us. But none of this discussion is saying that we can disregard all law, let alone does it mean we are subject to no law at all, as some believe.

Reading commentaries on the book of Galatians shows how frequently people make the mistake of concluding that Paul is teaching here that God's people are subject to no law at all. Other times they seem to admit that there are commands we must obey, yet the conclusion appears to be that our hope of eternal life is not affected by whether or not we obey those laws.

But Jesus does have a law. All commands in the gospel or New Testament are His law for us. We must fulfill that law, not ignore or dismiss it. One fundamental aspect of the law of Christ is that we must help others in need, even as He did.

See also John 13:34,35; 15:12-17; Ephesians 4:2,31-5:2; Philippians 2:2,3; 1 Thessalonians 3:12; 4:9,10; 2 Thessalonians 1:3; Hebrews 13:1; 1 Peter 1:22; 2:17; 3:8,9; 4:8; 1 John 2:7-11; 3:10-18,23; 4:8-5:3; Romans 15:1,2.

6:3 – If a man thinks he is something when he is nothing, he deceives himself.

Verse 3 is a warning against egotism, pride, and conceit. The danger is in thinking we are something when we are nothing – thinking more highly of ourselves than we ought to think. Such is self deception.

In the ultimate picture, compared to God, we are all nothing. Even compared to other people, we must not think we are "something" but other people are "nothing." We must recognize God as truly the great Ruler of all, and all men as our equals in importance.

Pride leads us to think we are important and deserve honor above others. We think we deserve to get our way or have our desires met more than do others. We think we deserve to be excused for our failures where others should be punished for their wrongs. These attitudes lead to strife and alienation.

Perhaps the emphasis in this context is that pride sometimes keeps us from helping others, or pride may keep us from restoring others with "meekness." If we think we are better than others and fail to see our own sins, then we may think we don't need to help others: let them solve their own problems like (we think) we have done.

Or pride may lead us to approach others with arrogance and condescension. But when we see ourselves as "nothing," we know we too have sinned and are subject to sin, and we too have problems with which we need help. This will lead us to help others in a humble, understanding manner.

See Romans 12:3-5; Philippians 2:2-5; Proverbs 6:16-19; 16:5,18; 13:10; 1 John 2:15-17; Romans 1:30,32; James 4:6; 1 Peter 5:5; 1 Corinthians 13:5; 2 Timothy 3:2; Luke 14:7-11; Galatians 6:1; Colossians 3:12,13.

6:4,5 – Each one should prove his own work that he may glory in himself and not in regard to others. Each one will bear his own burden.

Paul then admonishes each person to examine his own work. Compare 2 Corinthians 13:5. Each person has an individual responsibility before God. Each one must determine whether or not he will serve God faithfully on the basis of his own understanding of God's word, his own faith, and his own repentance. Each will be judged individually for his own life. Since that is true, each must consider his life to see whether he is pleasing to God and ready for that judgment.

We can bear one another's burden (verse 2) in the sense of helping one another. But ultimately each will be judged for his own life, bearing his own burden in that sense (verse 5). He will rejoice in his own work. Of course, he will also regret his own work if it is unacceptable. But the point is that each will be rewarded or punished for his own life, so each must examine his own work to make sure he is acceptable.

So, each must bear his own burden (verse 5). Yet verse 2 said we should bear one another's burdens. There is no contradiction. Verse 2 is talking about helping one another with his problems and hardships, where verse 5 is talking about individual judgment and responsibility before God, as in verse 4. Each one will bear his own judgment, so each must examine his own work.

See Matthew 25:31-46; John 12:48; Acts 10:42; 17:30,31; Romans 2:4-11; 14:10-12; 2 Corinthians 5:10; 2 Thessalonians 1:5-9; 2 Timothy 4:1; Hebrews 9:27; 10:26-31; Revelation 20:11-15; Ecclesiastes 12:13,14.

6:6 – Let him who is taught in the word share all good things with the one who teaches.

The teacher shares good things with those he teaches: spiritual nourishment and treasures from God's word. But the student should also share good things with the teacher. The laborer is worthy of his hire and deserves to be rewarded for his work in teaching.

This is true both from the view of the congregation and the individual. That is, the laborer works in a congregation, so the congregation supports him. But he also works with individuals, and they may and should be willing to support him. Luke 10:7, for example, refers more to individuals supporting a preacher than local churches. See also Matthew 27:55,56; Luke 8:2,3.

The context of Galatians 6:6 is individual activity (note verses 5,7-9, etc.). While other passages show that local churches can and should support preachers, and Galatians 6:6 might have some application there as a general principle, yet Galatians 6:6 has specific application, not to local churches, but to individual Christians.

3 John 5-8 describes the diligence of Gaius in his work of supporting and encouraging gospel preachers. We commonly think of such a need when a man is invited to come to preach a gospel meeting. Providing meals and a place to stay is exactly the kind of good work that John is describing here and is still needed even today.

Clearly receiving such teachers as described here is a form of fellowship. The passage says that, by supporting teachers in such a way, we become "fellow-workers" with them. In Philippians 4:14-16 Paul uses various fellowship terms to describe the sharing that the Christians in Philippi did to support his gospel preaching.

It is the responsibility of those who believe the truth to support the preaching of it. This is not the responsibility of those who are not saved. We should not solicit the community to support our work. We should rather freely give them the gospel that will save them so they will become believers and join with us in the work.

I have seen it stated that verses 6-10 refer to a Christian's use of his money. While money may be included, the teaching and application of the passage is far, far broader than simply money. The only verses that are even related at all closely to money are verse 6 and to a much lesser extent verse 10. The verses in between have no particular reference whatever to money. And we will see that verse 10 is far broader than money.

And even sharing with teachers, as here in verse 6, includes much more than money. The passage says we share "all good things." While this would include financial support, it would also include such things

Commentary on Galatians

as providing a place for him to stay as he travels: room and board. It may include providing him a ride to where he needs to go. It may even include sharing with him teaching materials that he can use in his work.

I know a brother who helped a visiting preacher by doing major repairs on his automobile. The passage in 3 John shows that Gaius supported preachers by furthering them in their travels. Many people over the years have helped me in my work by their prayers and words of encouragement. We share in all good things with preachers when we provide whatever they need to help encourage their work.

Other similar passages are described in Matthew 10:1ff; Romans 15:24; Titus 3:13; Acts 15:3; 21:5; 1 Corinthians 16:6,11; 2 Corinthians 1:16.

Consider also general passages about our responsibility to support those who preach the gospel: 1 Corinthians 9:4-14; 2 Corinthians 11:7-9; Philippians 4:14-18; 1 Timothy 5:18; Luke 10:7.

6:7-9 – Do not be deceived: God is not mocked, for whatever a man sows that is what he will reap. He who sows to his flesh will reap corruption, but he who sows to the Spirit will reap eternal life. Let us not be weary in well doing, for in due time we will reap if we do not faint.

Reaping what we sow

The concept of sowing and reaping is often used to illustrate Bible principles. Here is it used to illustrate the concept that our reward is determined by our lives. Paul states this as a general principle regarding service to God. The crop that a farmer harvests is determined by the seed that he sows. Likewise, the eternal reward a person receives is determined by the life he lives. So, a man reaps spiritually according to what he sows in this life.

Regarding this Paul says we should not be deceived. Some folks are fooled (or fool themselves) about this. They somehow convince themselves that they can live a life of sin, yet they will not be punished for it eternally but will receive eternal life anyway. They are fooling themselves, but not God. God is not mocked.

Some people teach as a matter of doctrine that you can live a life of sin, but God will still save you if you once believed in Jesus. Other people think they can fool God, hide from Him, deceive Him, lie or excuse themselves and get away with sin. Some try to blame other people or their circumstances for their misdeeds. Some claim God is simply so gracious and loving that He will not punish them for their sins.

But you cannot trick God. In this life people often get away with disobeying rules because their sins are not discovered or because those in authority do not enforce the rules. Perhaps the evildoer offers money or uses influence to escape punishment. But none of this will work with God. Don't be deceived. God is not mocked.

The illustration of sowing and reaping is based on the nature of creation: living things reproduce after their own kind (see Genesis 1). The word of God is compared to seed which, when a person hears, if he is receptive, it will produce in his life the faith and good works that lead to salvation (1 Peter 1:22-25; Luke 8:11). This shows that the seed sown must be the pure word of God; false doctrines are bad seed that also reproduce after their kind resulting in sinful conduct and eternal punishment.

Reaping as we sow is also used in 2 Corinthians 9:6-10 to teach lessons about proper use of our material possessions. We are rewarded spiritually according to our willingness to give generously. Some tie this to Matthew 6:19-21 and 1 Timothy 6:17-19, but neither of these passages mention sowing or reaping. They refer to laying up treasure in heaven. And the passage in Matthew 6 is not even referring primarily to use of material possessions. We lay up treasures in heaven by the good lives that we lead, not just by our use of money.

As Paul does here, the concept of sowing seed and reaping a harvest is used elsewhere in Scripture to illustrate sowing evil or righteousness and reaping consequences: Job 4:8; Proverbs 1:31; 6:14,19; 11:18; Hosea 8:7; 10:12. Sowing seed and reaping a harvest is also used to illustrate teaching and learning God's word: Luke 8:4-15 (compare Matthew 13:24-26; 1 Corinthians 3:6,7; 1 Peter 1:22-25; James 1:21).

There is also an indirect application here to evolution. If evolution were true, then given enough time, what one reaps would be different from what one sows. That is, evolution claims that over millions of years totally different kinds of living things result from previous kinds, so that all kinds came from one original kind. But if that were possible, then a life of sin might eventually lead to eternal life, or a life of righteousness might eventually lead to punishment. Such would totally defeat Paul's argument. Such consequences show how completely contrary to Scripture the doctrine of evolution is.

The spiritual rewards

Specifically, the application Paul makes is that our eternal rewards are determined by how we live. If we sow to the flesh, we reap corruption. If we sow to the Spirit, we reap eternal life. Please note that there are only two possible rewards in the end: corruption or everlasting life. Each one of us will receive one or the other. There are no other ultimate destinies.

Flesh and Spirit, in this context, must surely refer back to 5:16-26. Flesh refers to works of the flesh which a person does in fulfillment of fleshly lusts. So, sowing to the flesh means living a life according to the works of the flesh. Likewise, sowing to the Spirit means obeying the guidance of the Holy Spirit through the Scriptures, so one lives according to the fruit of the Spirit. (See 5:16,18,19-21,22-25.)

This being true, it follows that the context does not refer primarily or specifically to the use of money, although that would be included in general. Surely receiving eternal life requires much more than just proper use of money, and we can reap corruption in many other ways besides just misuse of money.

Living according to the flesh leads to the consequence of corruption. This surely refers to eternal death, since it is contrasted to eternal life. Eternal life, however, is the harvest to be reaped by those who follow the Spirit. These rewards are determined by God, and nothing can change it, for God is not mocked.

Many other Scriptures show that these are in fact the rewards we will receive at the judgment for our lives. See Romans 6:12-23; 2:3-11; Matthew 25:31-46; John 12:48; Acts 10:42; 17:30,31; Romans 2:4- 11; 14:10-12; 2 Corinthians 5:10; 2 Thessalonians 1:5-9; 2 Timothy 4:1; Hebrews 9:27; 10:26-31; Revelation 20:11-15; Ecclesiastes 12:13,14.

Do not grow weary

However, as with a farmer, so in this life, we do not reap at the time we sow. We must be patient till the harvest comes "in due season." There is a time for sowing and a time for reaping. The time for reaping spiritual rewards is after this life is over, not in this life. This means we must continue "doing good" for a lifetime.

Please note that this is a general encouragement to remain steadfast and faithful in doing the good works that God has instructed in His word. This is true of all the good works that God has given. Many passages tell us the good that God wants us to do. In all that good, we must be steadfast till the time of the harvest.

Unfortunately, many become weary in well doing, and they faint. They get discouraged and quit. Discouragement may come from hardships in life, suffering, persecution, health problems. Or it may come from years spent in laboring for the Lord, seeing little visible good that results. This tends to cause discouragement, so Christians consider quitting specific works that God wants them to do or they entirely give up serving God.

Many have done much good, but in the end they fail to reap eternal life because they are not steadfast till the end. What is needed is steadfastness and patience to keep on doing good. See Romans 2:3-11; 1 Corinthians 15:58.

Surely the reference here to doing good is much broader than just our use of money. Furthermore, it is much broader than just helping those around us who are physically needy. We must not grow weary in doing any good that God has instructed us to do.

Since the reward we reap according to the context is eternal life or corruption, it follows that those who faint will not receive eternal life.

And since this is addressed to children of God (3:26,27), the doctrine of "once saved, always saved" is thoroughly refuted here.

See also 2 Corinthians 4:1,16; 2 Thessalonians 3:13; Luke 18:1; Ephesians 3:13; Hebrews 12:3-11; Proverbs 24:10; Jonah 2:7; Numbers 21:4-7; Deuteronomy 20:1-3.

6:10 – As we have opportunity, let us do good to all men, especially to those of the household of faith.

Doing good as we have opportunity

Since we will be rewarded according to how we live (verse 8), we should not grow weary in doing good (verse 9). Specifically, then, we need to do good when we have the opportunity (verse 10). Paul draws the message of his letter to a close with this strong encouragement to do good toward others.

This good should be done toward all, but especially toward those of the household of faith. The Christian is concerned for all people, regardless of whether or not they are Christians (Luke 10:25-37; Matthew 25:31-46). But his special concern is for other Christians.

The church is elsewhere compared to a family. This concept is sometimes described by the expression the "household of faith" (1 Timothy 3:15; Ephesians 2:19). Family members care for one another in a special way beyond how they care for those outside the family. We should realize a responsibility to all people, but we have a special responsibility to our own family. And in the same way, since the church is described as a family, we have a special responsibility to other Christians.

Note that this good is to be accomplished "as we have opportunity." Often our opportunities are limited by lack of ability or lack of knowledge of needs. But we must be open and alert to the opportunities that we do have, seeking to do what good we can, not to avoid our responsibilities.

In this context, it may be that the emphasis is on the fact that we have opportunity in this life, but the time will come when life is ended and our opportunity is ended (verses 8,9). See John 9:4; Ephesians 5:16.

Application to Social Gospel and institutional issues

This verse has unfortunately become a battleground because some claim that it teaches the **church** to do good to all men. They then proceed to define "good" to mean nearly anything they believe to be good, including sending contributions to centralized organizations, caring for needy people, and providing recreation and entertainment. So, the verse becomes a catch-all argument to defend local churches becoming involved in caring for all the needs of all the people in the community, using man-made institutions through which to do the work.

But the passage must be understood and applied in light of other Scriptures, just as we do elsewhere in our study of the word of God. In specific, several aspects of these ideas need to be considered in light of Bible teaching elsewhere.

Church support of human institutions

Even if the passage were addressed to the church, it would not authorize support of institutions. The passage really says nothing about human institutions nor does the context anywhere refer to human institutions.

Other passages about church work and church organization show that the work of each local church should be supervised by its own elders. No passage teaches churches to make donations to other institutions so they can supervise the work of the local church. So, if this passage refers to the work of local churches, then that work must be supervised by local elders, not by the directors of some human institution. See Acts 14:23; 20:28; 1 Peter 5:1-4; Titus 1:5-9; 1 Timothy 3:1-7; 5:17; Hebrews 13:7,17,24.

Local churches or individual Christians?

But is this passage even discussing the work of the local church? The fact that the epistle is addressed to churches in the introduction does not prove this context refers to congregational work. Many epistles, even if they are addressed to local churches, yet they contain instructions that are to be carried out by the individual Christians in the church. For example, much of the letter to the Galatians discusses the subject of circumcision. Likewise, the discussion of the works of the flesh and the fruit of the Spirit in chapter 5 refers to individual responsibilities.

So is the context of 6:10 describing the work of individuals or of local churches? Note the following evidence that the context is discussing work of individuals, not local churches. "We" in verse 10 is defined to be:

Verse 3 – "a man … himself … he … he … himself"

Verse 4 – "every man … his … he … himself alone … not another"

Verse 5 – "every man … his own"

Verse 6 – "him … him"

Verse 7-9 – "a man … he … he … his … he … us … we … we"

Verses 7-9 discuss our eternal destinies, and that is determined individually, not congregationally.

The fact that "we" in verse 10 is plural does not prove that it refers to the local congregation. "We" is also used in the plural in verse 9 to refer to reaping as we have sown. Do we reap eternal rewards as a congregation or as individuals? Furthermore, 5:2 also uses the plural to refer to circumcision. Are people circumcised as a work of the church or as individuals?

So, this context discusses work which we should fulfill individually, not as a local church body. If we wish to learn what the local church should do, we must examine verses discussing church work.

Furthermore, the "good" we should do does not refer specifically or primarily to helping people physically needy.

I believe that one of the most overlooked aspects of this verse is that people automatically assume it is talking about helping people with ***physical*** needs. But doing "good" is a very general concept. How do we know what good is included? Only by context. But there is simply nothing in the context that would imply that the verse refers specifically or primarily to meeting physical needs.

Verses 1-5 discuss helping people spiritually. Is that "doing good"?

Verse 6 discusses supporting preachers in preaching. Is that "doing good"?

Verses 7,8 describe our eternal reward based on whether we sow to the flesh or sow to the Spirit. Is that talking specifically or primarily about helping people physically?

Verse 9 tells us to not be weary in doing good. Is that talking only or specifically about helping physically needy people or is it good of all kinds? The reference to doing good in verse 10 simply continues the admonition to not be weary in doing good in verse 9. Just as the doing good in verse 9 is broad and general, so the reference to doing good in verse 10 is also broad and general, not referring just to helping people who are physically needy.

Note the parallel language in 1 Thessalonians 5:15. Both passages say that we should do that which is good toward Christians and toward all. Is that talking only or specifically about helping physically needy people or is it good of all kinds?

John 5:29 says those who have done good will receive the resurrection of life, in contrast to those who have done evil who will receive the resurrection of condemnation. This is discussing eternal rewards, like the context of Galatians 6:10. Will we be rewarded only for helping physically needy people, or does it refer to all good in general?

Likewise in Romans 2:7, eternal life is for those who continue patiently in doing good. Is that just helping the physically needy, or is it good in general?

And 2 Corinthians 5:10 – At judgment each one will be rewarded according to what he has done, whether good or bad. Is that just helping the physically needy, or is it good in general?

Ephesians 6:8 – Whatever good anyone does, he will be rewarded by the Lord. Is that just helping the physically needy, or is it good in general?

1 Peter 20:15 – For this is the will of God, that by doing good you may put to silence the ignorance of foolish men. Is that just helping the physically needy, or is it good in general?

1 Peter 3:11 – Let him turn away from evil and do good... Is that just helping the physically needy, or is it good in general?

Many other examples can be considered.

So, why conclude that Galatians 6:10 is talking specifically or primarily about helping people physically? "Good" is whatever God defines it to be. When you understand the concept of doing good, you understand that there is no particular reference here to physical benevolence of those who are poor, sick, etc.

> "This general exhortation is in effect a summing up of the particular responsibilities of the preceding context. It is good to restore the erring, v. 1; to bear the burden of others, v. 2; to share temporal supplies with those who share spiritual supplies with us, v. 6; to sow in the eternal interest of the Spirit, v. 8; and to continue unwearyingly in all manner of well doing, v. 9." (Hogg and Vine)

Paul is drawing his letter to a close, and as he does he summarizes his message encouraging all to use their opportunities to practice what is good. This applies to all good that God teaches us in His word to do. The passage is intended, not to define good, but to encourage us in general to be committed to doing good. To know what works are "good," we must study other Scriptures.

The Scriptures provide us to all good works – 2 Timothy 3:16,17. We must never assume anything to be a good work unless the Scriptures say so. Galatians 6:10 and other similar passages encourage us to do good works but do not define what those good works are. In order to know whether any specific activity is a good work, we must find Scripture elsewhere to tell us so.

Conclusions and applications

Should local churches provide physical help for needy non-Christians? If so, we must have a passage somewhere that tells us so. Where is the passage? There is no such passage. Galatians 6:10 does not authorize such activity, because it is describing individual activity, not church activity, and because it does not define what good works it refers to. But when we study passages that do mention local churches helping needy people, they always show that the people helped were Christians. See Acts 2:44,45; 4:32-5:11; 6:1-6; 11:27-30; Romans 15:25-27; 1 Corinthians 16:1-4; 2 Corinthians 8:4; 9:1,12; 1 Timothy 5:16.

Should local churches send contributions to human institutions so the directors of those institutions can supervise the work God gave to the local churches? If so, we must have a passage somewhere that tells us so. Where is the passage? There is no such passage. Galatians 6:10 does not authorize such activity, because it is describing individual activity, not church activity, and because it does not define what good works it refers to. But when we study passages that do mention local churches doing their work, we find that the work must be supervised by men within that local church, not by leaders of some man-made institution. See the Scriptures listed above.

And note that if those people were correct who claim this passage authorizes local churches to do their work through human institutions, then it would authorize doing any and all of the church's work through human institutions. This would include spiritual work as well as caring for those who are needy: evangelism, edification, and benevolence. All of this is "doing good." So if the passage refers to the work of local churches, then churches are authorized to set up and support human institutions as missionary societies, benevolent institutions, and institutions to supervise edification of members in Bible study and worship assemblies. Those who originated the argument never intended to accept such conclusions, yet this is the logical conclusion of their argument.

6:11-18 - Concluding Remarks

6:11 – See with what large letters I have written to you with my own hand.

Verse 11 appears to begin concluding remarks. The language implies that Paul was now writing the concluding words himself. Whereas the previous portion was written by a copyist who wrote what Paul dictated, this portion was written with Paul's own hand in large letters. See the significance of Paul's own handwriting in 2 Thessalonians 3:17; 1 Corinthians 16:21; Colossians 4:18.

Some translations imply that it was the epistle itself that was large (KJV). But other translations imply that Paul had written the letters that make up the words in large handwriting. Hogg and Vine explain that, if this were a reference to the size of the epistle itself, Paul would have used a different word and a different case of the word. In any case, the reference to Paul's own hand proved that he was personally writing – as he often did in his letters – in order to prove the message to be genuine (see the above references).

But why would Paul write with large letters? This is not stated, so is a matter of pure speculation. It could be due to a physical problem of some kind or may simply have been his preferred way of writing. The reason is not stated.

Commentary on Galatians

***6:12,13 – Those who wanted to make a good showing in the
flesh were trying to compel the Galatians to be
circumcised so that they would not themselves be
persecuted for the cross of Christ. They themselves did
not keep the law, but they wanted the Galatians to be
circumcised so they may boast in their flesh.***

Paul's concluding comments include a few more remarks about
the Judaizing teachers. First, he states that they were compelling the
Galatians to be circumcised. This was their goal. Not only did they seek
to be subject to the law (4:21), but they insisted that the Gentile
converts also be circumcised as a sign of commitment to the law.

However, they did not do this out of real concern for the law itself.
Though they spoke of great commitment to the law, they themselves
did not really keep all of it (see notes on 5:3). Like many people today,
they kept and emphasized certain things in the law, but other aspects of
the law they ignored (this may have included animal sacrifices or other
such practices). Had they really believed the law was binding, they
should have kept it all. By not doing so they were in effect admitting
that the law itself was not their main motive.

What then was their concern? Paul said they wanted to boast and
glory in the flesh so they could avoid persecution. The "flesh" here
surely refers to the act of circumcision as a physical outward sign of
commitment to the law (compare Philippians 3:4-7). If the Gentile
converts were not circumcised, then people of Jewish background
would suffer persecution at the hands of other Jews for associating
with uncircumcised Gentiles and treating them as though they were
acceptable to God (see on 2:14ff). But if the Gentiles would be
circumcised, then the Jews could associate with them with no
opposition from Jewish friends.

Some commentators also believe that persecution may have come
at the hands of the Gentiles, especially the Roman government. Some
believe that the Roman government was tolerant of many religions as
long as they were religions that the government officially approved.
Judaism was an officially recognized religion. So if the Christians
would be circumcised, they would be recognized by the government as
simply a sect or denomination of the recognized Jewish religion. But if
they refused to be circumcised, that would make them a separate
religion which would bring persecution, not just from the Jews, but
from the Roman government as an unauthorized religion.

That persecution was a serious concern in this discussion had been
stated or implied in 3:4; 4:29; 5:11. Paul's lifetime of preaching the
gospel had repeatedly stirred up storms of opposition from Jews,
especially because he preached to Gentiles (see Acts 22:21,22).
Doubtless other Christians suffered likewise. This persecution would

end if all Gentile converts were circumcised. This was a real concern of the Judaizers.

As is often the case, what people argued differed from what really concerned them. If it was simply a matter of personal convenience to avoid persecution, one could understand the concern. But if Gentiles were required to be circumcised when the gospel did not require it, that would drive many Gentiles from the faith for no Scriptural reason. For Judaizers to bind circumcision as a matter of salvation, such that they would treat Gentiles as unfaithful and unworthy of fellowship if they had not been circumcised, that was intolerable. And to argue it on the basis that the law was still in effect was deceitful. The Judaizers were willing to cause many Gentiles to be lost for the sake of their own convenience!

6:14-16 – Paul never sought to boast except in the cross of Christ through which the world had been crucified to him and he to the world. Neither circumcision nor uncircumcision is anything, but a new creature. So Paul sought peace and mercy to be on all who walk by that rule, upon the Israel of God.

Crucified to the world

Judaizers might boast in the fleshly act of circumcision, but Paul refused to boast in anything except the cross of Christ (compare 1 Corinthians 1:29,31). He did not trust or glory in any outward act which was unrelated to Christ's death and was not in any way essential to that death. Jesus' death is what saves from sin. Circumcision could not save but was part of the system which condemned because it had no sacrifice for sin. Jesus' death was part of the gospel and was the grounds on which we truly can be forgiven. We ought to glory in that which saves, not that which condemns!

But the cross not only saves from sin, it also crucifies us to the world and the world to us – see notes on 2:20; 5:24; Colossians 2:20; Romans 6:2,6. Death again is the symbol of separation. Crucifixion also ended one's life and power. So, when we are forgiven, we ought to separate from the world so its allurements have no power in our lives, even as a dead man has no power to act. When we do, the world will also separate itself from us (1 Peter 4:3,4). We will mutually repulse one another.

"World" here refers to the society of those around us who live for this life rather than to serve God. It includes all who oppose or are indifferent to Jesus and His gospel.

What avails in Christ is neither circumcision nor uncircumcision, but a new creature.

In particular, the cross separates us from the Judaistic belief that we must perform the purely outward physical act of circumcision. The

Commentary on Galatians

gospel teaches, as Paul has throughout this epistle, that neither circumcision nor uncircumcision matters in our relationship to Jesus (compare 5:6).

What does matter is being a new creature in Christ. This is another expression for being born again as a child of God. In this relationship we inherit the promise offered to all nations through Abraham's descendants. Forgiveness by the cross makes us new people, cleansed from sin and dedicated to Jesus' service. Gentiles can do this the same as Jews, but circumcision has no spiritual value.

So, if any man is in Christ he is a new creature – 2 Corinthians 5:17. This is what matters. But if this is what matters, then we need to know how one comes into Christ so he can be a new creature. As described in our notes on 3:26,27, the Bible answer is that one comes into Christ when he is baptized on the basis of faith. As a result of being baptized into Christ, he walks in newness of life – Romans 6:3,4.

It is a shame to see commentators and other Bible students use the book of Galatians to try to claim that obedience to the gospel conditions of salvation is not necessary, since they claim one is saved by faith alone. In effect they claim that in Christ neither circumcision nor uncircumcision nor baptism avails anything as long as one professes faith. Yet here as well as repeatedly in this epistle as well as elsewhere in Scripture, we are plainly told that the gospel requires men to have obedient faith in order to receive the blessings of salvation in Christ. This includes baptism; it does not exclude it.

See our notes on 3:26,27; 4:28; 3:29. Compare 2 Corinthians 5:17; Ephesians 2:10,15; 4:24; Colossians 3:10; John 3:3,5; 1 Peter 1:22-25; etc.

Peace and mercy on those who walk according to this rule

"This rule" refers to the gospel message and all it teaches. It is a standard of authority, which we must follow (walk according to). All who do so receive God's blessings, but those who follow the law receive no such blessing.

Note that the gospel message is a "***rule***" or standard of authority. It is not just a "love letter" or conglomeration of suggestions which can be ignored with impunity. Furthermore, to receive the blessings of the gospel we must ***walk*** according to this rule. Our walk repeatedly in Scripture refers to our manner of life: our conduct. Those who want God's blessings must recognize the gospel is a "rule" which must be followed.

So, as Paul draws his letter to a close, he once again emphasizes that obedience to the gospel is necessary to salvation. The gospel is a rule or pattern which we must follow. When people believe or teach that the New Testament here or anywhere else teaches that obedience is not necessary to salvation, they do so to the peril of their own souls.

These blessings are for those who follow that rule and upon the Israel of God. It seems that both of these terms refer to the same group ("and" here may carry the significance of "even"). "Israel" here is spiritual in application and refers to the church or all who accept the gospel. See Romans 9:6; Galatians 3:29; 4:28; Philippians 3:3; compare "Jerusalem" in 4:26.

Finally note the application to the premillennial view that, when Jesus comes again, physical Jews will once again become God's special people with special blessings. This flatly contradicts Paul's teaching. God says neither circumcision nor uncircumcision matters. All that matters is being a new creature in Christ.

"Rule" (κανων) – "... 1 a means to determine the quality of someth., *rule, standard* ... 2 set of directions or formulation for an activity, *assignment, formulation...*" – Bauer-Danker-Arndt-Gingrich.

6:17,18 – *Paul urged that no one should trouble him since he bore the marks of Jesus on his body. He concludes by calling for the grace of the Lord Jesus Christ to be with their spirit.*

Paul concludes the epistle by reminding the Galatians of all that he had suffered for the cause of Christ. Some evidently doubted his authority as an apostle (chapter 1) and questioned his stand for truth. Paul says no one should trouble him with such accusations. His body bore marks of suffering for Christ.

I am told that slaves in that day were branded to identify who their masters were. Paul is saying that in a similar way his faithfulness to his master was demonstrated by the scars and wounds he had received as a result of persecution for the cause of Christ. His sacrifices spoke for themselves. To question his devotion to truth was foolish. Contrast Paul's record of service to that of the Judaizers (see verse 12).

He concludes by calling for the grace of Jesus to be on their spirits. This was his hope for them. He had expressed doubts of the outcome of their struggles with the Judaizers, but his sincere hope was that they would continue to receive the benefits of Jesus' grace.

Sources Frequently Cited in These Notes

Ancient Christian Commentary on Scripture. InterVarsity Academic, Downers Grove, IL, 2006. WORD*search* CROSS e-book

Bauer, Danker, Arndt, and Gingrich, *A Greek-English Lexicon of the New Testament and Other Early Christian Literature*, 3rd Edition. University of Chicago Press; Chicago, IL, 2001

Hogg, C.F. and W.E. Vine, *The Epistle to the Galatians*. Kregel Publications, Grand Rapids, MI 49503, 1921

Horne, Thomas, *Introduction to the Critical Study and Knowledge of the Holy Scriptures*, 4 volumes; T. Cadwell, Strand, London, 1828 (public domain)

McGarvey, J.W. and Philip Y. Pendleton, *Thessalonians, Corinthians, Galatians, and Romans*; Gospel Light Publishing Co. (no date)

Thayer, Joseph Henry, *Greek-English Lexicon of the New Testament* (original material prepared by Grimm and Wilke, translated, revised, and enlarged by Thayer); Zondervan's Publishing House, Grand Rapids, MI (public domain)

Vine, W.E., *Vine's Expository Dictionary of New Testament Words*; MacDonald Publishing Co., McLean, VA

Willis, Mike, *Truth Commentaries: Galatians*. Guardian of Truth Foundation, Bowling Green, KY, 1994

Addenda

Are We Saved by Law?

Not Saved or Justified by Law?

Romans 3:20,21 – Therefore by **the deeds of (the) law** no flesh will be justified in His sight, for by the law is the knowledge of sin. But now the righteousness of God **apart from (the) law** is revealed, being witnessed by the Law and the Prophets

Romans 3:27,28 – Where is boasting then? It is excluded. **By what law? Of works**? No, but by **(the) law of faith**. Therefore we conclude that a man is justified by faith apart from **the deeds of (the) law**.

Galatians 2:16 – knowing that a man is not justified by **the works of (the) law** but by faith in Jesus Christ, even we have believed in Christ Jesus, that we might be justified by faith in Christ and **not by the works of (the) law; for by the works of (the) law** no flesh shall be justified.

Acts 13:39 – and by Him everyone who believes is justified from all things from which you **could not be justified by the law of Moses**.

Galatians 3:10-12 – For as many as are of **the works of (the) law** are under the curse; for it is written, "Cursed is everyone who does not continue in all things which are **written in the book of the law**, to do them." But that **no one is justified by (the) law** in the sight of God *is* evident, for *"the just shall live by faith."* Yet **the law** is not of faith, but *"the man who **does** them shall live by them."* [Context defines what law is being referred to and the sense in which it does not justify. It is the law written in the book of the law and the only way to be justified by it was to continue in all things which are written in it.]

Galatians 5:2-4 – Indeed I, Paul, say to you that if you become circumcised, Christ will profit you nothing. And I testify again to every man who becomes circumcised that he is a debtor to keep the whole law. You have become estranged from Christ, you who *attempt to* be **justified by law**; you have fallen from grace. [Again, context defines the law to which Paul refers. It is a whole law which includes circumcision.]

This is a complete list of passages to my knowledge make statements to the effect that we are not saved or justified by law. Many other passages refer specifically to the Old Testament law saying it has been removed or that it was inadequate in some way.

Saved or Justified by Law

Law simply means a command, rule, or precept (or a collection of commands) that a person is expected to obey. Now notice that, in addition to the passages that talk about the Old Testament law or that say we are not justified by the deeds of the law, the New Testament mentions several **other kinds** of law.

The law of Christ - Galatians 6:2. Is it proper to say we are not saved by the law of Christ? When passages like those listed above say we are not saved by the deeds of the law, are they talking about the law of Christ?

The law of God – Romans 8:7 Is it proper to say we are not saved by the law of God? When passages like those listed above say we are not saved by the deeds of the law, are they talking about the law of God to which Paul refers here?

The perfect law of liberty – James 1:25; 2:12 – One who continues in the perfect law of liberty and is a doer of the work, this one will When passages like those listed above say we are not saved by the deeds of the law, are they talking about the perfect law of liberty?

The law of faith – Romans 3:27 – The law of faith is contrasted to the law of works, and boasting is excluded by the law of faith. 1 John 3:23 – Faith is a **command.** So faith is a law, a command. Are we saved by faith? If so, then here is a law, a command, by which we are saved.

The law of love – James 2:8 — Love your neighbor is the **royal law**. Matthew 22:37-39 — Love for God and man are the two greatest

commands. So love is a law, a command. Are we saved by love? If so, then here is a law, a command, by which we are saved.

The law of the Spirit of life in Christ Jesus – Romans 8:2 – The law of the Spirit of life in Christ Jesus has made me free from the law of sin and death. If the law of the Spirit of life makes us free from the law of sin and death, then is this not a law by which we are saved?

Obeying the truth – 1 Peter 1:22 – You have purified your souls in obeying the truth. If the truth referred to here must be obeyed, is that truth not a law or a command? And if we purify our souls in obeying that truth, then are we not saved by law?

Justified by works – James 2:14-26 – The passage repeatedly states that we are justified by works, not by faith only. The works described in the context refer to acts of obedience. Are these works not a law or command? And if we are justified by these works, then are we not saved by law?

Working righteousness – Acts 10:35 – Whoever fears Him and works righteousness is accepted by Him. Does working righteousness not refer to obedience to divine commands, and if so then are those commands not law? Peter is here telling Cornelius what he must do to be saved – Acts 11:14. And if we must work righteousness to be accepted, does that not mean that we are saved by law?

The gospel is the power of God to salvation – Romans 1:16 – Does the gospel contain commands? If so, it is a law. In fact, is it not the law of Christ, the law of faith, the perfect law liberty, and the law of the Spirit of life described in the passages above? But if the gospel is the power of God to salvation, and the gospel is a law, then are we not saved by law?

Baptism now saves us – 1 Peter 3:21 – There is also an antitype which now saves us—baptism. Baptism is a **command** (Acts 10:47,48) by which we are saved and our sins are washed away (see also Mark 16:16; Acts 22:16). If baptism is a command, then is it not a law? And if it saves us and our sins are washed away in baptism, then are we not saved by law?

So far as I can tell, all of these passages refer to law, command, or works of obedience to which we must submit in order to be saved.

Observations and Conclusions

1. We have some passages that say we are not saved by the deeds of the law, but other passages say we are saved by obedience to God's law. It follows that these are referring to different laws and even to different kinds of law.

Often people become confused because they assume there is only one kind of law. They read passages saying we are not saved by a law of works (like the Old Testament), then they assume that this means that we are not saved by any law at all or that no commands are required for salvation. When we realize there are ***different kinds of law***, then we see how we may ***not*** be saved by one kind of law, yet there still may be a very real sense in which we are saved by obedience to a different kind of law or commands.

We may compare this to the Bible teaching about works, faith, and other subjects. Some passages say we are saved by works, but others say we are not saved by works. The explanation is that they are talking about different kinds of works. Likewise, some passages say we are saved by faith, but other passages describe people who have faith yet are not saved. Obviously, they are referring to different kinds of faith. The same is true in regard to the different kinds of law required for our salvation.

2. Observe closely the passages that are often cited to claim that we are not saved by law and you will see that almost invariably what they really say is that we are not saved by the ***deeds or works*** of the law. And the few passages that may sound like we are not saved by law are all found in the immediate context (within a verse or two) of statements that show clearly that what is referred to are the ***deeds or works*** of the law, or specifically to the Old Testament law. No passage that I can find says we are not saved by law in any unlimited or general sense. Always the point is clearly made that it is the ***deeds or works*** of the law that do not save.

This distinction is significant. In order to be justified by our own deeds under the law, we would have to live our whole life without sin. This is true because any sin would cause us to stand condemned, and then we cannot cleanse the guilt of sin by ourselves (note again specifically Galatians 3:10-12).

So, when passages say we are not saved by the deeds of the law, the point is that we are not saved by earning our own salvation by living a sinless life. We are not saved by living an entire life in which we never violate the law. This is the significance of every passage cited to show that we are not saved by law. This point is made clear when we recognize that the verses refer to the ***deeds*** of the law, not to law in a general or universal sense.

3. Different systems of law not only contain different requirements, but they may also involve various conditions one must satisfy if he fails to live up to the requirements of the law. Some laws provide grace and mercy whereby those who have violated the law may receive forgiveness. Other kinds of law contain no such conditions. (Consider, for example, a 30-day grace period in an insurance policy

that allows a person to reinstate a policy if he has failed to make a payment on time.)

Hebrews 10:1-18 explains clearly that this is one of the differences between the Old Testament and the New Testament. The Old Testament contained laws or commands, but the only sacrifices it provided when a person sinned were animal sacrifices, which were not adequate to ultimately take away sins. The New Testament, however has perfect and complete forgiveness by the sacrifice of the blood of Jesus Christ. Both of the covenants included grace in a sense; but the grace offered in the New Testament is adequate to meet the need for forgiveness whereas that under the Old Testament was not adequate. Both covenants also included commands and therefore constitute laws. But the New Testament has adequate means to provide forgiveness for those who violate any of its requirements, if they meet the terms or conditions of forgiveness.

This is the sense in which we are not saved by law under the Old Testament or any law which, like the Old Testament, does not provide adequate forgiveness. Nevertheless, we are saved by the New Testament – even though it does constitute a system of laws – because it does provide adequate forgiveness.

Are People Today Required to Keep Old Testament Laws?

Introduction:

Exactly what is our relationship to the Old Testament law today?

The Old Testament contains many commandments not found in the New Testament, such as the seventh-day Sabbath, animal sacrifices, the Levitical priesthood, circumcision, special holy days, burning incense, tithing, instrumental music and dancing in worship, etc. Many people wonder whether we must obey these commands today.

I have met some people who claimed to keep all the Old Testament commands (including animal sacrifices). Other people disregard them all and keep only what they find in the New Testament. Still others try to keep some Old Testament commands but disregard others. To please God and to be united religiously, we must determine which Old Testament laws, if any, apply to us today. The purpose of this study is to consider exactly what the Bible itself says about these issues.

Consider some introductory questions:

Does God intend for people today to obey every command God has ever given?

People sometimes talk as if they believe that we today must practice everything that God ever commanded anybody in the Bible to practice, or must keep "holy" everything God ever told people to keep holy. But just a few Bible examples should convince us that this is not the case:

Noah's ark (Genesis 6:13-7:5)

God made a covenant with Noah (6:18), involving commands Noah had to obey (6:22; 7:5). But after the flood, God promised He would never again destroy all flesh by a flood (9:11-17). Must people today build arks like Noah? (God also commanded Abraham to offer his son as a sacrifice – Genesis 22:1-19. Must we today offer our sons as sacrifices like Abraham?)

Circumcision (Genesis 17:9-14)

Circumcision was both a covenant and a command given by God to Abraham and his descendants (compare 21:1-4; Leviticus 12:3). We today must keep the commands God has given us, but the command of circumcision no longer applies (1 Corinthians 7:18-20; Galatians 5:1-8; 6:12-16; Acts 15:1-29).

Levitical priesthood (Exodus 40:12-16; 29:1-9)

Under the covenant made at Mt. Sinai, God commanded only Aaron and his descendants to serve as priests (Numbers 3:10; 18:1-7; 16:40). But today Jesus is High Priest, though He was not a descendant of Aaron. This proves there has been a ***change in the law*** (Hebrews 7:11-18; compare 1 Peter 2:5,9).

Animal sacrifices (Numbers 15:1-6)

Throughout the Old Testament God commanded people to offer animal sacrifices (compare Genesis 4:1-5; Leviticus chapters 1-7). But today Jesus is our perfect sacrifice. Animal sacrifices have ceased to be offered because they are no longer needed (Hebrews 10:1-18).

Holy days/Feast days (Exodus 12:1-28; 13:3-10; Leviticus Chapter 23)

God commanded Israel to keep various holy feast days, but we today should not keep them (Colossians 2:14-17; Galatians 4:10,11). Note that there have been holy days, including days of rest, which God at times commanded certain people to observe, yet He later changed and no longer requires men to keep them.

Undeniably, God has given different laws to different people at different times. God is the same yesterday, today, and forever (Hebrews 13:8), but this refers to God's character and nature, not to His laws for men. The above Scriptures clearly prove that God Himself has made changes in the laws He has commanded people to keep.

Why are these commands no longer binding?

There are two possible reasons why we may not be required to obey a command given by God:

1. God may give a command to a specific individual or group, never intending it to apply to all people everywhere.

Obvious examples are the command to Noah to build the ark, the command to Abraham to sacrifice his son, and the command to Abraham's descendants to circumcise all males. (Compare Romans 3:19.)

If God intended for certain commands to be limited to certain people, but we take those commands and apply them to other people to whom God never intended to apply them, then we are not demonstrating faithfulness to God. Rather, we are perverting His will!

2. God may give a command to serve a temporary purpose for a limited time. When it has fulfilled its purpose, it is no longer needed, so God removes it.

Examples are the Levitical priesthood, animal sacrifices, and circumcision. In fact, this is true of all the examples we have previously mentioned.

Please note that ***people*** do not have the right, on the basis of their own human authority, to declare a law of God to be annulled. But neither do we have the right to bind a law on people whom God never intended to obey it. The question is: What is ***God's*** intent regarding a command. If He intends that law to apply to us, then we are unfaithful if we do not obey it. But we are equally unfaithful if we condemn people for not following a law when God Himself does not intend for those people to follow that law.

Man-made covenants as an illustration

Galatians 3:15 and Hebrews 9:17 use human covenants (contracts, agreements) to illustrate the principle of covenants made between men and God. This illustration becomes helpful in understanding our relationship to the covenant God made with Israel through Moses, including the Ten Commands and the Sabbath.

In every day life everyone understands the concept of contracts/covenants. We have contracts to purchase products and services (house, car, computer software, telephone, electricity, Internet), etc. A covenant includes conditions, terms, or requirements to be fulfilled by the parties who participate in it. In particular:

* Each contract is binding only on the parties named as participating in it. Other people may have similar contracts, but no one is bound by anyone else's contract. No one may attempt to bind on you the terms of a contract if you were not a party to that contract.

* Each contract is binding only as long as the terms of the contract remain in effect. The contract may stipulate that it will expire at a certain time or under certain conditions (lease a car for 5 years, buy a house with a 30-year mortgage, etc.). When the terms of a contract have been fulfilled, the contract expires and is no longer binding on anyone, not even on the people who were originally bound by it.

* A new contract, covenant, or testament may replace or succeed a previous one. If so, the parties involved are bound by the terms of the new contract, not by the terms of the old one. For example, if a man makes a new will, it replaces his previous will entirely. The new contract may have some conditions that are similar or even identical to terms in the previous contract, and it may have some terms that differ. Nevertheless, no terms of the previous contract as such are still binding on the parties – not even if the terms existed in several previous contracts. The only binding terms are those that exist in the current contract.

Earlier in this introduction we listed some of God's laws or covenants that are not binding on us today. The principles we have just discussed explain why these are not binding. We intend to show that the covenant God made with Israel through Moses is not binding on anyone today just like all these previously discussed laws and covenants are no longer binding. This will apply to all the laws and terms of that covenant, including the Ten Commands and the Sabbath.

We now live under an entirely different covenant that replaced the one made through Moses. None of the laws revealed through Moses – nor any laws revealed before Moses – apply today as such. All such laws, terms, and conditions have been replaced by the gospel of Jesus Christ. As in our illustration, the gospel may include some specific requirements that are similar or even identical to some that went before, but none of those laws are in effect today simply because they were included in any previous covenant. The only laws or conditions that are required of us today are the ones that are included in the New Testament.

Please consider our evidence from the word of God.

Part 1: Did God Intend for Old Testament Laws to Be Binding Today?

Without question, the laws revealed in the Old Testament were decreed by God Himself. Likewise without question, God had the right to limit the application of those laws to certain people and then to remove those laws from power whenever He chose, as in the examples already studied. What does the Bible say God intended regarding the Old Testament laws?

A. God Bound the Laws Given through Moses Only on the Nation of Israel.

Note specifically:

The Ten Commands were given only to Israel.

Deuteronomy 4:1 – When he gave the Ten Commands, Moses said they were given to Israel to observe.

Deuteronomy 4:44,45 – Moses set the laws, statutes, etc., before the children of Israel after they came out of Egypt.

Deuteronomy 5:1,6 – Moses spoke to Israel – that nation whom God brought out of Egypt – and gave them the Ten Commands to observe.

Exodus 34:27,28 – The Lord made a covenant with Israel writing on tablets the words of the covenant, the Ten Commandments.

1 Kings 8:9,21 – The two tablets of stone contained the covenant the Lord made with the children of Israel, when they came out of the land of Egypt.

Deuteronomy 4:7-13 – No other nation had such a great law as the Ten Commandments.

We will see that God repeated most (not all) of these laws in **other** covenants. But the Ten Commands themselves were given to one specific nation (to the people of that nation and to those who lived in the territory of that nation), not to all men for all time.

[Compare Exodus 19:1-6; 20:2,22; Deuteronomy 6:4,10; 9:1,10; 2 Chronicles 6:11; Romans 9:4,5; 2:14; Ephesians 2:11,12; 1 Corinthians 9:20,21.]

The Sabbath was given only to Israel.

Deuteronomy 5:15 – Israel (verse 1) was a slave in the land of Egypt, God brought them out and commanded them to keep the Sabbath day.

Exodus 31:13,16,17 – The Sabbath was a "sign" between God and Israel. How could this have been a sign between God and Israel if He had given the same command to other nations too? If a man gave wedding rings to many women, would a ring be a sign of his special relationship with his wife?

Can we understand that circumcision was not required of all people, because it was the "token" of a covenant made with Abraham's descendants (Genesis 17; Romans 4:11)? If so, then likewise, the Sabbath did not apply to all people because it too was a "sign" of a covenant God made with Israel.

People in general today do not need to keep the commands revealed through Moses, including the Ten Commands and the Sabbath, for the same reason we do not need to build arks like Noah or sacrifice sons like Abraham. God did not address these commands to us. To bind them on people of nations other than Israel would be like binding on you a contract someone else made to buy a car or house. The Old Covenant does not apply to Gentiles in general because we were never parties to it.

[Compare Ezekiel 20:10-12; Hosea 1:10; 2:11.]

B. God Removed the Old Law Because It Fulfilled Its Purpose.

Note the evidence:

These laws were in effect "throughout Israel's generations."

Since the law was addressed to Israel, God repeatedly said its provisions were to last "throughout their generations." This expression is used regarding the following practices:

Genesis 17:9,10 – Circumcision

Exodus 12:14; Leviticus 23:21,31,41 – Holy feast days

Exodus 29:42; 30:10 – Animal sacrifices

Exodus 30:8 – Incense

Exodus 30:31 – Holy anointing oil

Exodus 31:13-17 – Sabbath observance

Exodus 40:15; Numbers 18:23 – Levitical priests serving in the tabernacle.

[Compare Numbers 15:38; Exodus 30:21; Leviticus 7:36; Numbers 10:8; 35:29.]

All these practices would endure for the same length of time: throughout Israel's generations. Since they were all to endure the same length of time, if any of them have ceased, then they must all have ceased. But we have already proved that many of them have ceased; therefore, they must all have ceased.

All these requirements continued as long as Israel's special relationship to God continued. They all ended when that special relation ended, and that happened when the gospel came into effect. There is no more Jew or Gentile in God's plan (Galatians 3:28).

[Compare Ephesians 2:11-18; Acts 10:34,35; 15:7-11; Romans 10:12; Colossians 3:11.]

Hebrews chapters 7-10

7:11-14,18 – As shown earlier, only descendants of Aaron of the tribe of Levi were allowed to serve as priests under the law. But the law predicted that Christ would be a priest of the tribe of Judah. This required that the law be changed (verse 12) and disannulled (verse 18). The law itself implied this change would occur.

8:6-13 – These verses quote Jeremiah 31:31-34 which predicted God would make a new covenant different from the one He made with Israel when He led them out of Egypt. Christ has enacted this new covenant, so the first one is made old and is vanishing away (verse 13). Again, this fulfills the teaching of the Old Testament itself; it does not contradict it.

10:1-18 – Animal sacrifices under the first covenant could not completely remove sin. Jesus' death – the new covenant sacrifice – can completely forgive. So Christ **took away the first will and established the second**. This was in harmony with God's will, not contrary to it.

This explains the sense in which the law was weak and unprofitable: it told men they were sinners but could not permanently forgive them (7:11,18; 8:6,7). This does not mean the law was evil or a mistake. It perfectly accomplished its purpose, but from the beginning that purpose was intended to be temporary. When the new law came, the old was no longer needed, so it was removed.

Note that what was removed was the old covenant itself, not just the condemnation it brought nor just man-made traditions about it.

2 Corinthians 3:6-11

As in Hebrews, the Old Covenant (verse 14) is contrasted to the New (verse 6). The old was a ministration of death because it proved men deserved death. Even so, it came with glory. But the new covenant is a ministration of righteousness and is more glorious (verse 9).

Note verse 11 – That which was with glory (the old covenant – verse 7) was **done away,** so that which has more glory (the new covenant) may remain. Note that it is not just the glory that was done away, but **that which was glorious** – the Old Testament itself – was done away.

Galatians chapters 3-5

As in Hebrews, the law resulted in man's being cursed, because the law showed men were sinners but could not completely remove the guilt (3:10; 2:16). This contrasts to salvation by faith in Christ under the gospel (1:11,12; 3:26-28).

3:24,25 – The law was a tutor to bring us to Christ. But now that faith in Christ has come, we are **no longer under the tutor.**

To be "under" a law means to be subject to it or under obligation to obey it – note 4:4,21 (not just that we are condemned by it). (Compare 1 Corinthians 9:20,21; Matthew 8:9; Romans 3:19.) We are freed, not just from condemnation of the law, but from the law itself, which was the tutor. [Compare 3:16,19.]

5:1-6 – Since we are no longer under the law (5:18), circumcision no longer matters. Those who follow the old law are **entangled in a yoke of bondage, Christ profits them nothing, and is of no effect to them**. They are **fallen from grace**.

5:18 – We are **not under the law**.

Romans 7:1-6

Here again Paul contrasts the gospel to the Old Testament. The law showed men they were sinners (3:20,23). This brought condemnation (5:12; 6:23), but the law could not permanently remove that guilt. (This does not prove the law was bad, but only that the people were bad – 7:7-24; compare 7:5). Nevertheless, God did not want all men lost, so He offered the gospel (1:16).

7:2,3 – Illustration: a woman is bound to her husband as long as he lives, so if she marries another man she is an adulteress. She may remarry only if her husband has died.

7:4-6 – Likewise, we are **dead to the law and delivered from it**, just like the woman was released from the law of the first husband (verse 2). Note that we are freed, not just from condemnation or traditions about the law, but from the law itself. [Compare 6:14.]

And just as the woman could then be joined to a different man, so we are now joined to Christ. Note that **we should not follow both the Old Testament and the law of Christ**. We have a different law, just like the woman has "another man." To follow both laws at once would be like the woman having two husbands at once. It would be spiritual adultery!

Ephesians 2:11-16

Gentiles had formerly been separated from the covenant relationship enjoyed by Israelites. By His death, Jesus made peace between Jew and Gentile.

But to do this, Jesus had to **abolish the law of commandments**, which was a wall of partition between Jew and Gentile. The law (as we have shown) was given only to Israel and thus signified their favored position. To grant favor to men of every nation, God had to remove that law (compare Galatians 3:28; Acts 10:34,35; Matthew 28:19; etc.).

If we try to bind the Old Law again today, we rebuild the wall of partition that Jesus died to destroy. We are attempting to defeat the death of Christ!

Colossians 2:13-17

This is parallel to Ephesians 2. Paul tells uncircumcised Gentiles (verse 13) **not to allow people to condemn them for not keeping the Old Law** (verse 16). The reason is that Christ **blotted out** the handwriting of ordinances and **took it out of the way, nailing it to his cross**.

(Note again that the law was "against" men in the sense that it showed they were guilty of sin but could not forgive them.)

Matthew 5:17,18

Some say this passage proves the old law is still binding: Jesus did not come to destroy it, but it would stand till heaven and earth pass away.

But note that the passage says not one jot or tittle would pass away. This includes both the law and prophets (verse 17), even the least commandments (verse 19). If this means Jesus did not remove the law, then the **whole law** still stands (including animal sacrifices, circumcision, holy days, etc.). Yet we already proved that many of these things were removed. So, there must be a better explanation of this passage.

A parallel passage in Luke 16:17 shows that "Till heaven and earth pass away" means "It is easier for heaven and earth to pass away." So, it would be easier for heaven and earth to pass away than for the law to pass away **"till all be fulfilled"** (verse 18). But Jesus came to fulfill it!

So the passage actually teaches that all the law passed away when Jesus fulfilled it. (Compare Matthew 24:34.)

A contract can be rendered void in one of two ways: illegally by destroying it (as by tearing it up), or legally by fulfilling it. For example, if you hire me to build you a house for a certain fee, it would be illegal for you or me to destroy the contract. But if we fulfilled the contract (I build the house and you pay me), it would no longer be binding.

So Jesus said He did not come to destroy the law (remove it illegally contrary to its provisions). But He came to fulfill the law, and He did fulfill it (Luke 24:44-47; Acts 13:29). When it was fulfilled, it ceased to be binding, so He replaced it with a new law, completely in harmony with the provisions and intent of the law itself.

So, the Old Testament laws are not in effect on people in general today for two reasons: (1) They were given to the nation of Israel and never did apply to other nations. (2) God gave them to accomplish a purpose. They accomplished that purpose, so God removed them. We may no longer require people to keep those laws today for the same reasons that animal sacrifices, circumcision, the Levitical priesthood, etc., are no longer in effect.

Part 2: Is Any Part of the Old Testament Binding Today?

Some people agree that many Old Testament laws are no longer in effect, but they still bind some of those laws, such as the Sabbath or tithing or instrumental music, etc. Let us consider this approach.

Consider Some Possible Rules for Determining What May Be Still Binding.

We have learned that the Old Covenant has ceased to be binding. That would include all Old Testament practices unless it can be shown by the Scriptures that God intended for certain laws to continue. It is improper to just assume without proof that certain laws are still in effect and others are not. Consider some rules people sometimes suggest for making such distinctions:

"Law of God" vs. "Law of Moses"; "Moral law" vs. "Ceremonial law"

Some say the Ten Commands (including the Sabbath) are the "Law of God," the "Moral law" (or "spiritual law"), and this is still binding. But the other Old Testament commands are the "Law of Moses," the "Ceremonial law," and these are what was removed. However:

What *Scriptural proof* is there that these distinctions are valid?

How do we know that only the law of Moses or ceremonial law was done away, but not the law of God, etc.? What Scripture tells us which laws are included in the "law of God," so they remain in effect, and which laws are "ceremonial," so they were removed? (Note that the terms "moral law" and "ceremonial law" are nowhere mentioned in the Bible.)

The Sabbath, for example, was one of the Ten Commands, so some claim it is "moral" and the "Law of God," so it continues today. But it is also listed in other parts of the Old Testament besides the Ten Commands and in contexts with laws that have been done away (Exodus 31:13ff; Leviticus 19:3&30). In Leviticus 23:1-44 the Sabbath is listed right along with other feast days that are no longer in effect, so why doesn't this prove the Sabbath was "ceremonial," so it was done away? Wherein is the Sabbath any less "ceremonial" than these other feasts, many of which included sabbath rests?

Furthermore, when people seek to practice the Sabbath today because they claim it is "moral law" and the "Law of God", they usually also practice tithing, instrumental music, and even dietary laws. But these are not in the Ten Commands, nor is their nature any more "moral" than other "ceremonial" laws which have been done away. So, these folks violate their own distinction and apparently just "pick and choose" which laws to bind.

The Law of Moses and the Law of God are the same, not different.

The Bible shows that the law of God and the law of Moses are just ***different terms for the same law***, and the law of God included things that have clearly been done away. For example:

Nehemiah 8:1,8,14 – Here the same "book of the law" is called the book of the law of Moses (verse 1) and the book of the law of God (verses 8,18). God commanded it by Moses (verse 14), so both terms refer to the same law.

Luke 2:21-24,39 – The same law is called the law of Moses (verse 22) and the law of the Lord (verses 23,24,39). And this law was a purification rite, including animal sacrifices, which was clearly done away (compare Leviticus 12:2-8). So, the law of the Lord is the same as the Law of Moses, and it contains things that were done away.

(Other similar passages are Ezra 7:6,12; and 2 Chronicles 34:14,15,21,31; 35:12.)

2 Chronicles 31:2-4 – The law of God included animal sacrifices, new moons, and feast days.

So the Scriptures themselves prove that there is no distinction between the law of God and the law of Moses. The Old Testament was called God's law because He originated it, but it was called the law of

Moses because it was revealed through him (Nehemiah 10:29). This is true also of the Ten Commands and the Sabbath (Deuteronomy 5:1ff; John 7:18,19; Exodus 24:3-8; 35:1-3; 16:22-30; 31:12-17; Nehemiah 9:14; compare Mark 7:10 to Matthew 15:4).

Likewise, the Bible nowhere distinguishes moral law that continues from ceremonial law that ended. This whole distinction is a man-made rule having no sanction from God (Matthew 15:9; Galatians 1:8,9; 2 John 9-11).

Laws given before Sinai vs. laws given at Sinai

Some say that the laws Jesus abolished were the ones that originated at Sinai, but laws given before Sinai were not abolished (and this includes the Sabbath, which they say was given at creation – Genesis 2:2,3).

Again, where does the Bible say that laws are still binding if they were first given before Sinai? In fact, there are many commands that were first given before Sinai, yet we know they are no longer binding. This includes animal sacrifices (Genesis 4:4; 8:20; etc.), circumcision (Genesis 17:9-14), the Passover (Exodus 12), and laws of unclean animals (Genesis 7:2).

Further, there is no real proof that God bound the Sabbath on men from creation. No passage states that Noah, Abraham, Jacob, or any of the patriarchs kept the Sabbath.

Ezekiel 20:10-12 says God gave Israel the Sabbath as a sign between Him and them when He led them out of Egypt, and Deuteronomy 5:15 says it was a memorial of that event (compare Nehemiah 9:13,14; Exodus 31:13-17). How could it be a sign between Him and one nation if everyone since creation had the same sign? And how could it be a memorial of an event before that event occurred?

Genesis 2:3 says only that God Himself rested on the seventh day, and it says that is the reason **why** He blessed and sanctified it. But that does not tell us **when** He began to require **men** to keep it, nor **who** was required to keep it. Remember that Moses wrote the book of Genesis many years after Israel left Egypt and had been given the Sabbath. He mentions the Sabbath in connection with the Creation so men would see the purpose of it, not necessarily to tell when people began to keep it. Similar language is found in Genesis 3:20 and Matthew 10:4.

Everlasting laws vs. other laws.

Some say the Sabbath is still in effect because Exodus 31:16,17 says it was to be kept "forever," "everlasting," "perpetual."

But again, this passage says the Sabbath was a sign only between God and Israel, so why should it be bound on anyone else? And the penalty for violating this "everlasting" law was death. If this law is still in effect today, then it must be kept without change. Those who believe the law is still in effect must believe violators should be slain; otherwise they admit the law is not really in effect today.

The Old Testament terms "forever," "everlasting," etc., do not necessarily mean they have no end. We can prove this by noting many other practices that God said were "forever," etc., but which definitely have ceased. Examples are:

The Passover (Exodus 12:14)

Incense (Exodus 30:8)

Feast days (Leviticus 23:14,21,31,41)

Animal sacrifices (Leviticus 16:29-34; 6:19-23; 2 Chronicles 2:4)

The Levitical priesthood (Exodus 40:15; 29:9,26-28; 28:40-43; Numbers 25:13; Deuteronomy 18:5)

Tabernacle worship (Exodus 27:21; 30:8,17-21; Leviticus 24:5-9)

Circumcision (Genesis 17:9-14)

All God's commands and ordinances (Psalm 111:7; 119:151,152,160).

We have earlier given the evidence that all these practices have ceased, despite the fact they were "forever," "everlasting," etc. "Forever," in these passages simply refers to an indefinite period of time: "age lasting."

The context of Exodus 31:13,16 demonstrates that these terms mean "throughout Israel's generations." This expression was also used for many of the other above practices, and we earlier learned that it proves these practices, including the Sabbath, have all ceased because Israel's generations as God's chosen nation have ceased.

All these efforts to justify binding parts of the Old Testament today are doomed to fail. This conclusion will be confirmed further as we proceed.

The Verses We Previously Studied Prove that the Whole Law Was Removed, Including the Ten Commands.

Let us review the passages we used to show the Old Testament was removed, and we will show how each one proves that even the Ten Commands, including the Sabbath, were removed.

Hebrews chapters 7-10

Jesus took away the covenant that God made with Israel when He led them out of Egypt (8:9; 10:9,10). That covenant is here viewed as one covenant, the first covenant (8:7,13; 9:1,15,18; 10:9), in contrast to the second or new covenant. It was just one covenant, not two covenants: one that was removed and another that remained. But what did that first covenant include?

Hebrews 9:18-20 – The first covenant was dedicated by blood and included *every* command spoken by Moses. Exodus 24:3-8 explains more fully and shows this included *all* the words the Lord spoke (verses 3,4,7), including the Ten Commands given in Exodus 20:3-17.

Commentary on Galatians

Hebrews 9:1-4 – The covenant that was removed included the **tables of the covenant** that were inside the ark of the covenant. But the tables of the covenant were a record of the Ten Commands – Exodus 34:27,28; Deuteronomy 4:13; 5:2,22; 9:9,11.

So, the covenant that Jesus took away included all the laws given by Moses, including the Ten Commands and the Sabbath.

2 Corinthians 3:6-11

The old covenant would "pass away," in contrast to the new covenant that would "remain." What covenant was this that would pass away? It was the one written and engraved on stones (verse 7). But we just showed by the Scriptures that this was the Ten Commands.

Further, the covenant that passed away was the law which, when Moses delivered it, his face shone so he had to wear a veil (verses 7,13). But Exodus 34:27-35 shows this happened when he delivered the Ten Commands. So the old covenant that passed away included the Ten Commands, which included the Sabbath.

Galatians chapters 3-5

The law brought men to Christ, but now that Jesus has come we are no longer under (subject to) that law (3:24,25; 5:4). What law is this to which we are no longer subject?

3:17 – It is the law given 430 years after the promise to Abraham. Exodus 12:41 shows this refers to the time when Israel left Egypt. So, this is the covenant – **one** covenant – given at Mt. Sinai (Galatians 4:24), which we have seen includes the Ten Commands.

3:10 – The law refers to "all things written in the book of the Law." But we just showed in Hebrews 9:18-20 and Exodus 24:3-8 that this included the Ten Commands.

5:3 – If we bind part of the law, we are debtors to keep the **whole** law. The law is a whole. You cannot take part and leave part. You must follow it all or else realize that none of it is still in effect. But if we follow it, we fall from grace (5:2,3,4).

So, the law to which we are no longer subject includes the whole law given by Moses, including the Ten Commands and the Sabbath.

Romans 7:1-7

We are discharged from the law like a woman is freed from a husband who dies.

But what law is this from which we have been set free? It is the one that commands "Thou shalt not covet" (verse 7). But this is one of the Ten Commands. So, the law that was removed includes the Ten Commands, which included the Sabbath.

To try to bind the Ten Commands and the Sabbath and the law of Christ at the same time would be spiritual adultery, just like it is adultery for a woman to be married to two men at the same time.

Ephesians 2:11-18

Jesus abolished the law, because it was a wall of partition between Jew and Gentile. What law was that? As studied earlier, it was the Ten Commandments. That law was a wall between Jew and Gentile because God gave it to the Jews because of their special favored status. In particular, the Sabbath was a sign of God's special relation with Israel (Exodus 31:13-17).

Had Jesus left the Ten Commands or the Sabbath in effect, He would have left a barrier between Jew and Gentile. To accomplish His purpose of uniting Jew and Gentile, He had to remove the Sabbath and the Ten Commands along with the whole Old Testament law.

Colossians 2:13-17

Christ blotted out the handwriting of ordinances. To what law does this refer?

2:16 – The point is that, since the law was removed, we need not keep the laws regarding foods, holy days, or the **Sabbath**. So the Sabbath was blotted out!

Some claim the "Sabbath" here refers to the annual feast days, not the seventh-day Sabbath, because the Greek word is plural. However, "sabbath" is also plural (in the original text) in all the following passages, yet it clearly refers to the seventh day: Exodus 31:13; Luke 4:16; Acts 13:14; 16:13; etc. In Matthew 12:1-14 and Luke 13:10-17, the plural and singular forms are used interchangeably, all referring to the seventh day. In the Ten Commands themselves in Exodus 20:8 and Deuteronomy 5:12, the plural is used in the Greek Septuagint, as in Colossians 2:16.

Altogether, the New Testament refers to the "Sabbath" 59 times. Not one of these instances can be clearly shown to exclude the seventh-day Sabbath. And sabbath-keepers acknowledge that the word, even in its plural form, refers to the seventh-day Sabbath everywhere except in one verse: Colossians 2:16, which says that the Sabbath is no longer binding!

In fact, Colossians 2:16 lists the Sabbath separately from the new moons and the feast days purposely to specify the seventh day in addition to the feast days. Examination of the Old Testament references to Sabbaths, new moons, and feast days will show that this is a standard formula to refer to weekly, monthly, and annual holy days, just like in Colossians 2:16. Study 1 Chronicles 23:31; 2 Chronicles 2:4; 8:13; 31:3; Nehemiah 10:33; Ezekiel 45:17; and Hosea 2:11.

So, Colossians 2:14-16 carefully and specifically identifies the Sabbath as a practice that has been blotted out, just like the annual and monthly holy days were. We should not allow people today to require us to keep the dietary laws, the holy days, or the seventh-day Sabbath. And since the Sabbath was one of the Ten Commands, it follows that all the Old Testament laws were removed, including the Ten Commands.

Matthew 5:17,18

Jesus fulfilled the law so that it passed away. What did this include? It included the law and the prophets, every jot and tittle. Clearly that includes the Ten Commands and the Sabbath.

There is no proof that any part of the law, as such, is binding now. The law was a whole. It could not be removed only in part. To remove it, Jesus had to remove it all. And that's exactly what He did. We cannot go to the Old Law for authority for any practice now.

Part 3: What Law Should We Follow Today?

Some people ask, "If the Ten Commands were removed, wouldn't that make it all right to steal, lie, murder, etc.?" So, consider what the Bible says about the law we today should follow.

A. Today We Must Obey the New Testament Commands.

Jesus not only removed the Old Covenant, He replaced it with the New Covenant.

The reason the Old Covenant is not needed now is that a different law has taken its place.

Hebrews 10:9,10 – Jesus took away the first will **that He might establish the second.** It is a **new covenant** not like the one made with Israel at Sinai (8:6-9). (Compare 7:22; 2 Corinthians 3:6.)

Romans 7:4 – We are freed from the law **that we might be joined to Christ.**

Galatians 3:24-27 – The law was a tutor to bring us to **Christ.** Now that the gospel system of faith has come, we are no longer under the tutor (compare 1:11,12).

An illustration: The area we now call the United States was once under British law, then under the Articles of Confederation, but now we are subject to the Constitution. We are no longer subject to British law or to the Articles of Confederation because they have been replaced by the Constitution.

Similarly, God gave patriarchal rule, then the laws at Sinai, and now the gospel or New Testament. People today are no more subject to the Old Covenant than Americans are subject to the Articles of Confederation. But we are still subject to law: the laws contained in the New Testament.

This change occurred as a result of the death of Jesus.

Colossians 2:14 – Jesus removed the first ordinances nailing them to His **cross.**

Ephesians 2:13-16 – He abolished the law through His **blood** shed on the **cross** (verses 13,16).

Hebrews 9:16,17 – As with any will or testament, Jesus had to **die** to bring His testament into force.

The old law was in effect until Jesus died, then it was replaced by the New Covenant.

(Compare Galatians 3:13; Romans 7:4.)

The New Testament also contains commands and laws we must obey.

Matthew 28:18-20 – Jesus possesses all **authority** so we must obey all His **commands.**

1 Corinthians 14:37 – The message written by the New Testament apostles and prophets are the **commands** of the Lord.

1 Corinthians 9:20,21 – Though Paul was not under the law of the Jews, he was not without law but was **under law to Christ**.

James 1:18,25 – The gospel is the **perfect law of liberty,** by which we will be judged.

God removed the old law, not so we might be without law, but so we would serve Him under the terms of the New Testament. There are commands for us to obey, but these are the commands of the New Testament, not those of the Old Testament.

(John 12:48; compare 1 Peter 1:22-25; Romans 6:17,18; Acts 3:20-23; Isaiah 2:1-4)

The New Testament will never be replaced by any law on earth.

We have learned that, even while the Old Testament was in effect, God had plans to eventually replace it. Will the New Testament likewise be replaced by some other system of commands for men on earth?

2 Corinthians 3:6-11 – The first covenant passed away so that it could be replaced by that which **remains** (does not pass away).

Hebrews 12:26-28 (compare verses 18-29) – The Old Testament predicted that the law given at Sinai would be shaken (removed) that it might be replaced by another (the New Testament). But from the perspective of the Old Testament, this removal would happen only "once more." It would be replaced by a kingdom which **cannot be shaken** but will **remain.**

Jude 3 – The gospel faith was delivered to the saints **once** ("once for all" – NKJV, ASV). This word "once" is the same word used for Jesus' death in contrast to animal sacrifices (Hebrews 10:10-14; 7:27; 9:12,25-28).

The reason the Old Testament had to be replaced was that it had only animal sacrifices that had to be offered repeatedly because they could not permanently remove guilt (Hebrews 10:1-4). Jesus' sacrifice, in contrast, was perfect so it does not need to be repeated or replaced.

Likewise, the gospel was given to men "once." It is God's last word to man. It is so perfect, it will never be changed nor replaced by God while the world stands. (compare James 1:25; 1 Corinthians 13:8-13).

The New Testament has the sacrifice of Jesus, which can remove all sins so they are remembered no more. This sacrifice was offered by the sinless and eternal High Priest, Jesus Christ Himself (Hebrews 10:1-18; 7:11-28; 8:6-9; 9:11-28; Romans 1:16; Mark 16:15,16).

B. Some New Testament Commands Are Similar to Old Testament Commands, but Others Are Not.

Nine of the Ten Commands are repeated in the New Testament.

Note the evidence that most of the commands are included in the New Testament.

1. No God but Jehovah – 1 Corinthians 8:4; Acts 14:15
2. No graven images – Galatians 5:19-21; Romans 1:22,23; 1 John 5:21
3. Don't take God's name in vain – James 5:12
4. Remember the Sabbath – This command is the only one of the ten which is nowhere repeated in the New Testament. The only Sabbath rest promised in the New Testament is eternal life (Hebrews 4:9-11).
5. Honor your parents – Ephesians 6:2,3
6. Don't kill – Romans 13:8-10
7. Don't commit adultery – Romans 13:8-10; 1 Corinthians 6:9,10
8. Don't steal – Romans 13:8-10; Ephesians 4:28
9. Don't bear false witness – Revelation 21:8; 22:15; Colossians 3:9
10. Don't covet – Romans 13:8-10; Ephesians 5:3.

We obey the commands that were repeated in the New Testament, not because they were in the Old Testament, but because they are in the Old Testament.

Many New Testament practices differ from Old Testament practices.

Old Testament	New Testament
Animal sacrifices	Sacrifice of Jesus (Hebrews 10:9ff)
Human high priest	Jesus is high priest (Hebrews 9:11f)
Physical temple	Spiritual temple (church – 1 Cor. 3:16)
Fleshly circumcision	Circumcision of heart (Rom. 2:28f)
Instrumental music (Psa. 150)	Singing (Eph. 5:19; Col. 3:16)
Tithing (Hebrews 7:5)	Give as prospered (1 Cor. 16:1f)
Sabbath & holy days	First day of week (Acts 20:7; 1 Corinthians 16:1,2)

Compare Romans 7:2-6 – A woman is not subject to the authority of two husbands at once. If her first husband dies, the expectations of the first husband are no longer binding on the woman. The expectations of her second husband may in some ways be similar to those of her first husband, but they may be different in other ways. If she does things similar to what she used to do, it is because the second husband wants them, not because the first husband wanted them.

Likewise, we are now under the New Covenant, not the Old Covenant (including the Ten Commands). The laws we have now are in some ways similar to, and in some ways different from, the Old Law (compare Hebrews 8:9). But none of the requirements of the First Covenant have any power at all now as law. Wherever the laws are different, we follow the second covenant, not the first. Wherever the laws are similar, we obey, not because the first law said to, but because the New Covenant says to.

C. Specifically Our Special Day of Worship Is the First Day of the Week, Not the Seventh.

Many major New Testament events occurred on the first day of the week.

* On the first day of the week Jesus arose from the dead (Mark 16:9; Matthew 28:1,6; etc.).

* On the first day of the week Jesus first appeared to men to prove He had been raised (John 20:19; Mark 16:2,9; Matthew 28:1,6-10; etc.). Note that, according to Scripture records, Jesus' first appearances occurred on a first day of the week; and the next day on which He appeared was a week later on the next first day of the week (John 20:26ff).

* On the day of Pentecost after Jesus' crucifixion many great events occurred: the Holy Spirit came on the apostles, the gospel was first preached as being in effect, people first obeyed the gospel, and the church began. All this occurred on Pentecost; but Pentecost also came on the first day of the week (Acts chapter 2; compare Leviticus 23:15,16).

All these major events occurred on the first day of the week. What event of major New Testament significance ever occurred on the seventh day of the week? None. So it should not surprise us to see that the first day of the week has special significance in the worship of the New Testament church.

In the New Testament, Christians took up the collection and met for the Lord's Supper on the first day of the week.

1 Corinthians 16:1,2 – The church was commanded to take up the collection on the first day of the week. What passage tells the church to take up collections on the seventh day or any other day of the week?

Acts 20:7 – The church assembled regularly to partake of the Lord's Supper (Acts 2:42; Hebrews 10:25; 1 Corinthians 11:17,18,20). When did they so this? The passage says "on the first day of the week."

Commentary on Galatians

What passage anywhere tells the New Testament church to partake of the Lord's Supper on the seventh day or any other day of the week? And note that "the first day of the week" cannot possibly be the same as the "seventh day of the week."

Some say "break bread" in Acts 20:7 refers to a common meal. But the term "break bread" is often used for the Lord's Supper (Matthew 26:26; Mark 16:22; Luke 22:19; 1 Corinthians 10:16; 11:23,24; Acts 2:42). We know Acts 20:7 refers to the Lord's Supper because the context clearly shows this was a worship assembly. And Paul, who preached on this occasion, had already taught that only the Lord's Supper, not common meals, should be eaten in the worship assembly (1 Corinthians 11:17-34).

The significance of the day is also implied by the fact Paul waited seven days to meet with the disciples on the first day of the week (verses 6,7). But he was in a hurry (verse 16), so much so that he left at daylight the next day even though he had been up all night with the church (verse 11).

If the church had met on the seventh day of the week to break bread, Paul could have saved all this trouble and left a day earlier. If the seventh day is the special day for Christian worship, and the first day has no significance, why is the first day mentioned but the seventh day is not? And why did Paul go to so much trouble to meet with the church on the first day instead of the seventh day?

The only day authorized for the New Testament church to have the Lord's supper and the collection is the first day of the week. No passage anywhere in the Bible authorizes Jesus' church to do these things on the seventh day or any other day of the week.

Some claim we should keep the Sabbath because Jesus did.

We already learned that the law was not removed until Jesus died. This means that throughout His life, the Old Testament law was in effect (Galatians 4:4), so of course He kept the Sabbath (Luke 4:16; etc.).

He was also circumcised (Luke 2:21), had animals offered for him (Luke 2:22-24), taught others to offer animals (Matthew 8:4; Mark 1:44; Luke 2:22ff; compare Leviticus 14:1-32), observed Old Testament feast days (Luke 2:41f; Matthew 26:17ff), and showed great zeal for the physical temple (John 2:13-17). He taught others to observe all things taught by those who sat on Moses' seat (Matthew 23:2,3). In fact, He kept it all because He said not one jot or tittle would pass from the law till He had fulfilled it all (Matthew 5:17,18). Are we today required to do keep all the Old Testament laws because He did?

*Some claim that Paul kept the Sabbath even after Jesus'
death.*

But there is no evidence that Paul or any other inspired man observed the Sabbath **as a Divine commandment** after Jesus' death. The passages people cite to try to prove that Paul kept the Sabbath are all referring to assemblies of **unconverted Jews** (Acts 13:14,42,44; 15:20,21; 16:13; 17:1-3; 18:4f). Not one of these refers to an assembly of **Christians**. But whenever any specific day is mentioned describing worship meetings of **Christians**, it is always a *first day of the week* – Acts 20:7 and 1 Corinthians 16:1,2.

The passages that mention Paul and the Sabbath are all describing Jewish meetings (usually in Jewish synagogues) which Paul attended for the purpose of **teaching the unconverted Jews** who had assembled (Acts 13:5,14-16ff,42,44; 14:1; 17:1-3; 18:4,5). Of course these Jews kept the Sabbath, as they had for generations (Acts 15:20,21), because they did not believe the Old Testament had been removed. Their assemblies offered an excellent opportunity for Paul to teach, but no passage says he attended for the purpose of observing the Sabbath. We have already cited several verses in which Paul himself taught that the law, including the Sabbath, is not binding.

Using an opportunity to teach is not the same as observing a religious day. Apostles taught other times and places too (Acts 5:42; 17:17,22; 19:9f; 20:31). Does this mean we today must religiously observe all these other times and places too?

If Sabbath-keepers will allow us to do so, we will gladly attend their Sabbath meetings to teach them about the first day of the week, but we would not be doing it to observe the Sabbath. (If they attended our assembly on Sunday to teach us their views, would that prove they had become Sunday keepers?)

Sabbath-keepers sometimes belittle the evidence for the special significance in the gospel for the first day of the week. But the power of this evidence becomes especially convincing when it is compared to the lack of evidence for worship meetings of Christians on the seventh day. The truth is that Sabbath-keepers would dearly love to have verses like Acts 20:7 and 1 Corinthians 16:1,2 as evidence if those verses were talking about the seventh day of the week. And if those verses did refer to the seventh day of the week, Sabbath-keepers would consider them to be very convincing proof. But there are no such proof texts for the seventh day of the week. The only day of special significance for the worship of Christians is the first day of the week.

Finally, note that we do not say that the first day of the week is the "Christian Sabbath." A sabbath is a day of rest, and no New Testament passage tells us to **rest** on the first day or any other particular day. There is no "Christian Sabbath." But the first day is a special day of worship, on which we do acts of worship that are authorized for no other day.

Conclusion

The Bible teaches that the entire Old Testament law was removed by God Himself. None of it is binding today as law or as authority for any religious practice. This includes the Ten Commands and the Sabbath.

We now live under the New Testament. Every practice for the church must be authorized by the gospel. If no authority can be found in the New Testament for a practice, then it should be abandoned regardless of whether or not it was practiced in the Old Testament.

Why does it matter?

* Many practices were required under the Old Testament but are not included in the New Testament. This includes the seventh-day Sabbath, animal sacrifices, the Levitical priesthood, circumcision, special holy days, burning incense, tithing, instrumental music and dancing in worship, etc. If the Old Law is no longer in effect, then none of these practices is authorized for Christians today.

* So important was this issue to Christians in the New Testament that they conducted a major meeting in Jerusalem to discuss the issue (Acts 15; Galatians 2). This issue is the major theme of several New Testament epistles (Romans, Galatians, and Hebrews) and is also a lesser theme in other books (2 Corinthians, Ephesians, and Colossians).

* Jesus died to give us this better covenant. To return to the Old Testament would defeat a major purpose of His death.

* Inspired writers concluded that the New Testament is better than the Old in all the following ways. It has:

A better hope – Hebrews 7:19

A better covenant – Hebrews 7:22; 8:6

A more excellent ministry established on better promises – Hebrews 8:6

Better sacrifices – Hebrews 9:23

Why then should we be entangled again in the bondage of the Old Law?

Made in the USA
Middletown, DE
12 November 2021

52284891R00113